Riders on the Storm

BASED ON A TRUE STORY

OTHER BOOKS BY SHERRI KUKLA

Stay connected on
www.sherrikukla.com
www.instagram.com/sherri.kukla
Facebook.com/motomysteries

Riders on the Storm

BASED ON A TRUE STORY

SHERRI KUKLA

S&S Publishing Inc.
www.sspublishinginc.com

RIDERS ON THE STORM

© 2026 Sherri Kukla

Published by S&S Publishing, Inc.

www.sherrikukla.com

www.sspublishinginc.com

ISBN: 979-8-9865670-9-9

All rights reserved. No part of this book may be reproduced in any form or by any electronic or mechanical means, including information storage and retrieval systems, without written permission from the author, except for the use of brief quotations in a book review.

This work of fiction is based on a true story and may not reflect the true historical events or characters. See *Separating Fact From Fiction* at the end of the book for clarification.

Library of Congress Control Number: 2025919291

Printed In The United States Of America

Do not be overcome by evil,
but overcome evil with good.
Romans 12:21

Riders on the Storm

BASED ON A TRUE STORY

SHERRI KUKLA

S&S Publishing Inc.
www.sspublishinginc.com

RIDERS ON THE STORM

© 2026 Sherri Kukla

Published by S&S Publishing, Inc.

www.sherrikukla.com

www.sspublishinginc.com

ISBN: 979-8-9865670-9-9

This work of fiction is based on a true story and may not reflect the true historical events or characters. See *Separating Fact From Fiction* at the end of the book for clarification.

Library of Congress Control Number: 2025919291

Printed In The United States Of America

Do not be overcome by evil,
but overcome evil with good.
Romans 12:21

For our grandson Wyatt Kukla
It was his idea to tell the story

CHAPTER 1

SUMMER 1941
JOPLIN, MISSOURI

The incessant ringing of the phone jarred the stillness of the midmorning air. Five rings, ten, twenty. Would the caller never give up?

Bertie Mae Adams dropped to the dirt, leaning against the rough unpainted wood of the old barn, her knees pulled up tight to her chest. She buried her face in the ever-present apron she gathered up from around her waist and let the sobs wrack her thin body.

Silence. Finally, blessed silence. Maybe the caller had given up.

Her sobs slowed until the return of the jangling phone opened the floodgates once again. She couldn't avoid this call forever. But *please, Lord*, she begged silently. She needed time to get her thoughts together. To explain her erratic behavior the night before. To ease her conscience and get herself out of the trouble she knew she'd brought on.

The wooden-framed screen door banged open across the yard.

"Momma Bertie! Momma Bertie!"

As much as she wanted to, she couldn't ignore the cries of Jackson, the fourteen-year-old who was like her own son.

"Momma Bertie!" His voice–caught somewhere between a boy and a man–grew fainter as he followed her usual morning path to the chickens. Not finding her there, she knew he'd check to see if she was hanging laundry.

Meanwhile, the disturbing ring persisted. He'd never think to look behind the rundown barn. This wasn't part of her morning routine until today, when she sought solace in the overgrown weeds and wildflowers out back.

She clucked her tongue and stood. She couldn't let that poor boy search in vain. No matter how much she ached to hide from the grief she'd caused the other boy. She stuffed the corner of her apron in her mouth and chomped down hard to stop from screaming out. But the words raged inside her. I couldn't take it, Lord. I just couldn't take it anymore. I thought he was going to kill Jackson the other night.

Bertie Mae stood, inhaled deeply and knew it was time to be strong. She had to for Jackson's sake.

"There you are, Momma!"

She hugged the boy as she stepped onto the unpainted porch. "I'm sorry. I took a little walk, and I guess I lost track of time." She rarely fibbed, but figured that would be easier for the boy to hear than that she was out back, leaning on the barn and crying her heart out.

"The phone has been ringing like crazy," Jackson said as he pulled open the screen, then stepped back to hold it for her.

Such a polite boy. She was fortunate to have him in her life. As if his words had summoned the caller, the phone began jangling again, louder now that she was closer to it. She couldn't put this off any longer.

"Hello? Bertie Mae here. Who's calling?" She didn't know what possessed her to be so formal. Her insides trembled, and she knew it would be the child services lady. She wondered if she would go to jail for what she'd done.

"Miss Adams, it's Verna Wilson, Child Services."

"I'm sorry, Miss Wilson. I'm sorry. I know I did wrong. I never should have left the boy out front at the Children's Home." She squeezed her eyes, praying silently for leniency.

"Miss Adams—"

"It's just that he seemed like a danger to my boy Jackson," Bertie heard herself rambling. She couldn't help interrupting. She had to get the story out now before she lost her nerve. "He was so angry when the finance company repossessed his bicycle. He loved that bicycle, then he didn't have it anymore, and he took out his anger on Jackson."

"Did he actually say he wanted to kill him?" Miss Wilson's tired voice came through the phone wires.

Bertie Mae hoped the good Lord would forgive her for exaggerating. But now she had to be honest. "Well, no, ma'am. He didn't actually say those words, but if you could see the anger in that boy's eyes, you just felt that's what he was thinking. I just

9

couldn't take it anymore. I was so afraid for my Jackson that I just loaded Billy up in the car and drove him to the Children's Home and figured they would know better than me how to take care of that angry boy."

"I see," Miss Wilson said.

"I know I'm probably in trouble for that," Bertie Mae hung her head, not wanting to make eye contact with Jackson, knowing he was probably hearing her side of the conversation. She didn't want to scare him.

"Miss Adams, ordinarily there would be some sort of reprimand for a foster parent abandoning a child, but in this case, well, we understand the difficulty. In fact, we already sent Billy to the State Training School for Boys in Boonville."

"Boonville? Isn't that the detention place? He's only twelve. Isn't that young for something like jail? Couldn't the Children's Home take care of him?" As much trouble as the boy gave her, she hated to cause him to go to a place like a jail.

"They were willing to try, but he ran off from there and stole a bicycle. It must be like you said. He was upset at losing his bicycle, but he can't go out and steal someone else's bicycle. We talked to him about coming back to your place."

Bertie Mae cringed at those words before relaxing at her next sentence.

"But he refused. Said he'd rather go to the boy's school."

"Oh my, Miss Wilson, I sure hope they can help that boy. I just feel it in my bones. He's headed for trouble."

CHAPTER 2

NINE YEARS LATER
JANUARY 1950
MISSOURI STATE PENITENTIARY

G o ahead and throw me in the dungeon!" Billy snarled at the
guards. "I lived in a cave as a kid. I'm used to being thrown
anywhere."

The chaplain watched, his heart aching at the scene that had
unfolded before him as he oversaw the inmate's softball game on
this chilly winter morning. He made a mental note to see if there
was any truth to Billy's claim of living in a cave. This angry
young man seemed determined to lash out at anyone who came
into his path and said or did the slightest thing to provoke him.
The chaplain watched as the guards hauled the angry prisoner
away while the medics worked on his victim.

Blood dripped from the head of the inmate who had insulted
Billy on the softball field.

Grabbing a nearby bat, Billy started swinging at the other
guy's head before anyone could stop him. The makeshift
weapon, now tossed aside, probably had blood splatters dried on

11

the wood. The chaplain noticed no other inmates dared pick up the bat as the yard was now filled with armed guards.

It had taken a couple of shots from the gun tower to get guards out here to pull Billy off the inmate and get the bat from his hands. Inmates gathered around to watch the fight, some cheering on Billy, others screaming for the guy getting beat to fight back, having long forgotten the game. Yet, no one intervened, probably because they knew the bat would be used against them next.

Reverend Edward Schlattmann was no novice at seeing to the spiritual and athletic needs of the prisoners he ministered to and while people knew him as the jolly prison chaplain who almost always had a smile, this type of incident did little to keep his smile in place. His heart hurt for the young man, and he was determined to find out what his situation in life was. What had brought him to prison at such a young age? He was already into the third year of his sentence, the rev knew, meaning he'd been a mere teenager when he'd arrived at the state prison.

"What can I do for you, Rev?"

Edward stepped inside the warden's office and looked around at the stacks of files on the desk and the credenza behind where he sat. He watched as Warden Ralph Eidson removed his glasses and rubbed his eyes before replacing the glasses and looking up, his elbows propped on his desk.

"It's William Cook, Ralph," Edward said. "I believe the others call him Billy."

"I just heard he's on his way to lockdown in the dungeon."
Ralph pulled out a file folder stacked about three files down on
the right side of his desk. He laid it open before him, studying the
file.

"This boy," he looked up at Edward, "I know he turned
twenty a few weeks ago, but I still think of him as a boy, see him
as a boy."

"Totally understand, Warden," Edward said. "He acts like a
boy, seems behind for his age."

"Not intellectually," Ralph said. "He tests at a normal level
or beyond, but a social awkwardness is present."

"Could be from his slight physical deformity, possibly? The
eyelid that doesn't seem to work right. I'm not sure exactly what
the problem is."

Ralph dropped his hands, palms down, on the open file. "It's
all here, Rev. You're welcome to look if you think it will help."

Ah, something to smile about. "Actually," Edward said,
"that's what I was coming around for. Hoping to learn something
of this boy's past."

"I can tell you right now, he has spent nearly half his life
incarcerated in one place or another."

Edward felt his tongue involuntarily clicking on the roof of
his mouth. "You don't say? That is a shame."

"He's scheduled for release this summer." Ralph closed the
file folder and pushed it across the desk toward Edward. "Best
to keep him in lockdown as much of that time as we can to keep
him out of trouble, so he can make it to his release date."

SHERRI KUKLA

"How long can I have the file?" Edward stood, holding the thick folder under his arm. "I'll try not to take too long with it."

"I trust you," Warden Eidson said. "I don't anticipate needing it again soon unless there is another incident with him. But that's not as likely with him in lockdown."

"Can he have visitors?"

"What visitors? No one has visited that young man in the almost three years he's been here."

"Myself is who I had in mind."

"You know, that's a rough walk down to the dungeon. Dark corners with no cameras. I've heard stories of inmates roaming and of so-called accidents happening."

"I'll remember that." Edward nodded his thanks and headed for the door, then turned back before exiting. "First, I'll study his file, then I'll make my way to the dungeon and study the boy."

"I wish you luck."

Rev. Edward Schlattmann touched the cross-shaped pendant hanging around his neck and dangling near his chest. "I don't rely on luck." He smiled. "Prayer. Now that's where the real power is, Warden."

Ralph nodded, maybe trying to smile, but not quite successful if that was the goal. He sighed instead and stared into the eyes of the reverend. "And I'll remember that, Rev."

The reverend stood just outside the warden's office, pondering whether to return to the chapel, his base of operations at the penitentiary, and dig into the file folder or should he first visit Billy, see if he could get him to open up to him, before he

14

read what the file had to say. His mind made up, he headed for his tiny office in the chapel to lock the folder in his file cabinet and grab the little penlight that would easily fit in his pocket. He'd never been to the dungeons before, but it was a well-known fact here in the prison that it was a very dark place. He wondered if Billy would be in a cell alone, or with others.

Down below A Hall, one of the buildings that housed regular prisoners, was the dreaded basement with the block walls and cell doors, many of them rusted from the musty air circulating down there for well over a hundred years. He wished he had brought along a larger flashlight, but figured the penlight was better than walking in the dark. Although he doubted any prisoners were roaming, just the same, he kept looking over his shoulder, in case someone should sneak up behind him. He wouldn't do Billy any good if he got himself killed down here in the darkness.

Shining the light on the rusty doors as he walked along the narrow aisle, bordered on one side by the heavy cold block wall, he found the cell he was looking for midway down the aisle. Reverend Edward could hear shuffling inside the cell, but no voices. He'd heard that some cells in the dungeon held up to six prisoners, a recipe for disaster in his mind, but he hoped to find Billy in a cell alone. The other prisoners in adjoining cells, though separated by the block walls, could most likely sense there was a light in the walkway. He'd been told they only see the light when the food door opens.

It seemed cold to house prisoners in the pitch black, and he wondered who had made that decision. That meant they couldn't even read if it was true. He could not imagine existing in a small space in the darkness with nothing to occupy his mind except his own thoughts. For him, he knew if he were in that situation, he would review all the Bible verses he'd memorized in his life and be thankful he had worked so hard to do that. He'd use his time also to commune with his Creator, the Lord Jesus. But these prisoners? What went on in their minds during the long hours locked away in the darkness? He could not imagine it would be anything helpful to their situation or their future betterment.

"Billy? Billy Cook?"

Reverend Ed spoke boldly, hoping to elicit a response. He couldn't see through the grimy steel with the tiny holes that lined the bars on the door. He didn't have the key the guards had to unlock the food door. But surely his voice would carry through the door.

"Are you in there, Billy?"

"Who wants to know?"

The low monotone sounded like it came from just the other side of the door. The proximity of the sound gave the reverend cause to believe Billy was interested in communicating.

"It's me, Reverend Ed."

"What d'ya want with me? I ain't done nothing to you."

"No, that's true," Rev said, encouraged he'd gotten a dialogue started. "You haven't done anything to me, but I thought you could use a friend."

"I never had any friends, and I don't need one now."

The reverend wished he could have seen into Billy's eyes when he uttered the words. He couldn't tell if truth was being spoken just by the tone of voice. But looking into a man's eyes while he spoke. There was the answer. Of course, just being face to face with a man didn't mean you could see into his eyes. He'd watched Billy interact with others, and saw that he often stared at the ground when he spoke.

"Is what you said out there on the ball field true?" Changing tactics might get him somewhere.

"I didn't say nothing."

"Yes, you did say something," Reverend Edward said. "Something that caught my attention, that brought me down here to visit you."

"Well, I sure didn't ask you to come visit me."

It sounded like he was moving farther away from the door.

"I just wondered if someone did leave you in a cave when you were young."

"It's what I said, ain't it?"

He had moved back closer. So he did remember saying that.

"What do you remember about that?"

"I don't know. Why you gotta ask all these questions? Ask my sister Betty. Ask my brother Tommy. They was there. Ask Pearl, ask Helen. They was all there."

"Where are your siblings now, Billy?"

"See, there you go with all the questions. Is that what being a friend is? Asking a body so many questions, their head spins?"

"Yes, I see." The reverend nodded, even though he doubted Billy could see him. "Maybe that's not a good way to start up a friendship." He was stumped. Normally, conversations flowed easily between him and the inmates, especially outside while he coached them with wrestling or boxing or playing softball. He'd learned quite a bit about the sports to give them pointers, and the ones interested always seemed to enjoy his input. But how to talk to an angry prisoner who didn't want any friends, that he was clueless about.

"Got any questions for me, Billy?"

"Yeah, why did you bother coming down here?"

"I thought you might want a visit from a friend."

"I told you, I got no friends."

CHAPTER 3

JUNE 16, 1950
MISSOURI STATE PENITENTIARY

Reverend Ed Schlattmann sat in a pew in the back of the empty chapel. He reflected on the rundown state of this house of God when he'd arrived at the prison to serve as chaplain five years earlier. Within two years, he'd had the privilege of overseeing the complete renovation of the building and the redecoration. It had been a personal joy and highlight of his career here to provide a place of worship for the inmates that reflected the respect God deserved. He hoped lives were changed by the time they spent in the chapel, learning more about God and how to draw close to Him.

His mind wandered to Billy Cook. If only renovating a human life were as easy as renovating a building. He looked at the file folder in his lap. Nearly six months had passed, and he'd never yet returned it to the warden.

He remembered holing up in his office after his visit that day in the dungeons with the surly prisoner. He'd spent the rest of the day devouring every word in the file folder. There had been nothing in there to confirm Billy's story of being left in a mine shaft, but there was certainly a paper trail to show the father had abandoned almost a half-dozen children after their mother died. According to the file, Billy had failed at several placements— from a foster home, to a group home, to the State Training facility for challenging boys. He'd chosen a path of crime from an early age, starting with truancy and advancing to armed robbery and auto theft.

One would wonder if his lack of a proper upbringing could have caused all of this, but even with a much older sister offering to take him in, he still committed crimes. The reverend opened the file and glanced through the papers. Yes, there it was. Besides the younger siblings abandoned along with him, there were older half-siblings who were already adults at the time of the mother's passing. One sister in particular had reached out to the troubled youth and given him a home. He thanked her by robbing a taxi driver and getting sent to jail, then trying to escape, thus incurring a longer sentence. Even while in MSP, they found him with illegal drugs and suspected that he sold them to other inmates. But with no proof, his sentence was not affected.

Try as he might, the reverend could not connect with the young man, even after visiting him several more times.

The reverend shook his head while closing the file folder and standing. He supposed the warden would need to get this file folder back to get it filed in the archives. Billy Cook had been released earlier that day.

Edward rapped lightly, then opened the door and stepped in to see the warden eating a sandwich at his desk. He glanced at his watch.

"Lunch at three?" Edward stepped over and placed the file folder on the warden's desk, on top of multiple others just like this one.

Ralph nodded. "You know how it is some days."

"There is that folder on Billy Cook I borrowed in January." Ed pointed toward the pile. "Sorry for the delay in getting it back to you."

"Did you read it all?"

"I did." He stared out the window beyond Ralph's desk, at the magnolia tree in full bloom. What a contrast, the delicate pink blossoms growing profusely on the grounds of a facility that held so much ugliness and sorrow.

"You know the softhearted types out there would say his crimes aren't his fault." The warden swiped a napkin across his mouth while chewing his last bite. "But that boy wasn't an only child. Those other kids were brought up in the same sorry way. There were at least three or four others abandoned with him and then parceled out to whoever would care for them. But I don't see them here in my prison."

The reverend nodded. "I hear you."

"He got out today, you know?" Ralph crumpled the wax paper from his sandwich and tossed it with the soiled napkin into an overflowing trash container next to his desk.

"What do you suppose he'll do now?"

"Well, believe it or not," Ralph said. "He told me he plans on joining the United States Army."

21

"Now that is a surprise," Reverend Ed said. "A good one. Maybe he will make something of himself."

Ralph shook his head, his mouth down-turned. "The Army won't take him because of his criminal history."

"That's a shame. Might be the first time he had a worthwhile goal. Did you tell him that?"

"No." Ralph picked up the Cook file and stepped over to a file cabinet in the corner of his office. "Why discourage him before he ever sets foot out of here?"

"Agreed. Well, let's hope he turns his life around and this is the last we ever hear of Billy Cook."

CHAPTER 4

DECEMBER 23, 1950
SEATTLE, WASHINGTON

Dad, I'm excited about seeing you, too," Robert Dewey spoke into the phone. He had been looking forward to time off from his job with the oil company. He loved being a sales rep, and he was good at it, but hunting and fishing and visiting his dad were high on his list of priorities for his downtime.

"Well, Son, I know I'll be seeing you soon, but I still wanted to call and tell you happy birthday and also tell you and Louise, Merry Christmas! Will she be coming along on your trip?"

Robert smiled at his wife, who sat nearby. That had been the plan until her sister sprang a surprise visit on them from her home in Illinois.

"No, Dad, not this trip," Robert said. "She actually had put in for the time off from her job, but then she found out her sister is coming to visit."

"Pauline is coming to Seattle?"

"Yes, they haven't seen each other since the last time we were in Illinois a couple of years ago. She's coming alone, so I guess this will be a fun girls time with me being on the road."

"Hi, Dad." Louise took the phone from Robert. "I'm sorry I can't come see you, but we hope to get down there again, maybe next fall." She looked at her husband. "That visit will be a real family visit, though, no hunting allowed." The couple shared a smile.

"Okay, you have fun with your sister. Tell Pauline I said hello."

"I'll miss you, Dad. Now, here's Robert. I'm giving him back the phone."

"Well, Dad, we should go now. I know this call is costing you a lot of money." Robert had been surprised when he answered the phone, but loved hearing his dad's voice and his annual singing of Happy Birthday. Hard to believe he was thirty-two already.

"Son, you're worth every cent the phone company charges. Just to hear your voice. Now you be safe driving. We'll expect you to arrive in a couple of weeks. Aerial is eager to see you, too."

Robert cringed. She was no replacement for his mom, who had died shortly after he had returned from the war. At least his mom had lived long enough to see him return safely. He remembered how scared his mother had been when he told her he'd joined the Cavalry Reserve.

His dad must have noticed the silence. "Now, Son, she's not trying to replace your mother."

"I know, Dad. I just... Well, I don't know what to say. But this call is costing you too much."

"Okay, Son. We..." he stopped, maybe reconsidering his words knowing Robert's hesitation to feel strong affection for Aerial. "I love you, Son. You be safe."

"Driving to California can't be as dangerous as fighting in WWII, Dad. I'll be fine."

"Okay, Captain, I'll trust you on that."

Robert smiled as he hung up the phone. Both of his parents had been so proud when he became captain before his service ended.

CHAPTER 5

DECEMBER 23, 1950
BLYTHE, CALIFORNIA

C ecilia watched her surly coworker as he washed the dishes the busboys delivered to him. Something seemed different about him today. Maybe he was relaxing. Or maybe he had a plan. She hoped it was a good plan for his life. He seemed to live by the slogan tattooed on his fingers: Hard Luck. She wondered what was in his past.

She guessed him to be about twenty or twenty-one. He didn't talk much. She knew nothing about his family. He seemed quite alone in the world. Should she ask what was on his mind?

"Cecilia!" The boss sounded none too happy. As a waitress, she didn't belong in the kitchen. She belonged out checking on the customers, taking orders, delivering food. But knowing she was the only one who ever had a pleasant word to say to Billy, she'd felt drawn to the kitchen to check on him. Before she could get a word in to him, the boss was chasing her back out to do her job. She supposed it was only fair. That was her job.

"It's my birthday today. Happy birthday to me."

She almost missed the muttered words coming from the dishwasher. He didn't seem to be talking to anyone, just staring down in the dishwater as he washed.

She'd have to do something about that, she determined, as she headed back to take orders from the new customers who had come in.

"People must stand outside and line up, so they can all come in at once," Cecilia thought as she rushed from one table to another to get the orders and check on the ones who were already eating. No wonder her boss had called for her to get back out here. She'd thought everything was under control when she headed back to check on Billy.

What could she do for his birthday? Billy didn't seem like the type of guy they would invite into their home. There was something about him that, while feeling sorry for him, almost made her uncomfortable. Normally, she and Homer would welcome visitors to their home. They both loved cooking, and hospitality seemed to be a gift for them. But even without asking Homer, she was sure this wouldn't be a good idea. Besides, he was on duty, and she never knew if he'd get off work on time if he was the only deputy on duty that day. Maybe she'd just treat him to a meal here.

After clearing it with her boss, he agreed to schedule both of their dinner breaks at the same time, and soon Cecilia and Billy were sitting together at a small table in the corner of the restaurant.

He looked unsure of himself. Like maybe he'd never sat in a diner across from another person.

"It's for your birthday," Cecilia said. "My treat. Order whatever you want."

He stared across the table without speaking. Didn't even open the menu.

"Do you know what you want?" Cecilia said.

"Fried chicken."

She'd thought this would be a good time to get to know more about the unhappy young man, but he wasn't proving to be a very good conversationalist. One or two-word answers at best. Finally, just before their food arrived, she asked, "How old are you today?"

"Twenty-one."

As they ate, Cecilia wondered what had happened in the last twenty-one years to bring this unhappy young man to be celebrating his birthday all alone washing dishes in a Blythe, California diner. She learned he was from Joplin, Missouri, but never how he came to be in their little town.

The next day, Cecilia discovered she'd lost her chance to ask any more questions. Billy didn't show up for work, and it seemed that was the last they'd see of the dour-faced young man with the droopy eyelid that didn't quite shut. At least she'd helped him celebrate his birthday. Maybe that was good for something.

CHAPTER 6

DECEMBER 23, 1950
EL CENTRO, CALIFORNIA

What do you think?" Forrest Damron swigged the last of the soda his friend James had offered him as they mapped out the destination for their upcoming mining trip shortly after the new year.

James Burke had his eyes glued to the map, following routes with his finger, then making notes on a pad next to the spread out map. He seemed oblivious to the question.

"Do you think you and Vivian will join the family tomorrow?"

James looked up, still holding his finger in place on the map. "What's that?"

"For Christmas Eve dinner and then the church service? I think the whole family will be there."

"Are you kidding me?" James said. "Everyone's coming to town?"

"My Aunt Lola, my Aunt Maggie, my Aunt Mamie, my..."

"No, stop. Your family is just too big."

The two laughed together. It was an ongoing joke between the two of them, since Forrest came from a long line of Damrons on his dad's side and his mom was from a large family as well. They had always treated James like one of the family, but he often got overwhelmed when they all came together. He'd grown up with very few extended family members around and was used to small family gatherings.

"I really miss your Uncle Virgle."

"Same," Forrest said. "This will be our third Christmas without him already."

James tapped the map spread out in front of him. "If it weren't for him, we might not have gotten into prospecting. We might not be planning this trip right now."

"You're right. I think he was my favorite relative."

"I'm going to pass on getting together with your family tomorrow. I think we'll actually take a run out to the cemetery and leave some Christmas flowers on Virgle's grave, then go out for a Christmas Eve meal."

Forrest nodded. "My mom would like that, knowing you're remembering her brother."

"Yeah, and it keeps us away from the chaos." He laughed as he stuck his pencil behind his ear, then looked over the notes he had jotted down about their route. "No doubt your brother and his brood will be along, too."

"Look," Forrest said, "it's not as bad as you make it seem, and the kids love getting together with all the cousins." He stood and gathered up both of their soda bottles to return to the kitchen.

"I can't wait for our trip to get here, but first I'm going to enjoy Christmas and New Year's with the family."

"Good idea, same here. So let's finish up the plans before the girls get back from shopping." James followed his friend into the kitchen. "I think starting out at Ogilby will be good, then we'll head into Mexico." James leaned on the kitchen counter. "Two more weeks of work and then three days of exploring if we leave on Saturday right after I get off work."

"I'm looking forward to it."

"So what do you think you're getting from Santa?"

"Hey, buddy, don't you know who Santa is around my house? It's me, and I'm getting just what I want."

"Did you put money down on that new Geiger counter?" James said. "I'm jealous."

"You could get yourself one."

"It's true I could, but why should I when I can use yours on this trip? Besides, I'm putting money into some new camping gear and going to get a tune-up on the car, maybe a new set of tires before we head out. Not to mention some gifts for the family."

"New tires? That Studebaker is only a year old," Forrest said. "What makes you think you need new tires already?"

"Safety first, I always say."

CHAPTER 7

DECEMBER 27, 1950
EL PASO, TEXAS

H ow much you want for this one?"
"That one there will set you back forty-five dollars."
Gus Madison, the gun store owner, didn't know how to take
the look this customer gave him. Especially with that one bad
eye. Was he glaring at him, or did that eye just not focus right?
Something wrong with the eyelid that was for sure. But whatever
it was, he was pretty sure the fellow did not like the price.

"Now, if you go with a standard model..."

"Did I ask for a standard model?" A snarl backed the clipped
words.

"No," Gus said, "you didn't. But you seemed unsure about
that price."

"Did I say something about the price?"

Well, he had him there. No, he didn't actually say anything,
not in so many words. But this young man sure had a way about
him with his looks. As they say, if looks could kill.

"I'll take it," the surly customer said as he began peeling off
five-dollar bills from the roll he pulled out of his pocket.

Gus pulled out his order pad, dated it, then looked up as the young man placed the money on the counter between the two of them. "I'll need your name and address."

"Name's Billy Cook. W.E. Cook if you want to be all legal like."

"And your address?"

"Ain't got one."

Gus looked up as he spoke, then over the young man's shoulder, out the window, wondering if he lived in his car. There was no car in the parking lot. "I see," he said, although he didn't. "So where are you from?"

"Nowhere. I roam." Billy tapped on the glass display case where the gun he was purchasing waited for the transaction to be complete. "Now I'll have me my gun. Just like I told my pa when I left him back in Joplin. I'm going to live by the gun and roam."

Gus turned the pad around and held out his pen. "Put your John Hancock here," he motioned to the signature line on the bottom of the pad.

Billy gave him a look with that eye. Again, Gus shivered inside, wondering what was going on in that guy's head, and was he really the kind of guy who needed a gun?

"What do you mean?"

Relieved there wasn't a more sinister reason for the look he gave him, Gus realized Billy Cook had never heard the phrase.

"Your signature." Gus said. "Sign the bottom of this form for me, and then we're all done."

Billy scrawled something that may have been his name, then looked around the store. "I need me some ammo, too."

33

While Gus gathered the .32 caliber ammo, he made small talk, as was his custom. "So, what do you plan on doing with that little snub nose?"

He looked up as he tore the customer copy of the receipt off his pad, then pulled the gun out from the display case.

"That's my business," Billy said. He shoved the receipt in his back pocket, loaded the gun, thrust it into his jacket pocket and left the store without another word.

CHAPTER 8

DECEMBER 29, 1950
ATWOOD, ILLINOIS

Thelma Mosser waited on the kids as they took turns getting in their last trips to the bathroom. She watched out the window as her husband Carl loaded suitcases into the trunk of their one-year-old Chevy sedan. The farm had been good to them for the last few years. They'd been able to save the money for the car. As soon as the 1950 models came out, she still remembered the smile on his face when he drove the new car home. Immediately they began putting money away for the after-Christmas trip to visit his twin brother, who was stationed in Albuquerque. She was glad Carl had chosen farming for a career rather than the military like his brother.

"Mommy, how long until we get to where Uncle Chris lives?" Ronnie finished his turn in the bathroom and adjusted his Hopalong Cassidy hat carefully on his head. He cinched up the string until it almost touched his chin but wasn't too tight. "Do you think he'll like our hats?"

"He'll love your hats." Thelma smiled as her other son Gary joined them in the kitchen, also wearing his hat. "Your dad told me when they were kids they had red cowboy hats and holsters with play guns. They used to play outside all day long, pretending they were real cowboys."

"Daddy did that?" Five-year-old Gary asked. "How could Daddy play outside? He has to go to work every day."

"You dummy," Ronnie said. "Daddy was a little boy once too."

"Oh, Ronnie, don't call your brother a dummy." She took him by the shoulder and hugged him close, then smiled at Gary. "Ronnie is right though, your daddy was a little boy just like you two."

Two-year-old Pamela Sue came running down the hall. "I all finished," she called out, proud of herself that she could take care of her own bathroom needs. "All finished."

Thelma leaned over and scooped up Pam in her arms, hugging her close, then resumed her conversation with the boys. "And did you know, Gary, your daddy and Uncle Chris were the very same age?"

"You mean, when his older brother was seven, then he could be seven too instead of being only five? I want to do that!"

"You're funny, Gary," Ronnie said. "But you can't do that. I'm the oldest, and I'll always be the oldest."

"That's not fair. How come Daddy and Uncle Chris got to be the same age?"

"Because they're twins. They were born on the same day, and they look just alike." Thelma said. "You haven't seen Uncle Chris in a long time, so you might not have remembered that."

"Yeah," Ronnie said, "be careful because when you're looking at Daddy when we get to their house, you won't know if it's really Daddy or if it's Uncle Chris."

Carl came through the doorway to a house filled with laughter. "Daddy! Daddy!" Gary ran to his father with big news. "Did you know Uncle Chris looks just like you?"

Ronnie slapped his forehead with his hand and looked at his mother. "Oh, brother!" Thelma smiled, glad he didn't call him dummy again, his newest term for his little brother.

Carl reached down and patted Gary on his head. "I had a feeling he might look like me, little buddy. I figured it out when I thought I was looking in the mirror but realized I was looking at my brother."

Thelma joined her husband, wrapping an arm around him as she stood by his side, surveying their young family. How blessed she was. "I think we're all ready to go, honey." She looked over at her husband, staring into his eyes where they stood shoulder to shoulder. She'd always been tall, and remembered as a young teen she thought she'd grow taller than all the boys. She'd found the perfect mate in Carl, who matched her height exactly. He leaned over and gave her a quick kiss.

"I'm proud of you all." Carl glanced at his wristwatch. "We're five minutes ahead of schedule."

"How long till we get there, Daddy?"

Thelma joined in her husband's laughter. "It's starting already, and we're not even in the car."

"Let me tell you, buddy," Carl looked down at Gary. "If we drive all day today and sleep tonight and then drive all day tomorrow, we might get there very late tomorrow."

"Where are we going to sleep, Daddy?" Ronnie said. "Can I take my pillow in the car? It might be kind of crowded to sleep there, but I'll try."

"Sure, you can take your pillow if you want, buddy," Carl said to his oldest son. "But we'll stop and get a room at a motor lodge somewhere along the way." He looked over to Thelma. "I'm hoping to get to our halfway point tonight."

"Somewhere in Oklahoma, maybe?" Thelma said. She'd studied the map along with Carl. From Illinois, they would next pass through Missouri and then on into Oklahoma.

"Yes, hopefully about the halfway point of Oklahoma."

"Did you see I had all the food packed and ready to go?" Thelma said.

"Sure did. Thanks for getting that all organized. It's all loaded. We won't go hungry on this trip," Carl said.

"I have little snack bags packed for the kids I'll carry with me, so they can have treats along the way."

"That's a grand plan, don't you think so, kids?" Carl smiled at their brood.

They all looked so innocent and happy now, but Thelma wondered how many hours they'd get into the trip before the irritability and impatience would start. Twenty-some hours in a car was a lot for young kids. She hoped she had packed enough activities.

"What about Jasper, Daddy?" Gary said. "Who will take care of Jasper while we're gone?"

Carl smiled as the little white family dog perked up from his bed in the corner of the living room at the mention of his name. "You can take care of Jasper on the first part of the trip, Gary," Carl said. "Jasper's coming along with us."

"Yay!" Pamela Sue clapped her hands. Doggie, come!"

"Everybody watered and walked?" Carl said.

Thelma nodded, recognizing the old question from her parents when they were growing up. She wasn't sure where the saying came from, but knew it meant, are we all ready to go?

"Just got all our bathroom trips taken care of. We can load up and hit the road."

CHAPTER 9

DECEMBER 30, 1950
TAHOKA, TEXAS

Lee Archer blew on his weather-beaten hands to warm them before scraping ice off the windshield. These hands had been through a lot in his fifty-some years of life, and the harsh winters often chapped and cracked the skin on his fingertips. He briefly thought about getting his gloves out of the trunk, but didn't want to take the time. A few quick swipes across the windshield with the metal scraper and he'd be out of this icy wind and on the road.

Inside the car, he grabbed the thermos of hot coffee he'd brought along and sipped it before cranking the car over. The smooth sound of the engine purring brought a smile to his face. Being a mechanic wasn't just his job, it was his hobby and when he wasn't at work, he could be found under the hood or all the way underneath the car, tweaking and modifying, always looking for a way to get better speed or smoother running.

He loved his job, but he also loved getting time off, and with his boss out of town, and the repair shop closed for the next few days, he planned to take a drive up to Tulsa to visit friends. He intended to leave Sunday morning, but when he couldn't sleep, he headed out at 1 a.m., a little earlier than his original plans called for.

A few miles into his drive, he spotted a hitchhiker. As he got closer, he downshifted to slow the car and prepare for a stop. He knew how cold it was outside and sure would hate to be that guy. He wondered how far the young man was going. Maybe he'd have company for a good portion of his trip. Could be some college kid trying to get back to the dorm after spending Christmas with family. Who knows, maybe he'd just change his route and head straight north. Texas Tech wasn't too far away, and he was still feeling the Christmas spirit.

CHAPTER 10

DECEMBER 30, 1950
TULSA, OKLAHOMA

Thelma Mosser looked over the selection of postcards in the travel center. As usual, she was having a hard time deciding. Whether it was a greeting card or a postcard, she read every single choice before choosing one.

She could hear the children oohing and ahhing over all the selections in the kids' area and knew Carl would most likely let them each pick out a toy or two to play with on the road.

She settled on the card that showed an aerial view of the city of Tulsa. She couldn't believe how big it was, and the info on the back said there were 250,000 people living here. Comparing that with their small town of five or six hundred, she decided she was content with small-town living, although she enjoyed getting out and seeing other areas.

After paying for her selection and buying a stamp, she joined her family, where the children still hadn't made up their minds. Good thing, that would give her time to get a note written to her aunt, so she could drop this in the mail before they got back on the road.

"Did you find one?" Carl asked while he watched the kids, who were so enthralled with the choices they didn't even notice their mother had joined them in the toy aisle.

"Yes, I'll be right over there at the counter near the window. Thanks for watching the kids so I could get this done. I promised Aunt Elsie I'd send her a card while we were on the road."

"Take your time," Carl said. She appreciated that about him. He wasn't in a hurry when they took road trips. He wanted the family to enjoy every minute of the trip, not just when they reached their destination. She remembered driving places with her family as a child. Her dad barely wanted to stop for bathroom visits and gas. He always felt the vacation didn't start til you reached the place you were going.

Aunt Elsie, we're already having so much fun. Look at this big city. I'll take my small town any day. We'll call you when we get to Carl's brother's house. Happy New Year to you all. Love Thelma.

Perfect timing. Just as she dropped the card in the mail slot by the counter, Carl and the children joined her.

"Well, family," Carl said, holding Pamela Sue while she held tight to her new little baby doll, "let's hit the road. Uncle Chris is waiting for us."

"And we're waiting to see him, too," Ronnie said.

"We sure are." Thelma took hold of Gary's hand and followed Carl and Ronnie to the car. "Brrr, it's cold out here. Let's hurry."

"Sure wasn't expecting it to be so much colder than home," Carl said as he unlocked the door.

Settling into the car, she looked over her shoulder at the children already occupied with their new toys, and it warmed her heart. She loved family vacations, and she'd been looking forward to this adventure since last summer.

CHAPTER 11

DECEMBER 30, 1950
LUTHER, OKLAHOMA

Driving nearly four hundred miles with his quiet passenger, he wondered about the gun he'd seen the guy pull out of his pocket. Looked like one of those little snub-nose pistols that were popular.

Guns didn't bother him much. He owned a few himself, as did most of his friends. He even had a few acquaintances in his social circle who'd done time along with him. A couple had been in Leavenworth, so even a criminal type didn't make him too nervous. Although the gun when it pointed in his direction occasionally gave him pause to wonder what the goal was for this man. The guy hadn't been much of a threat to his life so far, and it seemed he mainly wanted a ride a lot farther than Lee was feeling comfortable about.

Determined to stay calm, Lee figured it was wise not to get the guy riled up. Hopefully, once they reached wherever it was he wanted to go, the stranger would get out and be on his way. Lee just kept following his directions, occasionally sneaking a few looks at the passenger with the pistol in his lap. He looked to be in his early twenties, but his skin had the acne of a teen. Curly dark hair on top of his head, cut short on the sides, and one eyelid that didn't look right, but he couldn't quite figure out what was wrong with it. Looked like some lettering tattooed on his fingers, but while driving Lee wasn't able to make out what it said.

He'd been watching the gas gauge for some time, in between keeping an eye on the highway and the man in the passenger seat. He figured it was time.

"Say there, are we getting close to your destination?"

"What's it to you?"

"Well, we better be getting some gas here soon, and how about some food? Are you hungry?"

"Don't worry about me, none. How much gas we got?"

"Oh, I'd say maybe about a quarter of a tank," Lee said.

"That's plenty." He motioned with the gun to the right. "Just stop the car."

"Are you crazy?" Lee looked around the acres and acres of rolling grassy foothills with not a building in sight. He wasn't familiar with this part of the country and did not know how far they were from the nearest town.

"Just stop the car!" The gun waving almost in his face convinced him to obey.

Lee checked his rearview and side mirrors for traffic, saw none, and pulled to the side of the road. He edged off the pavement into the grassy area lining the roadway, not sure what the guy had in mind and hoping to be out of the way of cars that might come by.

"Shut it off and drop the keys here on the seat." Once again, using the gun as a pointer, he emphasized the directions.

Noticing that the man never took his finger off the trigger, Lee was all too willing to comply.

"Okay, get out."

Lee glanced over and saw the man pick up the keys, then slide closer to him in the driver's seat. As Lee stepped out, the man followed him out the same door and nudged him with the gun.

"Step around back."

Standing near the trunk, he was joined by the hitchhiker, who pointed the gun directly at him. "If you make one move, I'll kill you. I won't hesitate to kill you."

Lee could feel his insides quivering and knew the man meant just what he said. He inhaled quietly, determined to present a calm, obedient demeanor. If I don't panic, he thought, I might make it.

He watched as the man threw the keys onto the ground. "Pick them up and open the trunk."

Lee obeyed and watched the man looking inside the trunk, where the large spare tire rested.

"Get that tire out of there and crawl in."

Lee reached into his back pocket. "Look, how about if you just take my wallet and my car and leave me here?"

The gun pointed directly at him. "I told you to get that tire out of there and get in."

Lee pointed at the wrench in the trunk next to the spare. "I'll need to use that tool to get the tire out."

"All right," the man said, his gun still pointed at Lee. "But don't try to hit me with it or I'll kill you." He stepped away and watched Lee work from what he must have thought was a safe distance from the wrench.

Minutes later, the trunk lid slammed down, trapping Lee in the dark trunk. He heard a car door opening, then closing and the roar of the engine, the sound that usually gave him pleasure. As soon as the car started rolling, then picking up speed, Lee took the tire wrench and wedged it into the space between the trunk frame and lid. Wiggling the tool back and forth, he could feel the trunk lid breaking free. The sound of the tires against asphalt as the car continued to speed up, he hoped, covered the sound of him prying the lid.

Sweat rolled down his forehead, dripping into his eyes. He didn't know whether from the temperature in the trunk on this cold December day, or the fear that shook him. Now, to escape without the madman seeing him. Earlier he'd thought maybe the guy wasn't such a bad guy, but his opinion had changed.

Lee held the trunk lid down, not wanting it to fly open if they hit any rough spots in the road, notifying his captor what was about to happen. He waited, hoping that soon the car would slow down. Maybe they'd come upon a little town with stop signs. Every nerve in his body was poised for action, with the plan worked out in his mind. He wasn't sure how much time had passed, but it finally felt like the car was slowing.

"Stay cool," he whispered to himself, "you can do this. Keep your head and you'll make it." The time was here.

Lee inched the trunk lid up slowly, just enough to roll out through the small opening he allowed between the lid and the frame. With adrenaline flowing through him, he hit the ground, rolled, then leaped to his feet and sprinted across the road and toward a farm he could see off in the distance. He heard screeching tires as the kidnapper stopped the car. Lee never looked back, and angry words screaming at him pushed him forward faster. "Come back! Come back or I'll kill you."

Lee's feet dug into the tall grass with every step. He hoped there would be no gopher holes or obstacles to trip him up. Yelling back over his shoulder, "No! No!" he zigzagged as he ran, fully expecting bullets to fly. His breath came in ragged bursts as he continued running, propelled by fear of dying. Then the amazing, oh so very welcome, sound of his car driving away. He didn't even care if he never saw it again. He'd take his life any day over his car.

Running a few hundred yards more, he dove into the grass at the foot of a stand of trees that he'd been aiming for. Throwing himself spread-eagle down into the foot-tall grass, he lay on his back, gasping for air. Once he'd caught his breath, he sat up, looking around and couldn't believe his good fortune. These trees bordered the farm. He just had to make it to the farmhouse.

CHAPTER 12

DECEMBER 30, 1950
ROUTE 66 SOMEWHERE IN OKLAHOMA

Thelma."

No response. Carl took his eyes off the road to glance over at his wife. She was preoccupied with the kids in the back seat, settling a skirmish between the two older kids. He reached over and tapped her thigh.

"Did you need me?" his wife turned her attention away from the back seat.

Carl pointed to the road ahead.

"Yeah, I think I'm going to stop and check on that guy up ahead on the roadside." He dropped his speed as they approached. "Looks like he may have car trouble."

"Good idea," Thelma said. "Maybe we can give him a lift to the next town."

"Momma, can I hold Jasper now? You said it was my turn next." Thelma turned as Carl pulled the car over.

"When Daddy stops to help this man, we'll get out and walk Jasper and let him take a potty break, then it will be your turn, Ronnie." She turned back to Carl. "If we give him a ride, I'll just scoot over so he can ride up front with us instead of in the back with the kids and the dog."

"Sounds good." Carl pulled into the grassy area alongside the highway and shut off the engine. He looked at his wife. "Take the kids over there away from the traffic while I see what I can do to help."

Carl watched as his wife and kids headed to the grassy area away from the road. A broken fence post provided a gateway to explore the land that probably belonged to a local farmer. Their little dog scampered after them, stopping every few feet to wet the fence posts, bushes and boulders. He was glad they'd stopped. Not only could they help this guy who appeared to be stranded, but the kids and dog could get some much needed exercise. They'd been cooped up for hours on this trip, and even though they were just at the travel center, there wasn't anywhere for kids to just be kids and run around. He didn't mind stopping again at the next town. It would be an opportunity to top off the gas tank. He was a cautious traveler and never liked to let the gauge get below the halfway mark.

"Hello there." Carl stretched out his hand as he approached the man standing by the front fender of the car. The open hood signaled to passing motorists that this wasn't just a stop to stretch his legs. "I'm Carl."

The man grunted as he returned the handshake, but if he gave his name, Carl sure didn't understand what he said.

"What's going on with your car?"

The man stepped around to the front and looked under the hood with Carl. "Don't know, just quit running."

"We'd be glad to give you a lift to the next town." Carl motioned to his wife watching the children running around in the farmer's field. "If you don't mind the noise of kids and a dog."

Another grunt. But the man closed the hood and took a step or two toward their car, so Carl took that for agreement that they would travel together.

Carl's shrill whistle got the attention of the kids and Jasper, and the entire group came scampering back to the car. He watched his wife step carefully through the broken fence, while the kids and dog piled into the back seat.

"Who's our new friend, Daddy?" Gary asked as he climbed in. The man ignored the question.

Carl bent down where he stood to watch the kids settle into their places in the back seat, then whispered to them all. "He doesn't talk much, so we'll wait for him to tell us what his name is."

"Okay, Daddy," Gary said, then picked up the paint book he'd brought along. "Daddy, can I have some water to paint?"

Carl smiled, then shook his head. He wondered why Gary chose that to bring when they told them to gather toys to play with in the car. It didn't occur to him that he thought they would let him have water to mix with his paint set. "Ronnie, did you bring crayons?"

"But, Daddy," Gary pointed to the large words on the cover of the book. "It says paint. It doesn't say color."

Ronnie handed the crayons to his dad, then looked at his brother. "You can't even read yet, Gary."

"But it does say paint."

Carl could sense Thelma standing close by where he was bent over conversing with the kids, and he thought he heard some growling coming from their new passenger. "You're right, Gary, it does say paint. But it's okay if you use crayons in the book."

"Okay, Daddy."

Shutting their door, Carl headed around to the driver's side. He scooted in behind the wheel and watched as Thelma situated herself in the middle, then their nameless passenger got in and slammed his door.

He no sooner pulled back out onto the roadway than he felt Thelma squirm. "Carl!" she whispered.

Looking over, Carl spotted a pistol in the hand of his new passenger, then watched as he stuck it in his wife's side. "Just drive!" the man growled.

Carl stared ahead through the windshield, eyes wide, heart beating hard. The kids had gone silent in the back seat as if they sensed the danger. "Oh Lord," he breathed silently as he kept his foot steady on the accelerator. "What have I done? And what do I do now?"

CHAPTER 13

DECEMBER 30, 1950
LUTHER, OKLAHOMA

Deputy Sheriff Bob Turner looked over the car stuck in ruts that had dug into the grassy area alongside the highway. It was definitely the car they got the call about. The license plate and description matched.

He'd had his doubts at first when he ran a background check on the caller, a Lee Burd Archer, and discovered he had quite a criminal history himself. Five different stints in prison, but nothing in the last two years.

Only a few days away from being installed as sheriff of Oklahoma County, Bob figured this might be the last call of this type he'd go out on. Seemed to be a minor incident—no injury, theft of eighty-five dollars and with the car being recovered only a few miles from where it was stolen at least this portion of the crime was handled. Once Mr. Archer arrived and inspected the car, they'd take a thorough description of the perpetrator and put other law enforcement agencies on alert about a kidnapper and car thief in the area. Looking around at the flattened down grass behind the car, it looked like possibly the man got a ride with another traveler.

He watched as the patrol car with the deputy he'd sent to retrieve Mr. Archer pulled up behind the car.

"Yep, that's my car," Mr. Archer said. He went right to the trunk that wasn't latched properly. "I probably broke the latch when I pried this open."

He didn't know why, but Deputy Turner felt relieved at the physical proof of the man's story so far. You never knew with someone who had a background of being incarcerated multiple times if you were getting the truth, or some fabricated story hoping to explain away the predicament they were in.

"Can we see your identification, please?" Turner approached the man. He motioned for them to talk on the passenger side of the vehicle, away from traffic.

After verifying it was as the man had reported when he called from the farmhouse where he had escaped, he opened the passenger door. "Can you check through the car and see if anything is missing?"

"Well, I can tell you right off," Mr. Archer said, "this duffel bag here isn't mine." He picked up a bag from the front passenger floorboard and held it out for the deputy to see.

"Was the man carrying that when you picked him up?"

"I believe he was. To tell you the truth, I didn't pay that much attention, but as I recall, he was hitchhiking and he might have been carrying something when I spotted him on the road and pulled over."

Deputy Turner took hold of the handle as Mr. Archer offered it to him. "Can you check further and see if anything is missing or there is anything else that doesn't belong to you?"

Mr. Archer slid into the passenger seat and then leaned over, examining a piece of paper tucked into the crease of the driver's side. He pulled out a folded paper, opened it, and then looked back at the deputy. "This sure isn't mine."

Turner looked at the paper, now unfolded, that was handed to him. "W.E. Cook paid forty-five dollars for the purchase of a .32 snub-nose pistol in El Paso, Texas." He looked up at Mr. Archer. "Does that describe the pistol you say he was pointing at you?"

"Sure does."

Mr. Archer's story sounded more believable with each new discovery.

"El Paso!" his partner said. "That's over 700 miles away. This man has done some traveling in the last few days. Look at the date on that receipt."

"December 27." Turner nodded, then looked to Mr. Archer. "Was he by any chance standing near a disabled car when you picked him up?"

"No, sir. Just a hitchhiker, with no visible means of transportation."

"Suppose he hitchhiked from El Paso all the way to..." He looked at Archer. "Where did you say you picked him up?"

"Lubbock, Texas."

"So that's what, maybe about three hundred, four hundred miles," Turner said. "I suppose it could be done."

"So how did I get lucky enough to be the one he stole a car from?" Archer said, as he slipped his driver's license back into his wallet, then dangled it in front of the deputies. "And cleaned me out of all my cash, too."

"You have to wonder," the other deputy said, "did he do this to anyone else before you? We'll have to check the reports coming in and see if there are any other kidnapping or auto theft reports between El Paso and here."

"We've got a name," Turner said. "We can start by running that, although it's a pretty common name. Probably hundreds of Cooks in this part of the country."

Lee slid across the front seat over into the driver's seat. The keys dangled in the ignition.

"See if it starts."

He gave a thumbs-up to the deputy, then turned the key. Nothing at first. He tried again, still nothing. Either a dead battery or worse.

"Not only did he steal my money and my car, it sounds like he ran it out of gas or something broke." Walking around the car, he pointed to the small bearings in the grass near the rear wheel. "Look here," he said to the sheriff. "Looks like he burned out the wheel bearings."

"We'll get it towed to the sheriff's garage so we can go through the car to see if there are any more clues that will lead us to this kidnapper."

"Hope you hang him when you find him," Lee said.

"Well, hanging's not going to happen, but this has become a federal crime, bringing you against your will across a state line."

Deputy Turner pulled his wallet out and removed a ten-dollar bill. He turned back to Archer. "Hate to have you stranded so far from home with no money. So maybe you can take this, get a meal, get a bus ticket and get back home."

"And that is why you just got voted in to be our new sheriff," his partner said.

"Are you saying I buy votes?" Turner wasn't sure how to take that.

"No, not at all. You care. You really care about the people you serve."

"I'll second that," Archer said.

Turner picked up the duffel bag from where he had dropped it on the ground next to the car. "I'll load this into my patrol car." He turned to his partner. "Get Archer's phone number and address, just in case the dispatcher didn't get it, and then drop him off at the bus station." He reached out a hand to Archer, who grasped his in a nice firm handshake. "We'll be in touch with you if we have questions, and you call us if you remember anything else about this Cook fellow other than what you've already told us."

"I'll be glad to do that," Mr. Archer said. "And thanks again for the money."

CHAPTER 14

DECEMBER 30, 1950
WICHITA FALLS, TEXAS

Pull in here."

Carl felt Thelma cringe as the man sitting next to her motioned with his snub-nosed pistol toward the gas station they were approaching. He wanted to reassure her that they would be okay. He had a plan to get help at the gas station. If all went as planned, within ten or fifteen minutes, they would be safe.

As they eased up next to the gasoline pump, the gunman said, "Tell that old geezer to pump the gas and then bring us out some lunch meat."

Carl nodded, but hoped they'd get a chance to go inside the store. That would give him longer to get control of the man. He had it worked out to get behind him and grab him, knocking the gun out of his hand and pinning his arms to his side.

The attendant started the gas flowing into the car, then turned toward them. "Follow me inside. You'll have to come in to get your food. We don't sell it out here."

Carl could hear the gunman growling under his breath as the two of them followed side by side behind the older man.

As soon as they stepped inside, Carl hesitated a second, letting the gunman get a step or two ahead of him. The old man had slipped in behind the counter and stood near the cash register. As the gunman began looking around the store, Carl reached around him with both arms, squeezing him tight. "Help me!" he yelled.

Before the man behind the counter could react, the gunman wiggled free and the two men wrestled, falling against a window display. "Help me! He's going to kill my family!" Carl yelled as he heard breaking glass where they had crashed into the shelves on display by the window. Try as he might to knock the pistol out of the gunman's hand, the guy held tight.

"Get out of my store or I'll shoot you both! Get out right now!" Carl spotted what looked like a .44 caliber six-shooter in the store owner's hand and knew he meant business. He'd never get out of this alive with two guns threatening to shoot him.

The gunman dragged Carl to the door as he continued to yell. "You have to help me. He's going to kill my family!"

Carl heard a lock clicking on the door as soon as they were outside. His heart sank when he realized his plan had failed. He wondered if the man really would kill them all now that he had tried to escape.

Eldon Cornwell sank into his recliner that evening. At sixty-two years of age, he was ready to give up. *Lord, what have I done? Take me, just take me now. I sold that innocent family down the road. I will never get that out of my mind. I could have saved them. But I failed.*

He looked over as his wife joined him in the living room. She took her usual spot in the corner of the sofa. Her knitting basket sat untouched on the floor.

"Eldon, you okay?"

He stared blankly. He had no answer for her.

"You hardly spoke a word all through supper. Didn't you like the food?"

His faithful wife. Every night for nigh on forty years she had dinner waiting when he came home from his job at the gas station and market. Forty years. Wasn't it about time for a fellow to retire? How long can a man go on selling gas and bread and snacks? *How long, dear Lord?* Maybe until he condemns a family to death?

"Food was good, dear." He realized he needed to respond before she questioned him further.

She was a lucky soul. She had no clue about the evil going on out in the world. The news didn't interest her. She focused her time on keeping house, baking and cooking, taking care of him, and volunteering at church. Good things. Her mind was clear of evil. The evil that consumed his thoughts right now. He could see that man's face. The one with the damaged eyelid that hung down, so it wasn't quite closed, but wasn't quite open. The other man screaming for his help.

Now it was crystal clear who was the bad guy. Then, when he could have intervened and rescued the man, rescued his whole family, it was a blur. He recalled the men scuffling, a gun in the hand of one of them, but with arms flailing and bodies moving every which way, voices screaming out, it didn't occur to him one was a good guy. He figured they were putting on a ruse, probably going to rob him. Then they slammed through the window, breaking it and he remembered pulling out his .44 and screaming for them to "get on outta my store."

The other man's words haunted him the rest of the day and he couldn't get them out of his head even now. "He's going to kill me and take my wife." The words were on a ticker tape running through his mind over and over and over again.

He remembered rushing to lock the door behind the men after he had chased them out of the store while brandishing his own gun. He thought he'd feel safe once they were locked outside. But peering out the window as the men got back in the car, he could clearly see now that the one with the gun was the shorter man with the funny eye. He was behind the tall man, shoving the gun in his back, pushing him into the car, and then crawling in after him. But what got to him the most were those little faces looking out the back window.

Three little kids, staring out the back window as if they knew somehow, that he'd had the power to save their daddy. He could hear their cries in his head. But that was crazy. Even from the store, he couldn't really hear their cries, but he knew that's what was going on in that car. Even those kids knew their daddy was in danger. They all were in danger. And what had he, Eldon Owen Cornwell, done? He'd chased them out of the store, like the coward that he was. He fought to hold back the tears that formed. He couldn't let his wife see, so he leaned his head back, closing his eyes.

"I guess you had a rough day at work, Eldon." She must have risen from the sofa. He felt her hand on his shoulder. "I'll just let you rest. I've got some laundry to fold in the bedroom."

He sighed with relief as she left the room. Not a moment too soon. The tears rolled as he struggled to get the voices and images out of his head.

He remembered watching and praying as Claude Skinner, one of his regular customers who'd watched the entire scene, said he'd chase them down. He returned moments later.

"They shot at me!" Claude yelled as he shoved through the door. "Give me the phone."

Eldon had listened in once Claude got the police department on the phone. He could only guess what the person said on the other end of the line. But Claude's demeanor and agitated voice surely conveyed the urgency of his words.

"They came in here yelling and screaming, squabbling and waving a gun around."

He paused, then responded. "Yes, two men. Mr. Cornwell chased them out of the store, then we realized one man might be in danger, so I took off after them in my truck."

Another pause, "Yeah, it was a Chevy Sedan, blue. Looked to be about a '49 or '50. And there were kids and a woman in the back seat. But then, the one man started shooting at me. He was hanging out the passenger window."

Must have been more talking on the other end. "No," Claude had said, "I didn't get the license number, but that plate sure enough was from Illinois."

Eldon remembered the hat he'd found, and waved it in front of Claude as he talked, then motioned to the tag inside. He'd found the hat on the floor near where the men had scuffled.

"Yeah, the one man left a hat here, says it's from some store in Decatur, Illinois. That family is in danger. I just know it. You gotta find them."

It was the last thing he remembered hearing Claude say to the police dispatcher. After that, Eldon had gone into his back room and collapsed with the haunting picture of the kids in the back window staring at him, as if begging for help. And he'd failed. Oh, good Lord, he'd failed. He'd never forgive himself if something happened to them.

CHAPTER 15

DECEMBER 31, 1950
SOMEWHERE IN TEXAS

"Where were you headed?"

Startled, Carl realized the guy seemed to be making conversation. The only sense of normalcy since this craziness had started. Two days driving with this character and he didn't even know his name. Maybe it was time to try something new.

"Albuquerque," Carl said. "To visit my brother."

He glanced over and saw him nod briefly.

"Say, what's your name, anyway? I'm Carl."

He looked in the mirror to make eye contact with his wife when he heard her moan from the back seat. Of course she wouldn't want him befriending their kidnapper, but he had to try a new tactic. Maybe the guy needed a friend.

"Depends. Sometimes William, some call me Bill, some Billy."

He hadn't really expected an answer, and definitely not one that long. "Well, Bill, we were planning on stopping at Carlsbad Caverns along the way. Have you ever been there?"

Out of the corner of his eye, he could see the man looking at him before he finally answered. "Huh-uh." He gestured with his gun toward the windshield. "Let's go there then."

"Look, Mister."

Carl held his breath as his oldest son, Ronnie, held a brochure over the seat, extending it toward Bill. "You can read about it here."

The man surprised him when he took the brochure for the caverns and studied it briefly.

"They got bats," Gary said, and Carl winced inwardly, wondering how much his kids had been picking up on during this two-day nightmare. And wondering what was going on in their little minds right now. Listening to their dad carry on a conversation with the bad man, as if he were a friend. Was it possible they could befriend the man, help him with whatever struggles he had that caused him to kidnap and threaten his captives?

"Mommy brought food so we can eat in the lunchroom," Ronnie said. Carl remembered back to the days safely at home when they had planned the trip. Watched the television show about the caverns, read the brochure together as a family. Learned about the lunchroom, where visitors could stop and eat while hiking down into the caves. It seemed ages ago. His wife's voice shocked him.

"We have enough for you, Bill, if you'd like to join us in the lunchroom at the Caverns." He wondered if Bill could detect the tremor in Thelma's voice. He caught her eye in the mirror and winked, grateful for her strength, for her understanding that they were in this together and they had to work hard to escape, no matter what it took.

Carl could see the gun pointed his way and glanced over at the sounds of Bill's gruff voice. "Just drive."

It seemed the friendly conversation was over. As the miles ticked by, he was glad to see the kids drift off in the back seat. The last mileage marker he'd seen said the caverns were about sixty miles ahead. He needed a plan in case the one of friendship didn't work. And by the look of the gun perpetually pointed in his direction, he really didn't expect that would work. He began formulating a plan. He estimated Bill was a good three to four inches shorter than he was, and he could probably overtake him if he could get behind him. He probably had fifteen or twenty pounds on the guy, so surely he could overpower him. If he got behind him, the gun wouldn't be pointing at him. He needed to signal Thelma to keep away with the kids, in case the gun went off.

He glanced over at the lightweight jacket Bill wore, and an idea formed. Thankful he'd brought an extra jacket, he'd offer Bill his new leather jacket. Thelma might not like that, since she'd just given it to him for Christmas, but if he could entice Bill to wear that one, since it will be cold in the caverns, he might get the advantage while he's putting the jacket on.

CHAPTER 16

DECEMBER 31, 1950
ALBUQUERQUE, NEW MEXICO

First Lieutenant Chris Mosser paced the floor. His twin brother, Carl, and family should have been here by now. They should have arrived late last night or early this morning.

"Maybe they had car trouble," Mary said.

He looked over at his wife. He hadn't said a thing, but as always she seemed to read his mind. Chris stood at the window, watching for his brother and family to arrive. They all had plans to celebrate New Year's Eve together that evening, then attend the Watch Night service at church as midnight got close. Tomorrow, January 1, they would celebrate with friends. He wanted to introduce his brother to the neighborhood. No one believed he had a twin brother, and now he'd be able to show them that even at age thirty-three they still looked almost identical. He remembered fooling their schoolteachers growing up, but no matter how many times they tried to fool their mother, she could always tell them apart. She wouldn't tell them what her secret was.

Thinking of his mother reminded him of his concerns. He wouldn't want her to know Carl was late arriving. She'd be sick with worry.

Mary stepped closer and put an arm around his shoulder, while they both looked out over the front yard. "Do you think it could be car trouble?"

"No, not Carl. He's a stickler for keeping his automobile in top shape. Besides, if they broke down somewhere and were getting work done, he'd find a way to call and let me know." Chris looked over at his wife and felt himself nibbling on his inner lower lip, a habit he'd had since a youth when he was worried. "I just feel something isn't right. But I don't know what to do."

"I'm praying," Mary said. "I've been praying ever since they didn't arrive last night."

"Do you feel it too?"

"You mean you feel like something is wrong?" Mary didn't make eye contact when she responded. He knew. Even if she wouldn't say it, he knew her unwillingness to look him in the eye meant she was worried about his brother, too.

"You do, don't you?"

"I'm sorry, Chris," Mary turned to him. "I guess I have had an uncomfortable feeling. So I've been praying."

"I think I'll drive down to the police station and let them know my concern. Maybe they'll know if there have been any accidents along Highway 66 between here and Illinois."

"Do you know your brother's license plate number?" the officer on duty asked.

"I don't, but it's an Illinois license plate. He's driving a 1950 Chevy sedan, dark blue. They left home early on the 29th and expected to pull in here late last night. He said they'd be following Route 66 nearly the entire way." Chris looked at his watch. Almost noon. "He's at least twelve hours overdue. It's not like him. He's punctual. He stays in touch if there are problems. He never just leaves us hanging like this."

"I haven't heard of any accidents along the main thoroughfare between here and Illinois," the officer said. "I'll run this by my superior, but I should be able to put a message out to other law enforcement offices along the route to be on the watch for your brother's car." Carl watched as the officer wrote everything he had told him, including the number of occupants in the car and the names of his brother Carl and wife Thelma.

"I can't promise we'll hear anything soon, but we'll give it a try." The officer looked up at him. "You might also try reaching out to some radio stations. Maybe write up a little announcement about your brother and his family being overdue on their trip. Don't want to sound the alarm yet like there is foul play, but definitely alert people to be watching out for him. Maybe get word to your brother to get in touch with you and let you know what's going on. Something like that."

"That's a great idea," Chris said. "You know, I think I'll make up a flier, see if I can get some printed real fast, and if he isn't here by this afternoon, I might just head out along the highway and start handing out the fliers at some of the road stops where travelers get gas and food."

"Good idea," the officer said. "Maybe you can include a family photo. Someone out there is bound to have seen them or maybe even helped them if they're having trouble. Don't forget to put your phone number on it."

CHAPTER 17

DECEMBER 31, 1950
JOPLIN, MISSOURI

Detective Nutt held the flier that had come across the teletype late that afternoon. It was the first he'd heard of the missing family. Traveling from Illinois to Albuquerque, they very likely passed through his town. Or at least should have. Depends on whether they broke down before making it this far.

He would put out a notification to the officers in his department and contact the other law enforcement branches in the area in case they hadn't seen the flier yet.

Walking over to his desk, he settled in the high-backed office chair, examining the rough copy of the family photo. Nice family. His heart ached a bit, as it did every time he saw a photo of a young family. But he imagined not as much as Goldie's did. She'd wanted children from the moment they got married. He remembered her talking about her longing to be a mother even while they were dating. He supposed they'd begun trying to become parents right from the very start of their marriage almost four years earlier. Doctors gave them no hope. He'd watched Goldie smile through her hurt. It was her way. Always smiling.

He wondered if they had ever had children, what they would have been. This family was blessed with both. Two boys and a cute little girl. Bet she'll be spoiled, he guessed, knowing that's what he'd do if he had two older boys and then a sweet little baby girl came along.

Picking up the phone, he dialed the sheriff's office. Time to quit pondering the disappointment of childlessness in his and Goldie's lives and help this family get back on the road. Maybe a local law enforcement officer would find them broken down somewhere on the outskirts of Joplin. He hoped he could call Chris Mosser, the brother listed on the flier, to give him the good news that they had found their family.

CHAPTER 18

JANUARY 1, 1951
CARLSBAD CAVERNS, NEW MEXICO

C arl drove all night, adrenaline flowing the closer they got to their destination. He'd worked out his plan and rehearsed it over and over in his head. Occasional glances over at their captor never revealed whether or not he was actually asleep. While he slumped some, his right eye never closed. He hadn't asked the guy if something was wrong with it, but the droopy lid and the fact that it never closed led him to believe it was a deformity, maybe from birth.

Pulling into the nearly empty parking lot, he turned off the car, and as the monotonous rumble that had lulled his back seat passengers to sleep quieted, they began to stir.

Working hard to keep the friendly persona up and not scare the kids, Carl said, "Looks like we'll be having breakfast in the lunchroom." He did his best to smile and keep his voice sounding happy. Though he felt far from it. His stomach muscles tensed as he rehearsed again and again what his plan was to take control of this Bill character.

"Tell you what," Carl said, once Thelma and the children were fully awake. As he turned to look over the back seat, he could see Bill scanning the area outside their car. He thought the young man was enthralled with the desert landscaping, but he wasn't sure.

"It's cold out and it will be cold in the caverns, so I'm going to get coats out of the trunk for all of us and I want you kids to stay in the car with Mom, so you'll be warm until we get out." He stared hard into Thelma's eyes, doing his best to send a message to her that he had a plan and she needed to stay inside to keep the children safe. Her slight nod assured him she understood and would abide by what he'd said.

He turned to Bill. "I've got a leather jacket you're welcome to wear, if you think you might like it. Should be warmer than the one you have on."

"Carl." He knew Thelma would object to lending his new jacket, but one look at her, and she seemed to understand. Her tone changed. "That's a good idea," she said, looking toward Bill, who ignored her.

"Come on, Bill," Carl said as he opened his door, let's go around to the trunk and get the jacket.

Carl's heart beat hard as Bill exited the car the way he always did, sliding over to follow him out the driver's side door. He tried to keep from alternately squeezing his hands into fists and straightening them out, hoping Bill would not notice his nervousness. He saw Bill slip the gun into his pants pocket and knew that part of his plan wouldn't work now, but he'd still do his best. The goal had been to knock it out of his hand after gaining control of him.

Around back, Carl slipped the key in the lock, turned it and eased the heavy trunk lid open. He couldn't believe his good fortune. There was the leather jacket lying on top of the suitcase near the rear of the trunk. He pointed to Bill. "There it is. Why don't you grab it while I stretch the kinks out of my muscles?" Raising his arms high overhead felt good. He'd been in the same position for hours. As Bill leaned over to retrieve the jacket, Carl stepped behind him, throwing his arms around the shorter man and holding on tight. His plan to step backward and take him down to the ground went awry, as Bill reacted first, stepping back with his right foot, then turning his body. A quick bend over before Carl could react, and he had grasped Carl's legs by the back of the knees, tossing him up and over his shoulder almost effortlessly.

Carl's head slammed on the ground, and as he struggled to get back up, he saw Bill standing over him with the gun pointed at his head.

"Try something like that again, and you'll all die."

Bill motioned to Carl with the gun. "We need to get back on the road."

CHAPTER 19

JANUARY 1, 1951
WINTHROP, ARKANSAS

His brother had to know something was wrong by now. They were long overdue. If only his brother were with him, the two of them together could take out this lunatic. But alone, with his wife and children at risk, Carl hardly dared try anything else. Already twice he had failed at overtaking the stubby guy. He must have learned those wrestling moves in prison. He heard the guy say once he wasn't going back to prison again.

If only the old man in that store had been on his side, they'd be safe now. Instead, they'd been trapped in this car for days with this wild man. No sleep, just constant driving. It was a wonder he hadn't fallen asleep at the wheel and wrecked the car, killing them all.

He took occasional glances out the side of his eye as he drove, whenever the man barked out orders for which roads to take, which stores to stop at. But with the gun trained on his kids in the back seat, there was no way he was taking a chance at making this man angrier than he already was. He pondered attempting to grab the gun the next time they came to a stoplight, but even then it was too risky. One of his kids might get shot. Thankfully, they had slept through much of the journey, probably from the exhaustion of the constant traveling, not to mention the stress that fear played in their little bodies. He knew what it was doing to his insides, and couldn't imagine how scared the children were.

He'd heard Thelma whispering to them when they were awake, trying to quiet their tears, keeping them occupied. But the hardest thing for her was the questions. "Who is that man, Mommy? What does he want? Why does he have that gun? When are we going to get to our uncle's house?"

Carl nodded inside. He didn't dare show any body movement that would cause this crazy man to question his thoughts or his movements. But he wondered all the same things himself. And then he had a crazy thought. Should he try to reason with this man? Find out what his motive was. What was the goal in all of this? He was a farmer, though not a psychotherapist. He had no idea where to begin.

"Pull over at that cafe."

The man's words interrupted his thoughts.

"Gimme that thermos," he growled at Thelma. Tears of exhaustion and fear rolled down her cheeks as Carl watched her reaction to the man speaking to her.

"Now, lady, gimme the thermos."

"It's…it's…empty," she stuttered as the tears flowed, then sobs.

"Shut your mouth and give it to me. We're gonna get it filled here." He pointed the gun at Carl while keeping his eyes trained on her. "Don't you and those little brats try nothing while we're inside, or your husband's a dead man. You understand?"

Carl watched, immobilized with fear, as Thelma threw her hands up over her face, nodding her head and sobbing. Thankfully, the children kept sleeping. He didn't know how—maybe by the grace of God. Maybe sheer exhaustion from the intense fear.

Walking into the cafe ahead of the man with the gun in his jacket pocket, Carl knew it was aimed at him. He'd learned after three days with this madman to do what he was told or die. And then if he died, what would become of his wife and children? For their sake, he followed the orders. His goal, to keep himself alive so they weren't left alone with this evil man. And to keep watching for the moment he could get the jump on him. If he could just disarm him, he knew he could protect himself against the smaller man. But the gun put him at a definite disadvantage. He swore he would never go unarmed again if he escaped alive.

Back in the car, Carl watched as the man lit up a cigarette from the new package he just bought, then was stunned when he held out the pack to offer him one. Carl shook his head and then passed food back to Thelma that he'd managed to buy while inside the cafe, and also a jar of water. The children had to be thirsty. He watched them stirring as he climbed back behind the wheel, always knowing there was a gun pointed either at him or his family.

"Head north."

This man seemed to have a destination. Carl couldn't wait to arrive at whatever the destination was. And once this man was out of his car, he would never pick up another hitchhiker again in his life.

CHAPTER 20

JANUARY 1, 1951
TAHOKA, TEXAS

First day of the year and what a way to start it. Lee Archer realized he once again had not remembered to pay his phone bill before leaving on the trip that went haywire. So not only did he get kidnapped and his car stolen, but he came home to discover his phone service had been disconnected.

Now what to do? No car, no way to call anyone to help with transportation or to inquire about his car. He had left them the address of the auto shop where he worked. He wondered whether the sheriff would have his car towed there. That would make sense, because it was going to need work.

He wondered if they'd caught the guy who had kidnapped him and stolen his car. He hoped so before anyone else became a victim. But even with the challenges he had right now, at least he was alive. That guy very well could have shot him when he told him to climb in the trunk.

He briefly thought about hitchhiking to work, but that left a bad taste in his mouth after his experience with the hitchhiker a couple of days ago. Maybe he could talk his neighbor into giving him a lift so he could find out if his car was there. He didn't even have any money since that guy robbed him, too. He'd used up the last of the ten dollars the sheriff had given him to ride the bus home when he got something to eat after getting back into town the day before. With it being the weekend and then a holiday, the bank wasn't open, but if he could just hold out until the next day, he could get money out of the bank and then pay his phone bill.

Lee was thrilled to see his car parked to the side of the automotive repair shop where he worked. He had brought his extra set of car keys just in case. "Thanks, George," he said, then waved goodbye to the old man who lived next door to him. He couldn't wait to get to work on his car.

By tomorrow, he hoped to have it running again and in the next couple of days to get the phone turned back on. Then, he might give that sheriff a call to see if they found the guy and thank him for having his car towed back.

CHAPTER 21

JANUARY 1, 1951
OKMULGEE, OKLAHOMA

Three hours had passed since their last stop. Surely the children needed to relieve themselves. Would the man allow that? Carl felt like a defeated man at the thought that he had to get permission from another man for his children to tend to their bathroom needs. He fought back tears. He couldn't let his children know how scared he was and could not further embolden their captor by letting him see the fear that was growing larger and larger within himself.

Carl watched as their captor led his wife and children to the bathroom around the back side of this service station. The attendant filled the tank while he waited behind the wheel. He wanted to tell the man that they had been kidnapped. Tell the man to get help. To call the police. To do something.

Just as he got out of the car and headed around to speak in private to the man filling the gas tank, Bill appeared from the backside of the building. The gun was still in his pocket, but Carl knew he was aiming it at him, the awkward way the jacket was held up in his direction. And with him standing between Carl and his family, he couldn't risk it, could he? Oh Lord, he did not know what to do. He had never been in a situation like this before. And there seemed to be no answers. Even doing his best to protect his family didn't seem to be enough. What was this man's endgame? Was it to arrive at a destination and get out of their car…or was it worse?

CHAPTER 22

JANUARY 2, 1951
JOPLIN, MISSOURI

C arl glanced at his wristwatch. The illuminated dial showed
1:30 a.m. Surely his brother had alerted the authorities they
were missing by now. The road sign they just passed showed
Joplin, Missouri, forty-five miles ahead. Looking down at his
odometer, he saw they'd driven nearly a thousand miles since
leaving home, and yet they were nowhere near his brother's
house. In fact, not even on the route. So if Chris had people
out looking for them, it would be like hunting for a needle in a
haystack. How would they have a clue where to look? If he knew
Chris, he was probably out looking himself. If only there were a
way to let him know.

He heard the children stirring in the back and watched
Thelma comforting them as they woke up cranky and crying.

"Look, Momma, a police car," Ronnie's voice sounded from
the back seat, rising above the cries of the children.

"A police car, Carl!" Thelma's words could hardly be
understood through her sobbing.

"Shut them up right now!" Bill said. Three days together and Carl still did not know what his last name was. He should find out, so he could tell the authorities when they were finally rescued. But it didn't seem like the time to say, by the way, what is your last name, so I can report you? Carl felt himself snort at the ridiculous late-night humor he found in the midst of their nightmare.

He wanted to flash his lights at the patrol car as it passed them, do something to signal, but the gun was out and wedged into his side. The man must have realized that if he pointed it in the back at the children, the silhouette of a gun might be visible in the headlights of the passing patrol car.

Once the policeman passed them by, he watched as his wife appeared to lose all hope. Her hysterical cries ramped up the sobs of the children, and the noise in the car reached unbearable levels, not only to him, but to Bill as well, it seemed.

"Pull over! Pull over right now! I'm going to put an end to this!"

"No! No! No!" Thelma screamed, with the children joining in. Carl had no clue how to quiet her. He couldn't tell her everything would be okay because he was fully convinced that it would not be okay. He was starting to realize it would never be okay again.

After following directions, they found themselves down a dark side street off the two-lane highway that would lead them into Joplin, or home, as their captor called it.

"Get out your suitcase and give me some shirts," the man said.

"Not my suitcase, Carl, not my suitcase!" Thelma, still hysterical, squeaked the words out. Carl wondered, with their lives at risk, what was so special to Thelma about her suitcase that she didn't want the man getting into it. Maybe it was that something of hers needed to be protected from the man. If not her person and her children and her husband, then at least her clothes and personal items she had packed. Could something be safe? Maybe that's what his wife, in her delirious state, was thinking.

The man watched as he opened the trunk, popped open a suitcase, then pulled out a couple of his dress shirts. What difference did it make at this point if the man got hold of his good shirts or his play shirts? He wondered whether he would ever need these clothes again.

Bill pulled out a knife and jabbed a hole in the shirt, then ripped it into strips. Carl followed him as he went back around to the car, where the crying and screaming had ramped up another notch. Bill started with Thelma, grabbing her wrists and tying them together, she squirmed and screamed while he reached down and did the same to her ankles, then up to her mouth, the man held the gun up, "You hold still or I'll shoot you right now in front of the whole family."

"Thelma," Carl mouthed as she looked his way, fear in his eyes. "Please, shhhh."

That seemed to calm her, and she held still while he stuffed a wad of torn material into her mouth, then tied a strip around her mouth and cinched it tight in the back. Pamela Sue climbed onto her mother's lap, as if to comfort her, and Carl watched devastated as the man also tied his little daughter's wrists together, then her ankles and finished with a strip around her mouth, tied in the back of her head.

The boys watched, silent now, but shaking in fear, still wearing their Hopalong Cassidy hats they'd been so excited to show their Uncle Chris. The madman ripped the hats off their heads, pulled his knife back out and cut off the cords attached to the hats. He tied their hands with the cords, cinching them tight, then used strips from the shirt to finish their ankles and cover their mouths, tying them in the back of their heads. Thelma, looking almost catatonic, watched, her eyes dull and lifeless. Unable to scream because of the gag. She could embrace Pamela Sue, who still sat on her lap, by dropping her arms down over Pam's head. Pam seemed content as long as she was on her mommy's lap.

"Now, I can think," Bill said. He pulled the gun out of his pocket and motioned with it for Carl to get behind the wheel. "Let's get back on the road."

Thelma watched from the back seat as her husband followed the directions of their abductor. He'd referred to Joplin as his home. Would he be satisfied when they arrived? Could they drop him off at his house and finally be free of him? She clung to Pamela Sue in her lap, thankful the little girl was drifting to sleep in her arms. Why hadn't that police car noticed them? Surely Chris would have alerted the authorities that they were missing. Told them what kind of car to look for.

What are the chances there would be another patrol car on this lonely road in the middle of the night? She could hope, couldn't she? She thought she'd lost all hope back when he was tying them all up, but now, as they drove and the children fell back asleep, she was renewing her hope. Maybe, just maybe, another police car would come along and would spot them and pull them over. It had to happen. Please, Lord Jesus, let that happen, she whispered.

Thelma watched the gunman tense and sit up straight, staring into the distance at headlights coming their way. They hadn't passed another car in the last twenty minutes. Would this be the patrol car she prayed for? Would he spot their car and pull them over and rescue them? The closer the car got to them, Thelma could make out the silhouette of the police lights on top of the car. Her heart beat hard at the realization that this might be their rescuer. This police officer had to see them and know they were in trouble. She could not take much more of this. Three days of driving with a crazed kidnapper. If she had a gun, she'd shoot this man dead. Anything to free her family.

She could hardly contain herself as the car got closer.

"Keep your eyes straight ahead," the gunman barked at Carl. "Don't even look over when he passes, or you're a dead man."

The minute the car got even with them, Thelma struggled to scream, but with the gag in her mouth, she couldn't get much sound out. She was stunned when the policeman drove right on by without even looking. Working at the bonds around her wrists and feet, she screamed around the gag. She could not take this another minute.

Suddenly, Bill Cook turned and pointed the gun straight at her chest. No threats this time. She heard Carl hollering, "No-o-o-o-o," then a sharp snap like a firecracker.

Carl turned his head just in time to see his wife go limp. He yanked the wheel hard to the right and slammed on the brakes. Before he could disarm the man, three more shots rang out. Then the gun turned on him. The last thing he heard was the crack of the gun firing the fifth shot.

CHAPTER 23

JANUARY 3, 1951
OSAGE COUNTY, OKLAHOMA

Deputy?" Jed Wilson couldn't see his own face, but the Tulsa police officer knew it had to be white. He was near collapsing. He'd never seen anything like this in his years on the force. Jed had been called in to help the Osage County deputy sheriffs after reports brought them to the car that was found parked near a ditch on the border of the two counties. Apparently, passersby had been ignoring the car since yesterday, thinking it belonged to hunters. Finally, someone had called in the report of the abandoned vehicle that turned out to be key evidence in the multi-state manhunt going on.

The bullet-riddled car was drenched with blood. But where were the owners of the car? And where was the killer?

"Look here!" Jed pointed to the slugs embedded low in the back seat. Nearby was a child's paint book, stained with blood.

He was glad he wouldn't be the officer to report back to the family member who had reported them missing. There were still no answers as to the whereabouts of the family, but from the looks of this car, they had not survived. The maniac thousands of officers were hunting was indeed the evil killer they suspected he would become. How many more victims would he have before they found and stopped him?

Deputy Sheriff Warren Smith examined the area where the slugs were embedded. They'd be removed soon, as other officers joined in the inspection of the car. "Get me some evidence bags, Jed."

Slipping on protective gloves, Warren sifted through the debris on the floor, finding six exploded cartridges from a .32 caliber weapon. Handing them to Jed, who had returned with the bags, he continued searching the front seat area. He studied the bloody knife he found jammed in the seat behind where the driver would sit and wondered, did he stab them before shooting them? After looking around at the clothes with bloodstains, the children's toys and hats, he determined to leave everything as they found it until the car was towed to the garage. He felt sure that Lt. Chris Mosser, the brother, would want to examine the car just as they found it. He'd been told the man planned to drive all night to identify the car, although it was already pretty clear who the car belonged to. Scattered on the floor in the back seat, he found identification for Carl Mosser and his wife Thelma, along with Traveler's Checks made out to Mr. Mosser.

Warren stepped away from the car to approach the group of reporters standing behind the cordoned-off area, who were waiting for a statement. He owed it to them, he knew. This case had become a nationwide nightmare, and with hundreds, maybe thousands of people helping search, he owed it to them all to give some information. No matter how hard it was to talk about what he had just found out, and what it meant for the missing family.

"We're almost certain we've got a whole family dead somewhere." Warren looked around at the reporters, some wiping tears as they jotted notes. "It's just a question now of finding them."

"Deputy, can you tell us how you know this car belongs to the missing family?"

"Tomorrow we will have a definite identification from the victim's brother, Army Lt. Chris Mosser. He is driving all night to get here from Albuquerque, New Mexico, where he is stationed. But as of now, I can tell you the items we've seen are a good indication it belongs to the missing Mosser family."

He took a deep breath and scanned the evening skyline behind the reporters, then resumed his job.

After sharing the info about the items they'd found, he watched as most of them scurried away, most likely to get back to the newspaper offices so they could get this into the morning editions. He probably should have told them about the bloody clothing belonging to the man and woman and children, but he just couldn't bring himself to say all that right now. He'd prefer to let the man's brother see it for himself before reading about it in headlines.

CHAPTER 24

JANUARY 4, 1951
TULSA, OKLAHOMA

Two miles away from where the car had been recovered, Deputy Sheriff Warren Smith watched as Army Lieutenant Chris Mosser fought tears while he examined the car that gave evidence to the horrible end to his brother's life along with his young family

Chris reached in and touched the children's paint book, splattered with blood, and struggled to hold back sobs that squeaked out even as he worked hard to stay quiet.

"Mr. Mosser, I do want to let you know that we'll be giving reporters access to photograph the car after you've taken the time you need."

Chris nodded. "It's okay. So many people have helped. They deserve to know."

"Mr. Mosser, step over here and look at what we discovered," Warren said. With the driver's side door open, he pointed to the service station sticker. "It reads 15,500 miles were on the odometer on December 28, which we believe was the day before they left home." He stepped back and ushered Chris into the space between the door and the driver's seat. "Look at the odometer now. It's 16,600 miles."

Chris dipped his head in and checked what Warren pointed out, then looked back at the man. "Their home is only about six hundred miles from here," he said.

"So we have about five hundred miles unaccounted for," Deputy Warren shook his head. "If this car was driven anywhere as far as that difference shows, the bodies, if slain, could be hundreds of miles from here."

Chris stared transfixed at the bloody mess. "I'll get the man who did this," he whispered. Then swiped his hands across his eyes and cheeks and turned away. "It's okay, you can let the reporters in now."

CHAPTER 25

JANUARY 4, 1951
OKLAHOMA CITY, OKLAHOMA

Two days after taking the oath of office for Sheriff of Oklahoma County, Bob Turner sat at his desk studying the photo they had found in the duffel bag removed from Lee Archer's car five days earlier. This case had gone from being one of kidnapping and auto theft to murder. The missing Illinois family had passed through their state just a few days ago on their way to Albuquerque, New Mexico.

He stood holding the photo in his hands and wandered over to his window, staring outside at the chilly day. He watched as clouds rolled in and the trees in the courtyard swayed in the wind. Looked like the weatherman got the prediction right today. Turning his attention back to the photo, he wondered aloud, "Could this photo hold the key to who the man is?"

Just as he'd figured, there were thousands of Cooks in the Oklahoma and Texas areas they searched, and narrowing it down to the right W.E. Cook was not working for their investigation.

Once the car of the missing family had been found yesterday, the urgency of identifying this man ramped up a thousandfold.

Returning to his desk, he hit the intercom. "Harriet," he spoke into the box, wanting his secretary's attention.

"Yes?"

"Can you come in here?"

He handed the photo to her when she appeared on the opposite side of his desk. "The editor of *The Daily Oklahoman* inquired about the photo. They want to transmit it over the Associated Press wirephoto service to St. Louis. Can you run it over to their office for me?"

"Absolutely."

He appreciated that Harriet, just like every other law enforcement personnel, seemed to take this case personally and was determined to help find the missing man.

"Remind them this is not for publication. We're hoping the more eyes on the photo, the better chance we'll find someone who knows who the children are and who might have sent this photo to our W.E. Cook mystery man."

CHAPTER 26

JANUARY 4, 1951
ST. LOUIS, MISSOURI

FBI Agent Charles Miller stared at the photo they'd retrieved from the Associated Press. It was a wire transfer of the photo W.E. Cook was carrying in the duffel bag he'd left in Lee Archer's car. Charles read aloud the message on the back: "Love, Jackie, Vera Mae and Betty Jo."

"If only there had been a last name," he said to no one, but of course photos passed among family members didn't need full name identification. This W.E. Cook fellow would have known who these children were. Perhaps nieces and a nephew?

He turned the photo back over and considered the children. They looked to be around eight to twelve years old, the boy older than the two girls. In the lower right corner was the inscription, "Kirksville MO." What are the chances this studio could identify the photo and tell him who the person was who paid for it? He stared at the children, wondering if they had any idea what their uncle had done. If he was their uncle? Charles shook his head, pondering the fact that this man was hurting so many people.

Like a rock thrown in a pond, the ripples of grief and sadness were many and beyond comfort.

Glancing at the clock on the wall, he stood and walked across his office to the large map of the state of Missouri. Planning out the route with his finger from here to Kirksville, he figured he could be there early to mid-afternoon. He knew he could send another agent, but he felt driven to follow this lead to what he hoped would be a successful end. Providing the name of the killer. Once they knew that, they could run his name through the nationwide database. A guy who would kidnap travelers at gunpoint and kill an entire family most likely had a criminal history. He felt they were on the verge of discovering important information about the man they were hunting. The first step toward actually finding the man himself. And sending him to the gas chamber.

Four hours later, Agent Charles Miller had the name. William Edward Cook Jr. and a complete description came from the Missouri State Penitentiary, which had released him six months earlier. He read the notes aloud he had jotted down on his notepad while talking with the warden: "Age twenty-two, eyes blue, complexion medium sallow, height five feet four inches, weight one hundred forty, medium to small build, hair light brown and wavy and most notable, just what they'd received from Lee Archer, the drooping eyelid."

The proprietor of the studio had been hesitant to give out information until Charles showed his badge. Then he pulled his file folder and got the woman on the phone who had brought the children in. Maggie Potter had immediately identified W.E. Cook as her brother. She had sent the photo to him at Christmastime the year before. Said she sent it to Missouri State Penitentiary. And bingo, there was the next phone call to make to gather all the information they would need to put out an all-points bulletin across multiple states.

The next step was to get back in touch with the original victim, Lee Burd Archer, to have him identify the photo the prison would transmit by wire both to his office and the sheriff's office. "Marlene, patch me through to the sheriff in Oklahoma City," he said into his radio speaker.

Within minutes, she responded, "Here you go, sir."

"Sheriff Turner here."

"Thanks for taking my call. It's FBI Special Agent Miller, assigned to St. Louis. We just got confirmation on the W.E. Cook, as twenty-two-year-old William Edward Cook, recently released from the Missouri State Pen. I'd like to question the man who originally reported the crime, Lee Burd Archer."

"You and me both," Sheriff Turner said. "We haven't been able to locate him since he left us last week."

"You're kidding me."

"No, and the fact is that man also has a prison record."

"Do you suppose they're working together or Archer is involved somehow?"

"We're working on that now."

CHAPTER 27

JANUARY 5, 1951
WICHITA FALLS, TEXAS

Lee Archer carried his overnight bag into the lodge the Texas Rangers had brought him to. When he phoned the sheriff in Oklahoma after getting his phone service reconnected, he sure didn't expect to discover that he was now suspected of working with the man. Apparently more people had been kidnapped, and he wasn't sure, but it sounded like maybe they had been murdered. His previous prison sentences were catching up with him, making him a suspect in this case.

He rubbed his hands on his thighs, trying to wipe off sweat. He needed to be calm for the interview with the rangers, and they said an FBI agent from Oklahoma would come in as well. His heart beat hard. He didn't want to go back to prison. Especially for a crime he didn't commit. He'd done a lot of wrong things in his life, but he'd never killed anyone.

Two hours later, it appeared he had successfully completed the interrogation after he provided an almost minute by minute recitation of his whereabouts from the time he'd left the sheriff in Oklahoma until the Texas Rangers had picked him up at his house. He was glad he'd come into contact with so many people during these last few days who could verify his whereabouts.

When the FBI agent showed up with the photo, Lee started nodding his head the minute they held it up for him to view. "That's him! That's him!" He stood up, pointing at the photo. "I'll never forget that face."

"We thought so, but your confirmation makes it definite."

"What now? What can I do to help? My boss said to take all the time off I need."

"Well," the agent said, "we can use all the volunteers we can get to search. The Mosser family car was in Tulsa, but we know from the mileage counter on the car that man had them driving nearly a thousand miles in the days that he had them. They could be anywhere, in any number of states."

"I don't know how long I can stay here in this lodge they booked for me, but I can always go back and get my car. I want to help."

"We'll be coordinating with other law enforcement agencies so the searchers can be organized and cover as much territory as possible."

The agent stood to leave, and Lee walked with him to the door of his room at the motor lodge. "Look." Lee dropped his eyes to the floor, then fidgeted with his hat. "I know you know I've been in prison more than once." He looked back up at the FBI agent. "Well, thank you for trusting me to help."

CHAPTER 28

JANUARY 6, 1951
BLYTHE, CALIFORNIA

Six days into a new year," Deputy Sheriff Homer Waldrip said as he looked over his notes from his conversation the evening before with FBI Agent Oliver Nordmarken. "Can't we just start the year off peaceful like? Nope. Got the biggest manhunt since the days of John Dillinger going on in the nation."

A train whistle in the distance sounded, and Homer stepped to the window to watch the train that ran along the outskirts of town. He'd always loved the sound of train whistles. Reminded him of when he was a kid growing up in a small town in Texas. He recalled lying awake in bed at night at his grandparent's house with the windows open. He remembered hearing the trains as they banged together, with cars swapping engines and being moved about at the railroad switching station.

The Santa Fe Railway transported passengers and freight throughout the U.S. even through their small town. He could see over the tops of the buildings. This was a passenger train coming through town now, and he knew somewhere there were people waiting to greet their loved ones coming for a visit or possibly returning home from being out of town.

He loved this small desert town. It suited him just fine. Bordering the Colorado River, it didn't have the harsh cold or heat that other parts of the desert had. He'd moved here from his home state of Texas when he'd heard they had a need for law enforcement officers.

Homer turned back to his notes. The description the agent gave him of this William Edward Cook fellow sounded a lot like the young man who used to work at the diner with his wife. They knew him as Bill. In fact, when he'd checked at the diner the night before, the manager confirmed that Bill's full name was William Edward Cook Jr. and directed him to the Wood's Motel to talk to Bill's friend Paul to see if he was in town.

Not finding anyone home the night before, Homer figured he'd give it a go again today, to see if he could gather information for the FBI agent.

Deputy Waldrip pulled up outside the room, parked, pondered whether or not to draw his gun, then decided against it. When no one responded to his first knock, he opened the screen and knocked again.

"Yeah?" a voice sounded from within.

"Paul," Homer said. "I want to talk to you a minute."

The door swung open, and Bill Cook pointed a gun in his face. "Come in," he said.

Heart beating hard against his chest, Homer stepped inside. Cook again took him by surprise when he grabbed the gun from his holster and ordered him to sit on the bed.

Homer watched as Bill unloaded the pistol, bullets scattering across the floor.

"You're in serious trouble now," Cook said. "We're going for a ride, and you need to do what I say. I don't mind killing another one." He motioned for Homer to accompany him to the door.

Placing the empty gun back in the deputy's holster, Cook said, "We're going to walk outside as if nothing happened and get in the car and drive." Homer watched as Cook slipped the pistol he carried into his pocket.

Homer slid into the passenger side and followed directions to get behind the steering wheel as Billy slipped into the seat, not far from him. With the gun poking into his ribs, he followed the instructions to drive.

Several blocks away, they both spotted the diner at the same time where Billy and Homer's wife worked together. "Speed up," Billy ordered. "I don't want anybody to recognize us."

Going over in his mind as he followed the directions to head south, Homer Waldrip reviewed everything he'd done wrong in this situation. Starting with not following the FBI directions to wait for the team to arrive before beginning to search. Then it had never even entered his mind the thought that Billy would be in that room. He just came to get info from an acquaintance. He'd walked right into this like a rookie on his first day on the job.

He glanced out of the corner of his eye and saw the gun aiming his way. It would be a miracle if he got out of this alive. Everyone knew he had most likely killed all five members of the Mosser family. Was he to be number six? The only good thing he could think of in this situation was that at least his wife was safe. But whether he would ever return home to her again, he had no clue. And frankly, he didn't hold out much hope that he would. Oh Lord, please watch over her, he prayed silently as sweat poured from his brow while he followed the killer's orders on where to drive.

The only time the gun wasn't stuck in his side was when Billy used it to motion the direction he wanted him to drive. Homer pondered whether he would have been able to draw his gun fast enough to take this guy out if it had still been loaded. He knew that was a no-win bet. He'd be dead before the gun ever came out of his holster.

A gas station up ahead broke the monotony of the open road they'd been on since driving out of the town thirty miles back.

"You got any money?" Billy said.

"A dollar and some change." Homer kept his eyes on the road.

His captor pulled a ten-dollar bill from his pocket and waved it in his direction. "Pull over and get some gas."

As he navigated the car in among the gas pumps and shut off the engine, Homer watched the attendant head in their direction. Maybe he'd be able to signal the guy somehow.

"And don't get no ideas. I killed 'em all," his passenger said.

What do you say to a comment like that? Yet the gunman must want a reaction. He measured his words carefully. "How many were there?"

"Five. Five of them—three screaming brats, a crazy lady and a man who drove everywhere I told him to."

Homer nodded. He imagined those kids were screaming. What must that have been like for those little kids to be in a car with a killer brandishing a gun? His heart ached because of the nightmare the family had experienced. Oh Lord, someone needed to stop this man. And he didn't see any way that it would be him.

"What can I do for you folks?" the gas station attendant startled him. He'd been so focused on the killings he'd stopped watching him. Homer didn't feel the gun in his ribs and assumed it was hidden. He still hoped the attendant would figure out something was wrong.

"Fill it" was all the words he could get out as he gave the ten-dollar bill to the service station attendant. He winked at the attendant, hoping somehow that would signal him, then wondered how many hundreds of miles this journey was going to be for him. Would it be anything like the journey the Mosser family endured?

"How about you just give me a break?" Homer shocked himself at the boldness of his own question. But if you're facing death anyway, what can it hurt to be bold and beg for your life? Not that it did any good. There was no response.

He heard the gas pump nozzle being removed from the car and the gas cap being put back in place. Homer watched in the rearview mirror as the attendant approached his window, then counted out change from the coin dispenser on his belt, and peeled off some bills from the roll he took out of his pocket. He wondered if Billy Cook was watching and had any thoughts of robbing this guy.

"Here's your change. Thanks and come again."

Homer held his hand out to receive the change, then tried to hide the distress on his face as the attendant turned and walked away without ever noticing something amiss. He wondered, would that be the last man who would ever see him alive, besides the man who most likely would take his life at some point?

Once again, the gun was stuck in his ribs as they pulled back out onto the two-lane highway. "I want to keep going until we hit Highway 80," Cook said. "I guess I'm going to have to kill you. I hate to because I know your wife and your children."

"Just release me then," Homer said. "Take the car. Take my wallet."

"I told you," Cook said, "I already killed seven people since I left Blythe back at Christmas time." He nudged Homer with the gun, causing Homer to glance over his way. "I guess you'll have to be the eighth one."

Homer found his mind wandering as Bill rambled on about the family of five. He did not want to hear details about the children being killed. The highway heading south was empty. He longed to see another sheriff's vehicle or a highway patrol, someone to rescue him.

"Pull up over there," Billy motioned to a large turnout on the two-lane highway. "Pull over, then get out. It's time."

Homer's heart beat hard at the change in Billy's voice. He knew he only had moments to live. He checked his mirror as he slowed and pulled over. Maybe other motorists would drive by. Maybe someone could alert the local police. They were over forty miles from where they started in Blythe, so surely there were other officers in this area. But the roadway was empty.

The car no sooner came to a complete stop than Billy motioned for him to follow.

Billy opened his door and stepped out, watching while Homer slid along the front seat, exiting through the same door. "Put your hands on the roof and stretch your feet back here." Homer could feel the gun in his back as Bill reached into his rear pocket, pulling his wallet out.

"Got anything I can tie you up with?"

Homer's insides quivered. He hoped his voice didn't shake. The last thing he wanted was to show fear to this coward with the gun. "A blanket." He motioned toward the back seat with his head, keeping his words to a minimum.

Pulling the blanket out of the back seat, Cook shoved it into Homer's hands. "Tear some strips off of it."

"That's good enough," Cook said after three or four strips. Then grabbed his arm. "This way."

The pair headed out into the desert a couple hundred feet from the car, down a little embankment into a ditch.

"Spread that blanket out and get down on it," Cook said. "Face down."

Homer could feel Cook straddling him, the gun pointing into his back, but then it felt like Bill had dropped it onto his back, and reached around to grab both of Homer's hands, yanking them up behind him. He wrapped the strips around them, over and over, in and out, then cinched tight, almost too tight. Homer groaned with the pain, not only of the tightness around his wrists, but of yanking his arms up farther behind him than they moved naturally.

"I'm going to put a bullet in your head," Cook said.

Homer twisted to look up at the man and saw him going through the wallet he'd just filled with cash the day before at the bank, planning on taking the family out for dinner tonight. Would the cash satisfy the killer, or would the shot to the head come after he got all the money?

"Thought you were broke." Billy Cook laughed and tossed the wallet on the ground after emptying it.

"You can't blame a guy for trying," Homer said.

"Don't you move for thirty minutes."

Minutes later, the patrol car's engine roared to life and tires burned rubber pulling onto the highway.

Tears of relief flowed. He was still alive.

CHAPTER 29

JANUARY 6, 1951
PALO VERDE, CALIFORNIA

Robert Dewey spun the radio dial searching for an English-speaking station. He'd been driving close to the border for hours, since leaving his dad's home in San Diego and driving east into the desert. As the miles clicked by, he'd lose connection with a good station, only to search again for another one.

He was looking forward to visiting the desert site where he'd trained with General Patton and reconnecting with a few war buddies. He'd really enjoyed the time spent hunting and fishing with his dad. This was proving to be a great little vacation.

Leaning over to give it another try at finding an English-speaking station, he caught sight of a rotating red police light in his rearview mirror. A squealing siren accompanied the flashing light. Glancing around, he realized he was the only car on the road and wondered if he'd let his speed get too high while he fiddled with the radio dial.

The patrol car was closing in on him, so he eased off the gas pedal, watching for a wide spot to pull over.

He hoped the officer would just give him a warning. He didn't want to have to pay a fine that would dip into his vacation money. Until he knew what the outcome would be, he felt a damper on his so far successful trip. He wondered whether he should let the car idle or shut it off as he rolled to a stop, but before he could decide, there was a gun in his driver's window. Stunned, he noticed the man holding the small pistol wasn't wearing a uniform. He saw the red light continue spinning in his rearview mirror, and he could hear the rumble of the police car running behind his car.

"Do what I say, and maybe you'll be lucky enough to stay alive like the last guy." The gun moved with every few words as if to emphasize the owner meant business. Robert sat frozen in place, unable to speak, his insides cold and shaking.

The car door jerked open, and he felt the gun poke him in the arm. "Get out!"

As he stepped out of the car, he got a look at the man, who was a good three or four inches shorter than he was. His left eye drooped, his lip curled up in a snarl as he motioned with his gun. "Around there."

Robert followed the prompting to the other side of the car, where the man opened the passenger door and shoved him in, climbing in right behind him. He hadn't taken any chances, and Robert wished the man had let him stay in the car while he walked around to get in. He would have taken off, even if it meant hitting the guy. The gun prodded him until he had slid all the way over behind the wheel.

"Drive!" The gun pointed toward the highway. "Yuma. Take me to Yuma."

Robert knew if he ever wanted to get out of this alive, he'd have to think fast. He couldn't let fear freeze him. He had to overlook his insides shaking. As he sped up and pulled onto the road, making a U-turn to head back in the direction he'd just come from, he gripped the steering wheel hard, to keep his hands from shaking. He didn't want this man to see the effect he was having on him. Something in his eyes, even with the one bad eye, gave the sense of darkness, of pure evil.

"I've killed people," the unwanted passenger said.

Robert nodded to acknowledge he'd heard. No sense in angering the man by ignoring him. But he continued to work out a plan in his mind. The gun still pointed at him while he drove. He needed to end this quickly. He glanced out the side of his right eye, noticing that occasionally the man took his eyes off of him and looked out the windshield, as if watching where they were going before he looked right back over at him.

Robert would be ready the next time he had a second without the man staring right at him, he would reach out and knock the gun out of his hand. He could flail his right arm in the man's direction, contacting his hand, and slam on the brakes to knock him off guard.

"A family on a vacation. Isn't that sweet?" the voice dripped with anger. "Bam. Shot dead. Ever last one of them."

Robert cringed. Had this been on the news? He hadn't watched any news or read the papers since he'd left home. He'd been so focused on his hunting adventure and visit with his dad. If what this man was saying was true, it had to have made the headlines. Right now, the police, maybe even the FBI, had to be looking for this guy. He checked his rearview, hoping for traffic, hoping for another police car, one with an actual police officer in it. The roadway was empty.

Then, glancing over, he saw his chance. Tires squealed as he slammed on the brakes and threw his arm across the front seat, but instead of the gun flying out of the man's hand, it jarred his hand, causing him to pull the trigger. Robert felt a flash of sharp pain as a bullet entered his right side, down low, near his hip.

"You can't scare me," Robert said, anger boiling up inside. "I've been shot before."

He reversed his strategy and let off the brake. Pain seared through him as he lifted his foot, slamming it down on the accelerator. The car jerked forward, then suddenly veered to the right, going off the pavement and into the desert. The man had leaned over and jerked the steering wheel, taking control of the vehicle from Robert. He let off the gas, hoping they were going to take this fight outside of the car. He had the height and weight on this guy and was ready to take him down. Injury or no, he would not let the pain hold him back.

The armed man poked the gun in his side when the car came to a stop. "Get out!" Once again, just as they got in the car, they both exited through the same door. Robert limped out, feeling the gun in his back as the man followed closely behind. He couldn't wait another second. He had to make his move. But before he could follow through with sidestepping to the right to turn and take the man down in a chokehold, the gunman stuck a foot in front of him and shoved him hard. The loud crack of the pistol firing was the last sound he heard as his body slammed hard, face down into the asphalt.

Chapter 30

January 6, 1951
Midway Wells, California

As soon as he heard his patrol car drive away, Homer immediately rolled onto his side, sat up and scooted over to the edge of the ditch. Leaning against shrubs growing out of the ditch wall, he manipulated his hands so a stubby branch caught in between the blanket strips and his wrists. Moving his hands around, he could feel the strips loosening. Then, he jerked his arms hard and hollered out in triumph as the branch freed his hands.

Climbing out of the ditch, he looked south, relieved to see no sign of his patrol car with the killer driving it. Homer headed north, walking against what would be the flow of traffic if any cars were to come along. If he had to, he'd walk all the way back to Blythe, no matter how long it took him. That he was alive filled him with adrenaline.

Thirty minutes into his walk, he'd only been passed by a few vehicles. As much as he wished they had stopped to offer help, he could understand them not doing that, especially if they'd been watching the news about the hitchhiking killer.

Homer kept pressing forward, gaining strength as he walked. He was glad he wasn't fighting the heat of summer since he had no water.

He welcomed the welcome sight of a Border Patrol Jeep pulling alongside him. The two officers inside listened to his tale. Hopping into the back of the Jeep and eagerly downing the thermos of water they offered, the three of them headed south in search of Billy Cook and the patrol car.

Homer pointed out the spot to the two officers where he'd been left tied up, and they continued on for another fifteen miles when they came upon the patrol car parked haphazardly, blocking the southbound lane of the road. The red light was raised and glowing, unlike the way Homer had left it, pointed down and turned off. There was no sign of Cook.

With the keys still in the ignition, Homer started the car and followed the Border Patrol officers as the caravan headed south in search of the killer, who no doubt was in another stolen vehicle.

Five miles down the highway, they came upon a body lying face down in the road. Homer felt as if someone had punched him in the gut. That could have been him. Anger boiled inside him at this monster who randomly kidnapped and killed.

Though there was no visible proof yet that Cook had done this, they all knew. It had to be Cook, who no doubt was now driving around in the car belonging to Robert H. Dewey, bearing

Washington plates, according to the license they found in the man's wallet.

Homer Waldrip watched the sorrowful tick-tick of the watch on the dead man's wrist. It was a tragic commentary that the watch still had life, while the man did not.

CHAPTER 31

JANUARY 7, 1951
BAJA CALIFORNIA, MEXICO

The dusky deep blue of a morning not quite ready to receive the sun greeted Forrest and James as they headed across the border after driving around sightseeing most of the night. Once they'd changed their plans to go prospecting in Ogilby, they'd driven east toward Yuma, but ended up stopping in Winterhaven, without actually crossing the state line. After enjoying the sights, they headed back west to find a good place to cross the border into Mexico to check out the fishing facilities they'd heard about from friends.

"San Felipe, here we come," James said from behind the wheel of his 1950 Studebaker.

The miles clicked by as Forrest worked on finding some American music on the radio dial, then settled back to enjoy the tunes along with the scenery. This side of the border was still desert like his hometown, but had a different feel and look.

"We've already gone forty miles," James said. "We're making good time."

Forrest nodded, then pointed to a man standing on their side of the road, holding a gas can. "Look there." Then, his eyes traveled to the other side of the road. "He must be out of gas. There's his car on the roadside heading in the other direction."

James eased off the gas. "Suppose we should stop? He looks American."

"Sure," Forrest said. "We can give him a ride to the next gas station."

James pulled up next to the man.

"Do you need some help?"

"Yes." The man pointed to his small gas can.

"Would you like us to take you to San Felipe to find some help?" James said.

"All right, yes, I would."

Forrest hopped out of the car and approached the man. "Do you want us to push the car off the road first?"

"I think that would be a good idea," the stranger said.

Forrest watched as James maneuvered his car into the other lane. He guided James as he slowly matched the front bumper of the Studebaker to the front bumper of the Buick, then pushed the car off the road.

Forrest opened the back door, welcoming the stranger in, before returning to his place in the passenger seat.

James pulled back onto the southbound side of the road to resume the drive to San Felipe. With no sound from the back seat a few minutes into the journey, Forrest turned to check on their passenger.

A .38 caliber Smith & Wesson greeted him, pointed directly at his face. He froze, but could feel his stomach trembling. Beads of sweat formed on his forehead. "Jim," he said, without taking his eyes off the gun, "you better look around. I think we are in trouble."

Forrest glanced over as James took a quick look into the back seat, then looked back in the direction he was driving.

"What do you want us to do?" James directed his question to the unknown man in the back seat.

"Turn the car around," the man demanded. "We are going back to the Buick."

"Pull over here," the man said when they reached the disabled car. "You!" he pointed with the gun in James' direction when the car came to a stop. "Get out and walk 10 feet in that direction."

Forrest watched his friend follow the instructions. Then the man turned his way. "Now you get out on your side and walk 10 feet in the other direction and wait there."

"What next?" he dared to ask the man after he also exited the car.

"We are going a long ways and we're going to need some stuff from this car." He pointed at the Buick. "You fellows are going to unload it and put it in this car," he said, motioning to the Studebaker.

Both men walked toward the Buick. "Hold it right there," the man said. Approaching Forrest, he held the gun on him. "Take your jacket off. Hold your arms out." He patted him down with one hand, while continuing to keep the gun on him with the other. Forrest snuck a glance at James, who stood a few feet away, watching. Then it was his turn, and Forrest watched as the man did the same to his friend.

Once satisfied they weren't carrying weapons, the man turned back to Forrest. "Have you got the keys?" Forrest said.

"Open the door." He handed the keys to Forrest. "Get that stuff out of the back seat."

"Which stuff?"

"Dump those blankets there."

Forrest reached in to grab blankets, interrupted by the gruff orders from the stranger.

"Be careful with them, they have got some stuff in them that I want to take care of."

He could feel hard objects in the blankets that felt like shotguns or rifles. Forrest handed the blanketed items to James, who transferred them to his car.

The man rifled through the trunk, then looked up at them. "Do you guys smoke?"

"Yes," James said.

"Well, just take this carton of cigarettes, then. The guy that had them won't need them anymore." He turned to James. "Get that oil can and the things out of the car and put them in your trunk."

After transferring items from the Buick to the Studebaker, more orders followed. "Now, take those license plates off the Buick."

Finding a screwdriver in the trunk, Forrest struggled to get the rear license plate off. His shaking hands made it hard to line the Phillips screwdriver up with the head on the screw. James took the tool from his hand to assist. Together, the men struggled to break the corroded bolts free from the plate. Finally, Forrest handed the loose plate to James. "I'll undo the front." His words sounded shaky even to himself, and he wondered if the man had heard. "I think I can do it now." The two men moved to the front of the car to retrieve that plate, the stranger's gun trained on them the entire time. It seemed this man had a bold plan that involved them. All because they were nice enough to pull over to give him a hand. What a mistake that was.

"Put those plates in the back seat."

The man slid into the back seat, leaving the door open, and said, "Okay, now you," he pointed to Forrest. "You get back in the car."

He took his seat on the passenger side and watched as the man pointed his gun at James, ordering him to get back behind the wheel. "Now, head north." The man slammed his door shut. "We're going to Mexicali."

Forrest watched as James eased forward back onto the roadway, then picked up speed heading toward Mexicali. James kept his eyes mostly on the road, but glanced over at Forrest, sharing thoughts through their eyes. They had to figure a way to get out of this situation.

As they took the northbound route, the man in the back leaned forward. "In case you guys don't know it, I am William Edward Cook, and they are looking for me all over the United States."

Forrest turned his head slightly to get a look at Cook, only to acknowledge he was listening, then turned back toward the front.

"There is ten more dead heroes back there on the road," Cook said, "and two more won't make any difference to me."

The two men remained silent.

"If you don't believe what I say, I will show you." Forrest turned, watching the man pull out a wallet and hold it up, showing his ID card.

James glanced over. "What's it say, Forrest?"

Forrest nodded. "It says William Edward Cook."

"We're going to cooperate with you," James said. Forrest was sure he could tell the pistol was still aimed in their direction.

"I want to see what is in that glove compartment." He pointed his gun over the seat toward the dashboard. "Open it and let me see."

Forrest dropped the lid open and pulled out papers, then leaned back for the man to get a clear look into the compartment.

Ahead was a good-sized dirt area to the right of the roadway. "Pull over there." William Cook motioned with his gun after tapping James on the shoulder.

"Get out of the car just like I told you before," he said, once James shut the engine off. Forrest watched as James exited, then walked toward the back of the car. He got out next, approaching the front of the car. Once Cook joined them, he motioned for both of them to come to the passenger side of the car, with their backs to the road and the car in between them and the two-lane highway. "Take out your wallets and show me what money you have."

Forrest reached into his back pocket, watching James do the same. Between them, they had a lot of cash they'd brought along for their trip.

William Cook held out his hand, motioning for them to hand over their cash. Once done, he tapped the wallet James held. "Give me your identification." Forrest watched as James handed over the ID card. "I'm James Burke now," William said. He shoved the Burke identification into his wallet, and gave his to James, then took his jacket off and began unbuttoning his shirt. "Give me your shirt," he said to James.

When the two switched shirts, William said, "That's the last description they have of me, wearing that shirt. Now if we get pulled over, they'll think you're the man they're looking for."

As the shirts were buttoned, and his jacket replaced, William nodded toward the car. "Got any paperwork showing that I own this car, now that I'm James?"

"It's in the glove box," James said.

"Okay, back in the car, let's get back on the road."

While they drove, Cook tapped James on the shoulder with the barrel of his gun. "Keep both your hands on that steering wheel where I can see them."

James brought his right hand up from his lap and took hold of the top of the steering wheel close to his left. "Keep them there at all times," Cook said.

He tapped Forrest's shoulder next. "You put your right arm on the doorjamb of the door there. Keep your right hand up by the window and your left arm on the seat behind this fellow."

After getting his arms placed as ordered, Forrest saw Cook point the gun in his direction, then he heard the sharp click of the trigger being pulled, releasing the hammer. His heart beat hard, and his breathing increased beyond what he could control. He could not believe he was still alive. He had just come so close to dying. Could it be that the gun wasn't loaded?

"Just sit there and don't move," William Cook said. "It will go off the next time. You're lucky. It landed on the empty chamber from the last man I shot."

Forrest remained frozen in place, determined to follow the instructions exactly. As much as he wanted to look at his friend in the driver's seat, he stared forward, as if he were a statue, unable to move.

Miles clicked by them, and a guard station sign indicated they were getting close to Mexicali.

"Slow down for the guard station, don't stop, just pass it slowly. Just wave and keep on going." He slipped the gun into his pocket. "If they try to detain us, just step on the gas and get out of there."

Forrest hoped someone would rescue them at this place. If someone signaled them to stop and they tried to run, he knew they would chase them. Would the man shoot them during the chase, or would they get rescued? He desperately hoped someone would signal them to stop. But his heart dropped into his stomach when they passed through the guard station with no trouble.

CHAPTER 32

JANUARY 7, 1951
EL CENTRO, CALIFORNIA

Forty-one-year-old Guy Woodward pondered his seventeen-year law enforcement career that had seen him go from the coastal community of Oceanside, California, to the desert of Imperial County. The task before him today made him long for the carefree days as a rookie motorcycle cop. He remembered two years into his new career when he dared to pull over the famous crooner, Bing Crosby, for going fifty-five miles per hour in a twenty-five mile per hour zone. It seemed like a different lifetime. And though he was now barely in his forties, he had a feeling the call he was about to go out on, if successful, would age him beyond his years.

The all-points bulletin had gone out to every law enforcement branch in the Imperial Valley—local police departments, California Highway Patrol, sheriff's departments and U.S. Border Patrol. The nationwide manhunt for killer Billy Cook had solid proof now that he was in this area.

The report came through after Blythe, California Deputy Sheriff Homer Waldrip had been discovered walking along the roadside in Imperial County after being left tied up in the desert. The story he related to his rescuers and then local law enforcement definitely identified the five foot four-inch killer. It had been a miracle that the deputy escaped with his life, but together with his rescuers, a couple of Border Patrol agents, they discovered another victim, who was less fortunate.

Law enforcement officers were now scouring the area between the scene of the murder of Robert Dewey and the border. Guy was torn between wanting to find this killer and wanting to protect his own family. He assumed that was the case for most of the officers in the valley who had a family. Whether wife, kids, parents, or siblings. The word must be going out across the country. Do not stop for strangers, no matter what, he'd told his wife and sons before leaving for work. Teenagers. He remembered being one. They know so much more than their parents. He hoped against hope this would be a time his kids would listen. No one would be safe until this man was found.

Patrolling the area south of his city, he kept an eye out for suspicious activity on the main road leading to the Mexico border crossing. Debating crossing the border himself, it didn't take long for him to reach the decision to just go for it.

Guy switched on his overhead light and siren and headed for the border. He was determined to find that car even if it meant driving through Mexico all day. He patted the shotgun mounted on his dash. And when he found the driver of that car… he couldn't bring himself to put words to the desire in his heart.

Six dead now. This killing spree had to stop. This dark storm
of terror rolling through the nation, their state, and now on into
another country had to be stopped. Were they all just riders on
this storm? The victims, the officers, the bystanders wondering if
they were next. He couldn't just sit back and wait for the storm
to stop. He had to be a driving force to bring it to an end.

He clicked the outgoing button on his radio: "Chief
Woodward, heading south. Going to cross into Mexico in
pursuit."

Frequent potholes marred the asphalt sections of the dusty,
rutted dirt roads south of the border. Guy kept his eyes roaming
from side to side and straining to see as far in the distance as he
could. He didn't know what kind of car he was looking for, but
any car he saw, he planned to pull over to check the occupant.
Billy Cook, according to the reports, was distinguishable by his
eye with the deformed eyelid and his tattooed fingers. He hoped
and prayed he would find him before there were more victims of
his evil. He had to find him. No more bloodshed, please, Lord.
No more bloodshed. He found himself repeating the same prayer
over and over as he continued his search.

Coming to a fork in the road, he hesitated briefly, then stayed
to the right. Spotting a couple of cars heading in his direction,
he slowed, tempted to pull over and block the road, but as the
first car got closer, he saw an older Mexican man driving with a
woman sitting in the passenger seat. The car behind had similar
occupants, along with several adults in the back seat as well. The

two cars were going slowly enough on the rough road that he could tell no one matching the description of the fugitive was in those cars.

And still, no cars loomed ahead of him. Twenty more miles up ahead, Guy pulled into the rustic parking lot of a roadside market. Exiting the car, he stretched, then turned to survey the area. A few cars parked haphazardly at the other end of the lot. Glancing in the store, he didn't see anyone near the door who might be watching him, so he wandered over to check the license plates of the cars. No Washington plates. Still, he glanced inside the cars, looking for signs of blood or some kind of fight. With Mexico plates on these cars, that didn't mean Billy Cook didn't swap out the Washington plates. Finding nothing suspicious, he headed inside to check out the customers.

Roaming up and down the aisles, he spotted a few Mexican national shoppers and then some Americans, but no one matching the description of the man he was hunting for.

Grabbing some cold drinks and a couple of pieces of fruit, he paid and headed out to his car.

Starting up the car, he let the engine idle while he peeled his banana, ate a couple of bites, then took a long swig of the cold soda. His odometer showed he'd already traveled over a hundred miles. He breathed a deep sigh, recognizing defeat. He couldn't even check in, as he was out of radio contact this deep into Mexico. He'd have to head back. It had been a wasted trip.

Backing out and heading north, Guy swung his visor over to the left to block the bright sun shining in on him as it began its descent into the western sky. He came upon another fork in the road, veering right again, thinking to go back on a different road than he had driven down on. He passed occasional small houses, set back off the road, that some might even call shacks. A few children played in the dirt outside one of the houses, and it did him good to hear their laughter as he drove by. He hoped no evil came upon them in the form of the fugitive thousands were hunting for on both sides of the border.

Continuing on, he wondered if his eyes were deceiving him, as up ahead off to the right he saw what appeared to be from this distance an abandoned car. If it was abandoned? He couldn't see anyone inside from this vantage point. Closing the distance, he noticed it was a Buick with no license plates, his heart beating hard, wondering if William Cook would be asleep or hiding in this car. Maybe it broke down.

Guy pulled off to the right, hoping that if someone was in the car, they wouldn't hear his engine. He unholstered his gun, then slowly eased his door open and stepped out. He saw footprints and tire tracks in the dirt. Still hoping to apprehend the monster, he peered in through the windows. The car was empty inside, and what looked like a large blood splotch stained the front driver's seat. No one in the back. He saw the tracks where it looked like a car had pulled over. Footprints led to the car. But which way did they go when they left? North or south? From the footprints, he couldn't tell if there had been more than one person in this car when it pulled over. And the big question in his heart and mind right now? Was the owner of that car still alive?

131

CHAPTER 33

JANUARY 7, 1951
MEXICALI, BAJA CALIFORNIA

Forrest watched as the mid-sized town of Mexicali greeted them a few miles later. He wondered what the man had in mind with this destination. But before he could find out, James spoke up. "How about if you leave us off here in Mexicali? You can take the car and all the money. We just want out."

Forrest prayed silently that this guy would give in to the plea.

"No," Cook said. "You guys are going all the way with me."

"Where is that?" Relieved that James was doing the talking, Forrest was too afraid to move yet, even to open his mouth to form a question.

"A long ways," Cook said. "Don't worry about it. I will tell you more about it later on."

As they entered the town of Mexicali, he said, "How much gas have you got?"

"About half a tank," James said.

"We better pull in here and fill it up," Cook motioned with the gun to the gas station coming up on the right. "Pull in and get some gas."

As they approached the gas station, Forrest turned his head slightly, watching Cook slip the gun into his pocket, then hand over some money to pay for the gas. Most likely, the money he had taken from them.

"Do you know the way to Tijuana?" Bill said as they pulled out of the gas station.

James looked toward Forrest, who nodded. "I think we can find it." He pointed to the road ahead. "Head west up here at the next turn."

They settled into a quiet drive, following the road as it twisted and turned, coming upon the Tecate grade until William broke the silence. "You guys just watch yourselves and don't get nervous, don't do anything that I am not looking for, and don't speak, and you are going to be all right." Forrest glanced over his shoulder and nodded to acknowledge they'd heard the instructions. "The last guy I was with didn't do this, and he is on the road in the ditch."

Forrest glanced over at James, who kept his eyes on the road. That must have been the owner of the Buick who William was talking about. The guy from Washington. Forrest had wondered about him when they buried the license plates a few miles back, at William's instructions. He wondered how old the man was and whether he had a wife and children. Or parents. And were he and James going to end up just like that man? He could feel his insides shaking, but he was determined not to let the fear show. And truth be told, if they were going to end up that way, why not just get it over with? Why drag it out? But maybe, just maybe, they'd be the ones to escape this madman. Somehow. He went back to watching the roadway, knowing he was supposed to be navigating this journey to Tijuana.

"Take a turn up here," Forrest said, pointing to the construction at the side of the road where it looked like some new businesses were going in. "This should be the way."

The road climbed up what felt like sixteen hundred or seventeen hundred feet after they passed the construction zone. "I think we're going the wrong way," James said.

"Yeah, let's go back," Forrest turned in his seat to examine the terrain on both sides of the car, looking for signs that might indicate where they were.

"We passed the road we needed back there," William said. "It's back a mile before this construction. You need to go back there and take that road."

Forrest wondered if William knew that, why he didn't say something when they passed it the first time. He wasn't going to ask, though. You don't ask a guy anything when he has a gun pointed at you. James followed William's direction, but when they got to the road William said to turn on, James hesitated and looked over at Forrest, who shrugged. "Doesn't look right to me," Forrest said. "I saw a detour sign when we came through here before."

They looked around, and James pointed to a sign lying on the road, like someone had recently run over it. It was in Spanish. "What's it say?" William said.

"Detour," Forrest said. "That's what that word means."

"Turn back then." William motioned with the gun.

Once back at the construction site, James slowed, rolling his window down. "Tijuana," he called out to the construction workers. They all nodded and pointed in the same direction. Taking the left-hand turn heading southwest, they eventually arrived in Tijuana.

"We are going to need a map," William said. "I left the one that I had back in the other car. Stop at any service station here that you think you can get one at."

What exactly was this man's plan that he needed a map? He must have a specific destination in mind, Forrest figured. Would they be going deeper into Mexico, and at what point would he and James be able to sneak away? Perhaps at night.

After stopping at several gas stations with no luck finding a map, William snapped at them. "You guys get hold of yourselves and find a map pretty quick," he yelled. "You are leaving a trail for a baby to follow."

If only they could be that lucky, Forrest thought. He hoped all these inquiries would lead to someone coming to their rescue. Near the outskirts of town, they got lucky and found a map of Baja California that seemed to satisfy their captor.

William studied the map as they continued to drive, then tossed it up into the front seat. "We are going to Santa Rosalia," he said. "We are going to take a ferry for Guaymas, Mexico."

Forrest saw signs for Ensenada, indicating about forty miles. He wondered whether they could stop to eat once they got down there. They'd brought along plenty of food, but never imagined they'd have to get permission from a killer before they could eat.

Did their wives know about this fugitive? Or have any clue they might be in danger? He hoped they didn't.

His watch showed five p.m. when they rolled into Ensenada.

"We better get some gas here," Cook said.

Forrest thought it was interesting that a man who had killed people could keep such a keen eye out for things like did they have enough gas to keep traveling. But he supposed this man had been on the run for a while now. So he was probably used to knowing how to get away from the police. And running out of gas somewhere, being stranded, wouldn't do it. Although, as before, he could just hitch a ride with some other innocent people. But he supposed he'd killed them first. If that was the case, he was mighty glad they were keeping the car gassed up.

"Stop here at this store," William said after they gassed up the car. "No talking in the store."

Forrest's stomach rumbled, and he found it hard to believe it was just that morning, probably eleven hours ago now, they'd picked up this guy and–he hated to admit–they'd been kidnapped. It was about the only thing to call it. At least they were still alive. It felt more like a week had gone by than just a day. After getting snacks and drinks, William instructed them to pull around behind the store.

"We've got to hide these guns," William said.

Once out of the car, he motioned for James to open the hood, where they stashed the .270 Winchester rifle and the .22 caliber rifle William had told them to retrieve from the Buick. They were able to wedge them crosswise under the hood. He then ordered them back in the car and instructed James to keep following the road they'd been traveling on.

Darkness had settled in sometime back, and Forrest's body ached from exhaustion both mentally and physically but he didn't dare let his eyes close. He knew James couldn't and he wouldn't either. Every time he glanced around, he could see the revolver still pointed in their direction.

"I really don't know where this road goes," James said. "To tell you the truth, I think we're lost."

Forrest cringed inwardly, wondering if this would anger the man in the back seat. Instead, he told James to pull off the road, and they'd get some sleep, then figure out the directions in the morning.

When the engine shut off, William passed blankets up to the front seat. "You guys take these blankets and wrap up in them."

After struggling to get their bodies completely wrapped in the blankets, more instructions came. "Now, look around," William said. "I want to show you something."

Forrest and James looked behind them and, in the glare of the dome light, they could see the .38 revolver in his hand, cocked, with his finger on the trigger. "Now, I want you to remember that this thing is going to be pointed at you all night," William said. He lay down on the seat with the gun pointed at the back of the front seat. "Now, if you guys want to move during the night, you tell me first."

Forrest nodded and saw James doing the same.

"You stay absolutely still," William said, "and unless you tell me, if you don't, you are going to get shot. I can see up against the windshield pretty good."

The dome light shut off, and the car grew quiet. Forrest needed sleep badly, but his mind worked overtime, wondering how they were going to get out of this situation. It was apparent with those threats about getting shot for moving, sneaking away in the night was not an option. Finally, thankfully, sleep overtook his worried and fearful mind.

CHAPTER 34

JANUARY 8, 1951
SAN SALVADOR, BAJA CALIFORNIA

P ull over! Pull over!" The gruff voice coming from the back seat accompanied the motion of the gun pointing to the side of the road.

James turned his head slightly, watching as Forrest slowed and maneuvered the car over to the edge of the rough road. He had offered to drive this morning to give James a break. Even though they had come to Mexico several times on prospecting and hunting trips, they'd never ventured south using this dilapidated road. He suspected the guy was purposely staying off major roads to avoid being caught. He wondered if that was how he did it with the family he killed. And would they be next? And if so, when? He preferred it to be sooner rather than later. Not that he wanted to die, but this not knowing, driving around endlessly, was maddening. He figured it was going on thirty hours they'd been with him. He hadn't been able to talk privately with Forrest and wondered what was going on in his mind. Maybe it was much the same as what went on in his own mind.

He felt the gun barrel nudge his shoulder when the car rolled to a stop. "You drive." James turned to look at their passenger. "You drive, he can take care of the radio."

James cringed at the thought of the radio as he exited his side of the car. They were broadcasting news about the hitchhiker killer every couple of hours it seemed, maybe more often. Passing Forrest in the front of the car as they switched positions, they made eye contact, and he knew. Forrest felt the same thing. They didn't have much longer to live. He could not imagine what their wives were going through and Forrest's daughters.

Had he told his wife he loved her before he left? He felt ashamed about how excited he'd been to get going on this trip. It had been more than a year since they had got away on a prospecting trip. It's funny that something that seemed so important a few days ago, now is not important at all. In fact, what were most important were his wife and his life. He'd give anything to replay the past couple of weeks and not take this vacation. If he got out of this alive, he didn't think he'd be doing any prospecting in Mexico for a very long time to come. He didn't care if uranium was available on every street corner, he wasn't coming down here to hunt for it.

If they got out alive. That was a big if.

"Turn around and head back the way we came," the passenger said.

James looked to see that Forrest was safely in and his door shut as he cranked the key in the ignition. He made a U-turn and headed back. There seemed to be no rhyme or reason to the path they were taking. They just followed the directions of the man with the gun. He could feel his hands sweating as he gripped the steering wheel and focused on loosening his grip.

"Find a radio station."

James could see out of the corner of his right eye that, once again, the guy used his gun to tap the shoulder of the person he was speaking to.

He continued driving as he watched Forrest spinning the radio dial, listening to the static and chaos of Spanish-speaking channels switching from unintelligible jabbering to mariachi music. His stomach dropped as the tuner stopped on an English-speaking channel.

"The suspect is five feet, four inches, about one hundred forty, droopy eyelid. He is armed and dangerous. Do not engage with this man but notify authorities immediately if you see him."

James stared out the windshield, not daring to look in the rearview mirror, for fear he'd see the angry stare coming from the droopy-eyed man in the back seat holding them hostage. How many times had they heard the same report? It must be playing on every radio station in both countries. If only they had heard it before stopping to help the guy.

"That's enough," the voice ordered from the back seat. "Find some music we can understand."

Forrest kept spinning the dial.

"I killed them all, just like the man on the radio says. Six of them. Or was it eight?"

James snuck a peek in the mirror, wondering what the look on his face would be. He couldn't see it though, his head was hanging down as he talked, and James wondered, was he sorry?

Or was he hoping for ten? A shudder ripped through his body, and he saw Forrest look his way. He must have noticed.

"Take me to San Felipe, driver. I want to go to San Felipe."

James glanced at the gauges on the dash. "We're going to need more gas to make it that far."

"Stop when we come to a station. We can get some food, too. We're going to do some hunting on the way. Like friends. You know?"

This took James by surprise, and he saw Forrest's head jerk in his direction.

"Anyone sees us anywhere, we're friends. You guys got that?"

"Sure, whatever you say," Forrest mumbled.

"It better be what I say, because if it ain't, you're both dead."

Acting wasn't his thing, but James had a feeling he was going to learn how if he had to pretend this killer was his friend when they stopped for gas.

A few miles down the road, they came to a gas station with a store next door.

"We'll get some food after the gas," William said. "And no talking."

"Look, if they talk, it will be more suspicious if we don't answer."

"They don't speak English," William said.

"I can talk to them in Spanish," Forrest said.

"Nothing doing." William shook his head. "I don't

understand the language, and I can't tell what you say. I am not going to take a chance on it."

"What if they talk to us?" James said, backing up Forrest's attempt to get permission to communicate with the shop people.

"You can go ahead and talk if you want to, but I will probably have to shoot you for it."

"You can tell by watching the people's reaction as I talk to them what I have said to them," Forrest said, "and if I have given any information, you will see it in their faces."

"Well," William said, "I think that is right. You go ahead and talk with them, but there is one thing I want you to remember. If I am caught, if we are caught, if I make up my mind that you had anything to do with it by tipping off these people, you two are going to get the first two bullets."

James gripped the steering wheel tightly as he pulled into the gas station. As much as they wanted to notify someone of what was happening, he knew it would be certain death if they did. Without even asking his friend, he knew Forrest wouldn't even attempt it.

CHAPTER 35

JANUARY 9, 1951
SAN DIEGO, CALIFORNIA

FBI Special Agent E.C. Richardson reviewed the myriad stacks of notes and papers on his desk. Tips were coming in from across the nation about the highway killer. The most promising coming from Imperial County indicated there was a good chance he was still in Mexico. His office had been assigned to head up the manhunt since this had long ago stopped being a state matter and become a federal offense.

Clerks and fellow agents had been forwarding all the calls and tips to him, thankfully organizing them in stacks of very promising to not likely. But even the unlikely ones were not to be ignored. This guy had proven not to stay in any one place for very long, and the positive sightings in several states kept them all on the move. And not just the agents in his office, but from every branch of law enforcement across nearly ten states.

E.C. stepped over to look out the window of his third-floor office on Broadway in downtown San Diego. He'd always enjoyed being right in the center of the big city, but it seemed it might be time to relocate for a bit. Plans were in the works to set up a field office in El Centro, since that appeared to be closer to the action. The cloudless blue sky with bright sun reminded him of something else he liked about this assignment in Southern California. The weather. Rarely harsh and he imagined it would be the same in El Centro this time of year. Too early for the triple-digit heat that town was known for.

E.C. had never imagined he would coordinate a manhunt that would rival that of the 1934 search for John Dillinger. This was certainly the biggest manhunt the department had undertaken since the FBI had tracked and killed the infamous gangster. He'd only been an agent for two years when that happened. Now, fifteen years later, he was heading up the manhunt from this location and wondered, would it end similarly? In a shootout with one of his agents or any number of other law enforcement agencies involved? He hoped and prayed no officers would lose their lives tracking this killer and no more innocent travelers as well.

"Leona?" E.C. returned to his desk and pressed the intercom button. "Can you bring in your list of agencies and states involved in the search for Cook?"

She took a seat on the other side of his desk and began immediately. "Tulsa, Oklahoma definitely and throughout the state." She flipped through notes in a file folder. "Coble Gambill, the Oklahoma safety commissioner, said every foot of road between Winthrop, Arkansas and Tulsa would be combed. He reported that two carloads of FBI agents, twenty-four highway troopers, state crime bureau agents and more than one hundred county and city officers are involved."

E.C. nodded, he remembered reading all that, but it was good to hear the reminder. "And what about searching by air? Did I hear that the brother of one of the men killed was taking part in that?"

Leona flipped through a few more pages in her file, nodding as she looked. "Yes, Chris Mosser, First Lieutenant in the U.S. Army, is the brother of Carl Mosser, the missing husband and father. He arrived in Tulsa to identify his brother's car when they found it, and he has stayed there to work with search parties."

"Is he part of the flying team?"

"I don't believe he is part of the air team directly, but he has met with the searchers. There are approximately twenty-five planes flying over Oklahoma and Arkansas. Their goal is to locate the bodies of the family."

E.C. nodded.

"Then, sir," Leona continued.

He appreciated her thoroughness and hoped she'd be able to help him and the other agents in setting up the field office in El Centro.

"As you ordered, the all-points bulletin has been circulated. Radio stations are broadcasting descriptions of the killer periodically, and his picture has been flashed on television news reports multiple times and will continue until he is apprehended."

"Thank you for that confirmation."

"I'm also hearing reports that days off are being canceled for police, sheriff's deputies, highway patrol and FBI officers while this search is in progress and multiple roadblocks have been set up in numerous states."

E.C. inhaled deeply, fighting off the sorrow that he couldn't let himself dwell on. He had a job to do. His own son was only a couple of years older than the oldest Mosser boy. He could not even imagine the anguish of that father as he tried to protect his family in the presence of an armed killer. He wondered, did the father have to watch his children die, or was he shot first? Was it wrong to hope that the FBI got to engage in a shootout with this squatty little killer just as they had seventeen years earlier with Dillinger? He clenched his hands, wondering, could he shoot the man if he encountered him? Then he thought again of those three little children, and he knew, yes, he could. And probably a few hundred other officers could as well.

"Sir?"

E.C. shook his head to clear his mind, realizing his secretary had been watching him.

"Leona, how do you feel about assisting us with setting up an office in El Centro until we wrap this case up? The agency will pay for your transportation and lodging costs. Bring along your husband if he can get the time off work."

Leona nodded. "I'm sure he'll take the time off work. He is as committed as we are, as the rest of the nation, to finding this man and stopping him before he takes any more innocent lives. Have you read the comments in the newspapers? There are a lot of angry people out there, so angry that he would take the lives of little children."

Glad his secretary couldn't read his mind, he only said, "I understand how they feel."

"We have to catch him, E.C." Leona wiped tears away. "We just have to."

CHAPTER 36

JANUARY 9, 1951
EL MARMOL, BAJA CALIFORNIA

James, Forrest and William piled into the car after unsuccessfully trying to hunt quail for dinner. Just before pulling away, William stuck the rifle out the back window and fired.

"What did you shoot?" James asked.

William pointed, a proud look on his face. "Coyote. I bet that's two hundred yards out." They climbed back out of the car and headed out to check. Sure enough, the coyote lay dead. Behind the back of their captor, James made eye contact with Forrest, who was shaking his head. He felt the same way. What was the point? Killing just to kill. Was that to be their fate as well?

Back in the car, they continued their southbound journey. James drove, with Forrest manning the radio, just as Bill had ordered them to do earlier. James had no idea how far down into Mexico they were, but he knew it was hundreds of miles farther than their original destination of San Felipe.

"Slow down! Slow down!"

James let off the gas, surprised at the urgency in their captor's voice. He could see in the side mirror, Bill Cook, leaning out the window, waving at an oncoming car on the narrow roadway.

The northbound car, carrying two, what he assumed were local men in the front seat, stopped when it rolled even with them.

"What's the road ahead like? Can we get through okay?"

James listened without joining in. He rolled his window down to get a look at the men and thought he saw the man in the passenger seat staring over at him and Forrest.

"Where can we get something to eat?"

"Punta Prieta is a couple of hours ahead of you," the driver said. "You can find a restaurant there."

James watched as Bill slid back into the car and rolled his window up. James waved a thank you to the driver and followed suit, rolling his own window up, then slowly heading forward.

"Do what the man said." Bill Cook leaned over the seat, pointing toward the road with his pistol. James' stomach rumbled out an urgent request for food, and his foot grew heavy on the gas pedal, hoping to get to the restaurant soon.

CHAPTER 37

JANUARY 10, 1951
IMPERIAL COUNTY, CALFIFORNIA

I mperial County Sheriff's Clerk Liza Hodges felt her
stomach flip-flop and heart beat hard as she listened to the
woman's voice on the other end of the line.

Surely this couldn't be happening in their town. One murder
already in their county and now this. Two missing men. *Please,
God,* she prayed while listening to the man's wife, *don't let this
be connected to the killer on the loose.*

She jotted notes, glad for her proficiency in shorthand, as the
woman talked. It was hard to understand her through the tears.
Liza felt her own tears forming, but she had to stay professional.
She was the only one in the office at the moment, the others were
all out on patrol. The sheriff had issued an all-points bulletin
upon finding the body of the Seattle salesman dead on a deserted
desert road, dumped carelessly and the man's car missing.

She'd have to notify the sheriff immediately of this missing
person's report. She knew in her heart there was a very good

chance it was connected to the manhunt that she'd heard was going on in multiple states, and even into Mexico, according to the report that came through late the day before. She'd seen the notes on the board in the briefing room when she came in this morning.

"Ma'am, please know that we will do all in our power to find your husband and your friend's husband. I have your number, and we will keep you informed of anything we learn."

Liza squeezed the bridge of her nose to stop her own tears, as she listened to the wife sob harder while she continued to talk.

"We will broadcast that information immediately. A reward is a very good idea. I will let the sheriff know about the reward."

More unintelligible talking and sobbing, but she thought she understood enough to respond.

"Yes, eight hundred fifty dollars, I have that written down. Thank you, ma'am. We will do all in our power. Yes, we will be in touch."

She barely got the receiver back in the cradle before her own tears flowed. She had a terrible feeling that this missing person's report was definitely linked to the killing of Robert Dewey.

She looked at her notes. Forrest Damron, age thirty-two, and James Burke, age thirty-three, driving a 1950 maroon four-door Studebaker, traveling in Mexico. Wives have had no word in four days, and they were supposed to have been home by last night. Family offering an eight hundred fifty dollar reward for finding the men.

She picked up the radio to connect with the sheriff in his car, just as the door burst open and Sheriff Robert Ware rushed into her office. "I've heard through the grapevine about some missing men."

Liza wiped her eyes, holding her notes up and nodding. "I just took the report."

CHAPTER 38

JANUARY 10, 1951
PUNTA PRIETA, MEXICO

Forrest leaned back on the rough tree trunk, watching as James fired the .22 caliber rifle William had instructed them to take turns shooting. "We're just friends," he'd told them, "out target shooting." Then he pointed the pistol at them. "And you better make it look good."

Surprised they'd been trusted to shoot a gun in his presence, Forrest figured it was because there was no way they could get a shot at the man. The moment the rifle turned in his direction, they'd be dead. They were target shooting, but while they shot, they knew they were also the targets as William always had his finger on the trigger of the gun pointed in their direction.

Forrest had just taken his turn, then handed the rifle to James, barely making eye contact. It felt like they'd been with their kidnapper for weeks. His new watch showed him it had been three days since they picked him up. He studied the watch. It was his first time owning one that told the date and the time. His grandfather had given it to him for Christmas. He wondered if he would ever see him again? What must it be doing to the old man wondering if he was dead or alive? The chances of getting out of this alive were slim. Six people before them were killed. Were they the next two to go?

Studying his watch again, he imagined what Dorothy and the girls were doing right now? He fought tears that were welling up at the thought of his young family. On a normal Wednesday afternoon, Dorothy would prepare an early dinner. Sometimes they'd go to the midweek prayer service at church. The girls loved getting together with their friends. He inhaled deeply, squeezing his eyes shut to stop the tears. He did not want William to see him wiping away tears. Surely this would be a time to go to the prayer meeting. He imagined the whole town was praying for them. It would definitely take a miracle to get out of this predicament.

"You!"

Forrest looked up at the pistol pointing in his direction.

"Your turn to shoot again. We're friends. We take turns."

"Yeah, buddy," he thought. "We're friends. Glad I never had another friend like you."

He wondered, could they try to really become friends with the guy? Is that his problem? He's alone in the world. Could they somehow change his way of thinking? His desire to kidnap and kill?

"Now!"

He looked up at the demanding man. What was his goal here? What was the end plan? Was he hoping to get some sort of happiness out of whatever he was doing?

James headed in his direction, holding out the rifle. "Come on, buddy." He nodded, then motioned his head toward their captor as if to tell him, "You better do what he says before he kills us."

Forrest took aim at the targets William had placed for them to shoot at. But when he stared at the tin cans, instead of seeing the cans dotted with bullet holes, he saw the face of William, the kidnapper. William the murderer. He pulled the trigger back, let it up, then back again, let it up, then back again, until he had gone through all ten rounds within seconds.

"Hey, don't waste the bullets," William said. "Take your time."

Forrest looked over at him as he spoke and wondered. Could he really kill the guy if he had the chance?

Later that evening as they took their sleeping positions in the car, William said, "Tomorrow, we make up time. I want to roll into Santa Rosalia by dark."

Forrest looked over at James, waiting for him to respond.

"Sure thing," James said. "We'll have to get more gas somewhere."

"We get there by dark, then we have the weekend to explore the town, maybe take in a movie."

A movie? Forrest wanted to shout the words. Their lives were in danger. This guy was a fugitive killer, and he wants to play tourist.

"Sounds like a plan," James said, so Forrest chimed in. "Sure thing."

He stretched out as much as he could in the front seat of the
car and entertained himself by making useless plans of escape.
Was he destined to be under this guy's control for the rest of his
life? There had to be a way out. There had to be.

CHAPTER 39

JANUARY 10, 1951
OSAGE COUNTY, OKLAHOMA

I t's a done deal." County Attorney Russell Havens flipped
through newspaper clippings his secretary had placed on his
desk at his request.

The one on top had the photo of the Mosser family, then the
car with the front seat view, the child's book with blood splatter
clearly showing. His heart ached. He remembered when his
daughter was young. They had taken family trips and always
returned home safe. But this family never got the chance.

His law clerk watched him from across the desk. Russell looked
up at him.

"Five murder charges, Arthur," Russell said. "One for each
member of the family. This is just the start, it's what we need to
do to send that monster to the electric chair."

"He'll be the second murdering hitchhiker to get the electric
chair in our state this year if that happens," Arthur said. "Did you
follow the Max Kletke trial? They just executed him four days
ago."

Russell nodded. "That one wasn't in our county, but I followed it in the news."

"I'd never pick up a hitchhiker," Arthur said.

"You have to wonder if the Mosser man was aware of the Kletke trial. Would it have made a difference in his choosing to help someone who appeared to be stranded?"

"How do you know who to trust?" Arthur said. "Have we got to a point where we don't help anyone because of the chance of being murdered?"

"Hard decision," Russell said. "Just a small percentage of the people who need help, or a ride, are the bad guys, but does that help the Mosser family, knowing the chances of being killed were slim?"

"What if they find the bodies in another county?" Arthur said. "Will our murder charges stick?"

"The discovery of the car here gives our county a good claim to try the case. Even if they find the bodies in another county or even another state, based on how many miles that car had been driven, there won't be any actual proof to know where the killing actually took place. I'm going to push for the trial to be held here, and for the death penalty to be sought. It's the only acceptable form of punishment considering the evil he inflicted on those innocent people."

"Now, they just have to find him," Arthur said.

"They're pursuing him down into Baja California and Imperial County in California. The sheriff there said thirty carloads of officers are probing every corner of the county."

"Do you think those two men from there are still alive?"

"We can only hope and pray they are, but based on what's happened so far, it's doubtful. Six already dead at the hands of William Cook and two missing."

"Reports say that in at least one of the small towns across the border they've conducted a house by house search." Arthur pointed to the newspapers on his desk. "I think I've read every word that's been printed about this case."

"Same here," Russell said.

"Has it ever occurred to you it could be months or years before they find him?"

"Arthur," Russell stood, gathering up the newspapers on his desk and slipping them into the file folder his secretary provided. "I try not to think about that."

"One day at a time, right, boss?"

Arthur nodded. He'd done all he could at this point.

CHAPTER 40

JANUARY 11, 1951
BENITO JUAREZ, BAJA CALIFORNIA

P ull over right now!" The urgent nature of William's command caught them by surprise as they had driven in relative silence for the last couple of hours.

Forrest looked in the back seat to see the killer rolling down the window, then aiming the .22 rifle out the back window. He looked in the direction the rifle was pointed and saw a large hawk sitting atop a cactus, probably two hundred fifty yards off the roadside. At the crack of the rifle firing, the bird dropped to the ground. "Got him!" William said.

He stared around the landscape as if looking for more live targets, then tapped James on the shoulder with the pistol. "Keep going."

Forrest felt sick. They were hunters who killed to eat, not just for the sheer joy of watching an animal die. That looked like one of the large species of hawks he'd seen before down here, with a huge wingspan. But if a man would kill people randomly like this man had done, why not animals, too? He once again felt his insides shaking.

"A few more hours," William said. "Then we'll be there."

He sounded happy. If he was, he was the only one in the car happy.

"We'll camp on the beach."

"Sounds good," James said, his voice a monotone as he kept his eyes on the road. Forrest glanced over at his friend, understanding fully how he felt. James was likely as disgusted as he was at the hawk's killing.

Staring out his side window, he calculated how many days they'd been captives. If he was counting it right, this must be Thursday. He should have been at work right now. And yesterday, and the day before. He supposed this would be considered an excused absence. He could almost laugh if it weren't so tragic. Would he ever get to go back to work again?

He glanced over at James and caught his eye when he looked his way briefly. The determined look in James' eyes gave him hope. If James hadn't given up hope yet, he wouldn't either.

CHAPTER 41

JANUARY 11, 1951
EL CENTRO, CALIFORNIA

Vivian Burke sat alone, curled up in an overstuffed chair in the corner of the living room, desperately missing her husband James. She watched as family and friends milled about, low voices muffled. She knew they were here to support her and Dorothy, but honestly, it hurt even more. Their quiet voices resembled the way people sounded and acted at a funeral. No one quite knowing what to say. She wiped tears away, she hoped surreptitiously. She did not want to attract the attention of well-meaning folks who would attempt to comfort her with words that only hurt.

"God is with him," she'd heard. Well, then why doesn't God bring him home?

"I'm sure he's okay," was another one. How could they know? They can't know. No one knows. No one knows but James and Forrest whether they are okay.

"I just feel sure he will be home soon." That one really made her want to scream. But she just stayed quiet. She couldn't even bring herself to thank the people who she knew meant well.

Honestly, there wasn't a single thing anyone could say at this point that would help her. She just wanted to be left alone. Alone with her thoughts. Alone with her fears. Alone with her memories. Trying to remember what the last thing she had said to James was before he took off on his trip. Alone with her anger. Why did he have to leave? Why couldn't he be satisfied just staying home for once? Always out exploring. She wanted to scream out in anguish. But she sat quietly. Staring at the floor. Only occasionally glancing up at the people. So many people. She wished they would all leave. She wished she could leave. But she knew that would just draw more attention.

When Dorothy had invited her over today, she thought it would be just the two of them and Dorothy's little girls. She didn't know it would be a houseful. Are they already having a wake without the bodies? Tears flowed. She could not stop them, no matter how hard she tried. She dropped her head down onto the arm of the chair, exhaustion overtaking her.

Vivian didn't know how much time had gone by when she felt the presence of a small person next to her. She raised her head to see Dorothy's little daughter Sharon kneeling by her chair. She felt her hand resting on her knee. Vivian took hold of it, squeezing. This little one had to be hurting as much or more than she was. Her daddy was missing. She knew Dorothy was being strong for the sake of her children, not wanting to scare them. They had discussed it when they first realized their husbands were missing.

Sharon squeezed her hand back. "I'm praying for my daddy," she said. "And for Mr. Burke, too."

Vivian felt a fresh wave of tears. She apparently wasn't as strong as Dorothy. She leaned over to hug Sharon. "Thank you, precious." Wiping her tears, she looked into the little girl's eyes, glassy with her own tears. "I'm praying, too."

"I told God I really want Him to bring my daddy home."

"I want that too, honey," Vivian said. "We all do."

She scooted over as Sharon climbed into the chair next to her. This little one offered more comfort to her than all the adults in the room. Together, they could weep and hope and pray. Maybe tomorrow they would hear something.

CHAPTER 42

JANUARY 11, 1951
TUSCOLA, ILLINOIS

T *here is one thing that stands out like a beacon light in the career of William E. Cook, murderer. He is a parole convict. Thus, once again it becomes evident that there is something fundamentally wrong with our parole system when a man so vicious, so warped, so incensed against society, can gain freedom by official sanction. For William E. Cook is not an isolated figure in the world of violence. He has had many predecessors throughout the length and breadth of this land down through the years, with the result that police records are botched with crimes committed by ex-criminals who never should have been turned free.*

Judson W. Arnett, publisher of *The Tuscola Review,* had been a newspaperman most of his life. It was in his blood. The pen is mightier than the sword, he truly believed. He held the first copy off the press of today's paper, with the specific goal of rereading the editorial that would surely get tempers flared across the city. Whether those readers were angry with the murderer, angry with the parole board or angry with him for printing this editorial. They would demand to know who wrote it. It was their policy not to use bylines on the editorials. And he would refuse to tell them. He wouldn't admit or deny writing the words himself. Though he had read them enough, he could practically recite them.

There is a growing feeling in this country that parole boards should be manned by medical specialists rather than by political appointees, as is the case in too many instances. And there is also the feeling that there are some people who should never be released from prison regardless of the nature of their initial crime. This latter suggestion seems harsh, but it is a fact that there are men and women to whom violence becomes an obsession. Many times this obsession develops while the individuals in question are serving sentences for minor crimes. A parole board dominated by doctors and specialists would recognize this development and guard against it. Political appointees have no way of knowing whether or not a man is rational and ready for his return to society.

Without a doubt, Judson knew that William E. Cook Jr. had not been ready for his return to society. In fact, if the reports could be believed, a violent temper had controlled this young man since he was a child.

Not ten miles away was the one hundred sixty acre parcel that Carl Mosser would never again farm. A large grassy yard that his three children would never again romp and play in. A beautiful farmhouse where Thelma Mosser would never again stand on the front porch watching over her children. And they could thank the parole board for this. The one that determined that William E. Cook was ready to be let loose back in society. Fewer than seven months after he was released, he'd left a wake of death in his path. And who knew if there were more deaths to come? Word had it that two more men were missing and very possibly were his captives, if they were even, in fact, still alive.

He turned his attention back to the newspaper on his desk. The ending was powerful. He had to read it one more time before starting his day.

William E. Cook, murderer, had been a troublemaker since the age of eleven. But it was only during his last incarceration that he developed into a vicious killer. He had the obsession when he left prison after serving a few years for a felony, but no one recognized that here, indeed, was an enemy of society. And as a result a fine Atwood family has been wiped out.

William E. Cook, murderer, is more than a name in the headlines. He is the fearful symbol of a parole system that is archaic and loaded with danger.

All three phone lines simultaneously started ringing. He checked the time. Yes, right on schedule. Most readers knew the newspaper office opened at 8 a.m. every day of the week. And right on schedule, the angry readers were calling to weigh in on the *William E. Cook, murderer* piece. He certainly hoped they were calling in their support, for if not, if they in fact disagreed that the fault lies with the parole board, then it was his opinion they were just as much at fault, for catering to the criminal element that renders innocent people unsafe. It was a crying shame if that was the case.

CHAPTER 43

JANUARY 12, 1951
SANTA ROSALIA, BAJA CALIFORNIA

James shrugged off his blanket into the sand and stood, reaching his arms high in the air, working out his tired muscles. It had felt so good to sleep stretched out on the beach instead of cramped in the front seat of the car behind the steering wheel.

He watched William where he lay, maybe asleep, maybe awake. They could never quite tell with that one eye that didn't close all the way. With the ever-present pistol clutched in his hand, one finger ready at any moment to pull the trigger. Day six of their captivity.

He stood staring at the ocean, listening to the waves gently slapping against the shore, and thought about what a peaceful place this might be for a family vacation. But with the circumstances that had brought them here, it was anything but peaceful.

He wondered about his wife and family. Life had to be as difficult for them as it was for him and Forrest, just in a different way. He supposed they probably assumed they were dead. He imagined his wife mourning him, trying to figure out her life as a widow. He hoped and prayed that would not come true. Perhaps this might be the day they would be rescued, or they would escape or that Billy Cook, the killer, would be captured. *Please, Lord. Could this be the day that happens?*

Several hours later, they walked through town and headed for the movie theater. He wondered at the change in being secretive. On the trip down, they stayed on back roads and now, just walked around in plain sight without trying to hide. Although still not allowed to talk to anyone. Maybe he figured they were deep enough into Mexico that no one was looking for him here. And sadly, James wondered the same thing. Because even with this guy's noticeably messed up eyelid, and getting in and out of the maroon colored car, no one, not one person had stared at them in this town as if they were anything other than a few American tourists waiting for the ferry to take them deeper into Mexico. Oh Lord, what would happen when they got deeper? When he didn't need them anymore? William had his identification, and once they got over into Guaymas, chances are he'd feel like he had made his escape. He wouldn't need them, and they surely knew too much about him to just release them. They had until Monday for something to happen. He said they'd spend the weekend here in Santa Rosalia and take the ferry on Monday. *Please, Lord, let something happen before Monday to set us free.*

William kept the pistol in his jacket pocket as they walked around town. He directed them to the movie house, subtly reminding them he'd have the gun aimed at them the entire time.

He paid for the tickets and then directed them down an aisle to the first row of seats. William motioned for Forrest to take the third seat over from the aisle, then nodded at James. William took the aisle seat, then leaned over, pulling his jacket back so the two could see the gun under his jacket pointed in their direction.

Just about the time James was relaxing, mildly entertained by a movie that he couldn't follow, although it was helping to improve his limited knowledge of Spanish. William leaned over. "Come on, let's get out of here."

The man with the gun was in charge. They both stood as he stepped into the aisle, and motioned for them to walk ahead of him, knowing the ever-present gun was pointed at their backs as they exited the theater.

Back at the beach, William pulled out the rifles, checked to make sure they were unloaded, then handed one to each of them. He gestured towards the large rocks close to where they parked. A few scattered parties along the beach barely glanced their way. The locals probably saw hunters often.

"We'll just hang out here for a bit. You guys mess with the guns like you're cleaning them and getting ready to do some more hunting."

Nighttime couldn't come soon enough for him. As they wrapped up in their blankets on the beach near the parked car,

James sighed. Another day. They made it through another day still alive. Another day he did not get his wish or his prayer answered. They were still prisoners of the killer. He hadn't thought he could sleep, but the exhaustion of the week, both mental and physical, caught up with him, and he was soon, thankfully, sound asleep.

CHAPTER 44

JANUARY 13, 1951
EL CENTRO, CALIFORNIA

Police Chief Guy Woodward leaned his elbows on the desk, his fist propped against his chin, chewing on his lower lip, as he stared out the lone window in his office. Nearly sundown on another day with no answers. He'd heard a news broadcast on the radio earlier that day quoting Sheriff Robert Ware saying the investigation had "assumed a routine status." He cringed at the thought of how that must have made the wives of the missing men feel. It made him feel bad. It had been seven long days since he'd discovered the last car William Cook had abandoned. Having left a trail of six known dead within a matter of a few short days, it was highly likely these two men had also been killed. Routine? This was anything but routine. He questioned the choice of words the sheriff had uttered. If, in fact, that is what he said. He knew that sometimes reporters misunderstood or couldn't read their own notes.

The wives hadn't been at the station for the last couple of days. He could only imagine the grief and fear they were living with, and was glad they had each other and their family members to comfort them.

Guy looked up as the dispatch clerk entered the office, papers in hand.

"What do you have there, Miranda?"

"More info coming in across the wire about the manhunt."

He patted his desk and watched as she placed several pages on his desk pad.

"Thanks, Miranda, I'll go over them."

"Do you need anything else?"

"No thank you, just pull the door shut, please."

He needed to study these papers alone. He needed time to process and, most of all, he needed not to have any witnesses should the tears that threatened to fall as each day passed finally force their way out of his eyes. A police chief shouldn't cry, should he?

A thorough reading of the report showed they were in good company in the search. Hundreds, if not thousands, of law enforcement officers were searching not only for the killer, but for the killed. Five bodies they'd been looking for across a number of states for ten days already. The way that killer got around, he was likely long gone from California or Mexico.

Besides the state of Oklahoma, where the bloodstained car was found, there had been reports of sightings in Idaho, Montana, Wyoming, Georgia, Minnesota, North and South Dakota, Utah and their own state of California. Surely some of these were mistaken, but every tip, every lead had to be followed up on. He knew he wasn't the only law enforcement officer or even civilian lying awake nights, then spending long hours pursuing the case.

He noted farther down in the report the price on Billy's head was up to almost twenty-four hundred dollars now, with family and friends of the missing Illinois family offering fifteen hundred dollars and the family of the missing prospectors here in his town offering eight hundred fifty dollars. He hoped this would bring out hundreds more searchers.

Guy added the papers to the fat case file folder in his desk drawer and propped his head in hands. "Lord, please," he breathed out. "Show us where he is. Protect those men. Lead the searchers to the poor family who lost their lives. Please."

He'd managed to hold back the tears for another day. It was time to head home to his family. His safe family. It almost didn't seem fair.

CHAPTER 45

JANUARY 13, 1951
TIJUANA, BAJA CALIFORNIA

Tijuana Police Chief Franciso Kraus Morales reviewed the updated wire reports coming through about the United States FBI fugitive William Cook, the man also known as Billy. The man with the droopy eye. He'd also been called the Cockeyed Killer.

It was late in the day, a full week after they discovered evidence of him in Mexico, and after reading reports of sightings in various states, he doubted the man was nearby. But he knew, as did all the other officers on alert, you had to keep looking. You could never stop looking until the man was captured. He just hoped it was sooner, not later.

"Chief," his patrol officer Javier Hernandez approached with two men following. So lost in his thoughts, he hadn't even heard them come in. "They need to speak to you. This sounds big."

"Chief Morales here." He stood, reaching out to shake the stranger's hand.

"My name is Xavier Gonzales. I'm the paymaster at the lead mine in Santa Rosalia. I think we have seen the man you are hunting for, that William Cook fellow."

Morales motioned to Hernandez, who stood nearby listening. "Get the governor on the phone. We need his plane right away."

"Yes, tell me where and what you saw," Morales returned his attention to Xavier, eager to hear the rest of the story, hoping to verify its accuracy.

"My co-worker here, Jerry Grant, who is the mine engineer, and I were driving north on the highway and we spotted a car heading south. A man leaned out the back window and flagged us down. He looked just like the reports said, had that droopy eye, and there were two Americans in the front seat. Men. They looked scared to me."

"What did he say to you?" Francisco scribbled notes as the man talked, making sure he got their names and where they worked. If this panned out, he would need to reach them again to congratulate and offer gratitude for leading them to the killer.

"He asked us about the condition of the road up ahead and wanted to know what towns were ahead."

"Did you answer his questions?"

"We did. He asked about places to eat."

"Where did you direct him?" Francisco asked, still scribbling notes.

"We said Punta Prieta would be the best place to get some food, but we weren't too far from El Marmol."

Morales directed the men's attention to the fliers.

177

"Yes," both men said at once.

"That is definitely him," Xavier confirmed.

"And the car you saw," Morales said. "Tell me about it."

"It was maroon, maybe a Studebaker, don't know for sure though, but definitely maroon."

"That's our guy."

The office became a buzz of activity as flight arrangements were made. Morales shook hands once again. "Gentlemen, thank you. You may have saved the lives of the missing men. We will be in touch with you."

CHAPTER 46

JANUARY 14, 1951
OKEMAH, OKLAHOMA

Reverend Bertrand Simmons, or B.N., as he preferred to
be called, stepped to the pulpit as the choir finished the
opening hymn. He saw the surprised looks of the people in the
pews, for this was not the usual order of service. No, at this time,
Ken Hufman, the much-loved Music Director of First Baptist
Church, would stand in this place leading the congregation in the
worship time that preceded his message. But today, well, today
was different.

He stood before his people, almost short of words.
Something that rarely happened, in fact, he'd often been
embarrassed at the gloating praise the people gave him.
Dynamic. They said he was a dynamic preacher. And he loved
to share the gospel every chance he got. But today, his people
weren't going to listen to a message about the gospel. They
were going to go out and minister to the hurting. He believed
in searching they were ministering, even if they found nothing.
They were ministering to the hurting family members of the
Mosser family. Just two weeks ago, probably very few people

in the nation had heard of the Mosser family, other than close family and friends. But now, sadly, they were almost a household name.

"Brothers and sisters," he spoke, sensing the restlessness in the pews, as he stood before them for so long without speaking. "Today, my heart is heavy, as I'm sure yours is as well. Heavy, but at the same time, I'm feeling encouraged that we have been given something to do. I know many of you have been following the news reports of the Mosser family, who have lost their lives. And today, this very morning, I read in the newspaper that we are all being called upon to help."

He watched as men nodded, women dabbed at their eyes, children wiggled and tugged on their parents' sleeves, most likely asking what the preacher was talking about.

"For those of you who may not have read the morning newspaper, I'd like to share with you what is significant about today. Sheriff Dewey Smith," he stopped and looked over the folks listening intently. "For those of you who are lucky enough to have never encountered law enforcement officers," he enjoyed the few chuckles that gave a moment of levity to such a difficult topic. "Sheriff Smith is the sheriff of our county, and he is putting the word out that there has been a proclamation by the governors of both Oklahoma and Arkansas to residents to lend support to the county and state-wide search for the bodies of the missing Mosser family."

Whispers and low voices sounded throughout the congregation as people looked at their neighbors and most likely began considering what they could do to help.

"You'll see in your bulletins that I had a message planned for today, Pastor Ken had songs picked out, but I feel such a heaviness in my heart for the loved ones left behind. I can't imagine the hurt they are bearing, first in knowing that the lives have been taken of their family members, but then in not even knowing where they are. Being deprived of giving them a proper burial. So, my intention today is to urge all of us here to join in the search."

Heads nodding all across the sanctuary encouraged him and strengthened him, and he hoped in some small way they could all be an encouragement to the extended Mosser family.

"I'll read the statement our sheriff has put forth, then we will close in prayer and dismiss, so that we all may join in the search."

Reading right from the morning newspaper, B.N. shared the words of the sheriff.

To the people of Okfuskee County:

I, the sheriff of Okfuskee County, have been asked by the governor of the State of Oklahoma to direct a county-wide search on Sunday, January 14, 1951, for the bodies of the Mosser family.

Therefore, I am requesting in each public gathering Sunday morning that we would appreciate your making the announcement that we would like to have each individual in the county to thoroughly search his own premises.

We would suggest that people living in towns, would sometime in the afternoon take time to visit someone you know in the country, and aid them in searching out all possible hiding places.

If the bodies are found, please place a guard, and notify the sheriff's office immediately.

In appreciation of your cooperation, we are deeply thankful.
–Dewey Smith, Sheriff.

B.N. looked across the congregation and saw not only women, but now men too, wiping at tears, most likely knowing these just weren't adult bodies they were searching for but the bodies of three precious little children.

The words of this official announcement, calling on each of them from the highest level of government in their state to join in the search, made the crime more real, reached out to each one of them in this room and involved them. It warmed his heart to see the response and know that his people would follow the instructions and join in.

"And now, Lord God, we ask you to give us strength to follow the instructions we've just heard and to bring comfort to the family members who are grieving. In the name of Jesus we pray, amen."

CHAPTER 47

JANUARY 14, 1951
JUST OUTSIDE OF SANTA ROSALIA,
BAJA CALIFORNIA

James watched the sunrise from the makeshift camp and listened to his stomach rumble. He longed for a big breakfast–bacon and eggs, or steak and eggs, or ham and eggs, or all of the above. It had been days since they'd had a good meal. Subsisting on snacks and fruit they'd been able to pick up at roadside stands and little markets.

This was their seventh morning to wake up and still be in this nightmare. But the fact they were still alive was a good thing. He didn't know how long the family drove around with Cook before he killed them. Maybe that was still their fate. He wondered what his wife was doing. He was pretty sure it was Sunday, and he wondered if she would go to church. Maybe they were praying for them at church. Actually, no maybe about it. He knew for a fact they were. Who knows, maybe people all across the United States were praying for them. They could surely use it.

He saw Forrest stirring in the blankets he was wrapped in nearby. William, as usual, sat propped up against a tree, one eye closed, the other perpetually open. Surely he had to sleep at some point, but since there was no way to tell when he really was asleep, and with that gun always in his lap and his trigger-happy hand close by, there was no way of escape. Neither of them had been willing to try. He figured, and knew Forrest probably felt the same way, any attempt at escape would only hasten their death. Maybe if they kept cooperating, they'd get out of this alive. Just maybe. It was all they could hope and pray for.

"How about we go into town and find a restaurant?" James glanced at Forrest but spoke toward William. The man didn't move.

"Sounds like a good idea to me." Forrest stood, stretching his arms overhead, then bending over to touch his toes. James knew how he felt. Days in the car were wearing on him, too. He joined in the stretching.

Finally, Bill opened both eyes and stared in their direction. "Nothing's open today. It's Sunday." The words came out in a growl. Maybe this guy was tiring of this game, too.

"We could go check," Forrest said.

"It's a waste of time."

James almost laughed out loud. Time was all they had on their hands at this point. Why was this guy worried about wasting time? "I think it's worth a try."

"Get out your cooking stuff," William said. "Cook me up some of those eggs you brought."

So much for going into town for a real meal.

After breakfast, William brought out the tin cans for more target practice.

As the day wore on, the eggs and beef jerky that had satisfied him earlier were no longer holding his hunger at bay. He decided to try again.

"How about we go see if the restaurant has opened now?" James said. "You know, for the after-church crowd."

"I want some of those native oranges." Forrest rubbed his belly. "Those sure hit the spot."

James watched as Bill seemed to perk up. The mention of the oranges had gotten his attention. He remembered now when they got a bag at the roadside stand a few days ago, Bill had eaten half the bag himself. He wondered if Forrest really wanted the oranges himself or if he used that as bait to get Bill to agree to go into town.

"Do you think we could find some?" Bill said.

"Definitely," James said. "Practically every roadside stand has them. And then we can find a restaurant to get a decent meal while we're out looking for oranges."

"Pull over when you see the orange stands."

More instructions from the back seat driver. The orange stands would slow them down, but at least he knew eventually they would get a hot meal.

.

CHAPTER 48

JANUARY 14, 1951
SANTA ROSALIA, BAJA CALIFORNIA

Forrest inhaled the tantalizing smells of the restaurant as soon as they stepped out of the car. Even after munching on a few of the oranges they'd picked up on the way, his stomach still growled like he hadn't had a decent meal in a week. And he hadn't. His mind wandered to home, and all the meals he'd missed with his beautiful wife and little daughters. Would he ever see them again? He had to believe he would. They'd made it this long. Almost three times as long as the other family if the radio accounts were right.

James held the door open, and Forrest followed Bill inside with James bringing up the rear. A round table with four chairs near the back was open, and Bill took a seat first, his back toward the entrance. Forrest let James choose his seat, and he ended up in the middle of the two men.

The menu on the table featured both Mexican and American food, and when the waitress came to take their order, Bill pointed to the photo of the fried chicken platter.

Forrest looked over at James. "What do you think? Sounds good, doesn't it?"

"Anything sounds good at this point."

"We'll take the same," Forrest said, gathering all the menus and handing them to the waitress as she finished jotting down their requests.

Forrest wondered if anyone else in the restaurant had seen the pistol tucked in Bill's belt that showed below his leather jacket if he moved just right. No one was staring at them, so maybe not. He tapped his finger on his water glass, somewhat in time to the Mexican music playing, but more from a nervous tick.

Bill, as usual, stared down at the table, sometimes looking around at the floor, and Forrest focused on his own water glass as his mind pondered various scenarios for how they could get out of this mess. Maybe they could try again, offering their car to the man if he would just leave them here. He doubted that would work though, since Bill knew they could obviously identify him.

He felt James bump his foot under the table and ignored it at first. Floor space was at a premium under restaurant tables, and anyone stretching could easily bump the other person. But when it happened a second time, he looked over at James, who nodded toward the door.

Forrest felt his heartbeat speed up as he watched the three uniformed officers standing just inside the door, probably acclimating their eyesight to the dark interior. Then as they gazed around the room, their perusal stopped when it got to their table. All three men headed in their direction.

Forrest and James kept quiet, hoping and praying this was the rescue they'd been longing for. Bill was oblivious to the newcomers in the restaurant and just stared at the table waiting for his chicken.

Forrest pulled off the performance of his life as he kept a poker face while the men made a beeline for Bill Cook. The tallest of the three pressed his service revolver into their kidnapper's back. Bill sat up straight, his hand twitched as if he was going for his gun.

"Don't make a move for that gun in your belt." The booming voice silenced the restaurant as all the patrons watched the drama unfold.

Bill sat tense for a moment, then his shoulders slumped and he surrendered with no fight at all.

And just like that, their captivity was over. Forrest looked over at James and saw tears in his eyes, mirroring what Forrest knew his must look like. Tears of joy. *Thank you, Lord, thank you!* They were going to go home.

The two men accompanying the taller officer led Bill out of the restaurant after handcuffing him. The man who'd apprehended him turned to Forrest and James and held out his hand to shake.

"Chief Franciso Morales, from Tijuana, and you two must be Forrest and James, the prospectors?"

"I'm Forrest, he's James," he said as he returned the handshake. "Thank you, thank you so much for saving us."

"You can thank the two men the fugitive talked to on the road the other day. They came to our police station yesterday when they got to town. We flew down right away. Jose Navarro, the pilot for the governor, flew me and one of my officers down to El Marmol, then we followed your trail to Punto Prieta where people said they had seen you. We got into town here about the same time that you pulled in. We'll be flying him back to Tijuana, then will turn him over to the FBI in the U.S."

"I thought I saw the guy in the passenger seat looking at us, while the driver was talking to Cook."

"Same here," James said.

"You know, most people thought you two were dead," Chief Morales said. "Going to be some mighty happy people when they hear you're still alive."

The waitress appeared, balancing three chicken plate dinners. "Shall I still serve these?"

Forrest looked at the police chief. He wasn't sure what the game plan was now, but he sure was hungry.

"Go ahead," Chief Morales said. "You two eat while I step outside and we make arrangements to transport him. Then we'll make flight arrangements–on a different plane–for the two of you to fly to Tijuana so we can take your statements."

"What about our car?" James said, not that he was in the mood to drive the hundreds of miles back to the States.

"We'll transport that by freight at a later date. It needs to be searched."

Chief Morales left them to enjoy their meal.

"This is the best meal I've had in a long, long time," Forrest said, as he prepared to dig in.

"Our celebration meal." James lifted his water glass in a toast.

"Talking Bill Cook into getting oranges this afternoon was the smartest thing we've ever done in our lives."

CHAPTER 49

JANUARY 15, 1951
JOPLIN, Missouri

Detective Carl Nutt was a decorated World War II veteran and Purple Heart recipient who had served on the front lines of the war effort. He once shared with a friend that the details of the terrors he witnessed never left him. By the end of this cold day in January, an entirely new type of terror would be added to the memories he could never forget.

The thermometer outdoors hovered right around the forty-degree mark while Detective Nutt sipped hot coffee at his desk, occasionally glancing at the newly installed gas heater in the corner of his office. He enjoyed the warmth, but it was about the only joy in his day. He and his fellow officers had a hard task facing them.

Until twelve days ago, the family was considered kidnapped. But with the discovery of their bloody car filled with bullet holes in Tulsa, it was certain they were dead. The big question was what had William Cook done with their bodies? And did he kill the entire family, or was it possible some of them were still alive? Would even a madman kill children in cold blood?

He reached into his desk drawer to retrieve the photo of the Mosser family. The little boys in their Hopalong Cassidy hats, the little girl in the checked dress with one arm around her daddy's neck as he held her. A smiling mother standing between the boys. He'd kept the photo in plain sight on his desk, not knowing if it was recent or older until the day the description of the car came in. In the back seat, the boy's Hopalong Cassidy hats were found among the blood and bullet holes. The strings had been cut. Carl didn't imagine the boys or their father cut those strings. The photo he had must have been a recent one.

He set the photo aside and returned to studying the FBI wanted poster featuring the front and side headshots of William Cook. Slamming his fist down on his desk, he directed his question to the lifeless photo of the killer. "Where did you leave their bodies?!"

His raised voice brought fellow officer Walter Gamble from his office down the hall. Carl could tell by the look on Walter's face, he fully understood the frustration, the anger.

"He was from around here," Walter said. "You think he would have left the bodies nearby?"

"A hundred miles from where he shot them?" Carl stood to study the map on his wall. They'd marked all the places where there had been confirmed sightings. They couldn't mark the hundreds of tips that had come into the FBI, their map would be unreadable. It was one hundred fifteen miles between Tulsa, Oklahoma and Joplin, Missouri, where they were, where William Cook had lived his miserable life. And it was miserable. Carl Nutt knew that. But did that misery give him license to inflict worse misery on innocents? No! He screamed the word inside his head. One outburst on this day was enough.

"Suppose he killed them here, dumped their bodies somewhere..."

Carl cringed at the word dumped. It was so disrespectful. However, he knew it accurately described what they would most likely discover when they recovered the bodies. Whether it was their department here in Joplin, or somewhere else along the path of multiple states they had driven.

"He could have even shot them in Texas where that old gas station attendant chased them down." Carl threw his hands in the air and struggled to hold back the tears that wanted to fall every time he let himself think too much about those children. He took a deep breath.

"If only that old guy had just shot the man," Walter said.

"He didn't know." Carl offered a defense for the man who probably was aching with the pain of knowing he was the last to see that family alive and he'd let them get away.

"I'm going to get on the phone with that state evidence man in Tulsa and see what they've turned up, maybe something that can help us."

Carl felt his leg jiggling up and down uncontrollably, tense with nerves as he waited to be patched through to the evidence man. Something had to give. They needed a break in this case. How long could this drag out with no answers for the family? No answers for the nation who knew a madman was on the roam with a gun and a temper. And a precious family was missing.

About the time he finished his call, he saw Walter dart back down the hall to his office as the extension line jangled several rings.

He looked at the notes he'd scribbled on a scratch pad while listening. This clue just might point them in the right direction. And it's likely that their hunch from earlier in the day would pay off. Billy Cook may have returned to his hometown to dispose of the evidence of the most heinous crime this town had ever witnessed in its entire seventy-eight-year history.

"Carl!" Walter's voice reached him from his office, before he saw the man scurrying down the hallway, carrying his own piece of paper with handwritten notes. "This might be our key to finding that family."

"Who did you talk to?" Carl tapped his own notes as he questioned the officer. "And I've got some good intel from the state police in Tulsa. But let me know what you've got."

Walter read from the note he held. His hand shaking, and a quaver to his voice. "Guy says—"

"Did you get his name?" Carl interrupted.

"Harold Suman."

"What did he say?"

Walter continued, "Says he was in jail once with Billy Cook."

"Hmm, sounds like a reliable source if he knows him."

"Says Billy once bragged to him that he'd killed a man and stuffed his body down an abandoned mine shaft." Walter looked up as Carl nodded, a big smile on his face.

"Bingo! That goes right along with what I just learned."

"From the Tulsa State Police?"

"Yes. They did an analysis of the mud from the car and said it had heavy shale content."

Walter's eyes went wide. "They did shale and zinc mining over in that area near where Cook comes from."

An hour later, a group of detectives, police officers and firemen stared horrified down the mine shaft they'd just uncovered. Word had spread, and they'd had to cordon off the area as onlookers, reporters and photographers gathered. Detective Carl Nutt was tempted to send them all packing, but he knew this was a collective pain, not just in their town but across the nation. And since the killer was a native of Joplin, in some ways it hurt so much worse for all the citizens of this town than it might have for others across the United States who'd been following this case for the past two weeks.

He appreciated the orderliness and somber attitude of the bystanders as they waited for the officers to make their move. The 50 foot deep shaft flooded with murky water held the bodies of the Mosser family, their lifeless figures floating in a final disrespectful act of the killer with no regard for the lives of people who had done nothing to him even remotely deserving of this treatment. He'd taken out his anger on the world, on a family who had what he did not have.

This time Carl could not hold back the tears as he stared down at the shiny patent leather shoes and lace anklets of little

Pamela Sue. She must have been the last one carelessly tossed into this pit. Without looking around, he could tell by the sniffs and gasps that nearly everyone around him reacted with the same level of grief.

He looked over at the photographers waiting for permission to approach the crime scene. As much as he did not want their bodies photographed, he owed it to the nation who grieved for them to see the truth. And he hoped any person out there who might be called to serve on the jury to determine this man's fate, would see this photo and it would be indelibly etched in their mind as they made their decision on the final outcome of this man's trial. No matter what the rules were for the jury regarding media exposure.

"Detective," the fireman lifted his gas mask to speak as he came back up on the hoist with Pamela Sue's little body. "Even the family dog is down there."

Carl shook his head while wiping the tears that continued to flow. He watched as Pamela Sue's body was placed gently on the tarp spread out nearby to receive the bodies as they were recovered. The evil that could consume someone was beyond him. This poor family.

CHAPTER 50

JANUARY 16, 1951
OKLAHOMA CITY, OKLAHOMA

U.S. Attorney Robert Shelton stared transfixed out the window of his home office. Thick law books lay open on his desk, his glasses next to them. He'd read and re-read the passages about the federal kidnapping act and knew without a doubt the law applied to this case. He practically had the law memorized word for word. But he needed a break, both from straining his eyes and from straining his heart.

Lush trees surrounded the house, their leaves tapping against the window. He watched as green branches swayed in the icy wind that had been blowing most of the day. He wondered whether they'd get more snow this evening as predicted. A simple thought, the weather. One that gave him a welcome reprieve from the torment that had haunted his mind and prevented him from sleeping over the last few days.

He should have stayed at the office until his usual quitting time of five, but the pacing was distracting his law clerk and secretary, not to mention giving away his unrest. He preferred to keep his emotions in check, always presenting a confident demeanor, the look of a man who only expected success at whatever he set out to do. And in this case, that was to elicit the highest level of punishment a defendant could receive. The death penalty.

But before he could argue that, based on the Lindbergh Act that he could recite in his sleep, the law that gave him the right to demand the death penalty, he had to get the word that the case would be transferred to his jurisdiction. California and Missouri prosecutors were also vying for the right to try this killer, but the gun was first pulled on the victim Lee Archer right here in the county where he lived. He took a personal interest in protecting the citizens of his state, but even more so, of his own district. He'd followed the case in the newspapers, on the network broadcasts, through the FBI notices and legal notifications sent out daily. When Billy Cook had arrived in his district with Lee Archer on December 30, it was shortly after that he connected with the Mosser family.

He turned from the window and slammed a fist on his desk. By God, he knew this jurisdiction was the right one to try this case. And this jurisdiction was where the punishment of death would be meted out. He was driven to see that this madman paid for his heinous crimes.

"Dad?"

Startled to see his fifteen-year-old son standing at the office doorway, Robert struggled to get out of his legal battle mode and put his dad hat on.

"Hey, Joe. I didn't realize you were home from school already."

"Yeah, the coach canceled basketball practice today because of a meeting he had to attend. But what's going on with you? You're home early, and I thought I heard something hit your desk."

Robert stepped around his desk and dropped into the office chair, pondering how much to tell. He wanted to protect his son from the horrors of the world. There would be time enough for him to learn that. He shuddered at the thought of those little innocent children who learned about the evil all too young at the hands of the killer.

"Is it the Cook case? Everyone's talking about it at school. They said the guy kidnapped that family here in our town. Is that true?"

His son took him by surprise. Here he was, wanting to protect him, and Joe already knew about it. Maybe it was time to face the fact that his son was growing up. He'd be a sophomore next year and off to college in only a few more years. Robert wondered, but had never asked, if Joe would follow in his footsteps and get into the legal profession. He rather hoped he would. And if he did, he'd be the third-generation Shelton to practice law. He kept his dreams to himself, though. He remembered his dad often sharing his longing for them to set up a law practice together someday. And while he had enjoyed the profession, he wondered if he would have chosen something different without the influence. Although at the same time that influence had led him to do great things. He was torn between letting his son make his own decision, or guiding him as his father did.

"Dad?"

"I'm sorry, Joe." He stood and came around the desk, dropping his arm across his son's shoulders. "Let's go see when supper will be ready. I'll answer your questions on the way."

The aroma of beef stroganoff greeted them as they entered the kitchen a few moments later.

"You're not bringing your work home, are you, Robert?" Phyllis softened her chastisement with her always-present smile. He knew even more than his own desire, his wife longed to protect their son from the evil that sometimes invaded their lives because of his career.

"I asked him about it, Mom."

"And you had to give him all the details?" Her smile stayed, but he could hear a touch of sadness in his wife's voice that the innocence of childhood was becoming a thing of the past for their son.

"Mom, it's all everyone is talking about at school, and the kids expect me to have all the answers because of Dad's position. Should I tell them my mom says I'm too young to hear about it?" Like his mother, the smile on his son's face as he looked at her softened the words that could have sounded harsh coming from another teen.

Robert smiled. "He's got you there, Phyllis."

She pointed to the stack of plates and silverware on the counter. "Well, how about you two set the table for supper?" She put her finishing touches on the meal while they obliged, then said, "We might as well discuss it while we eat. I've wanted to know too, Robert, if you're going to try the case."

After grace, and passing of the food, before even taking a bite, Joe jumped right back into the conversation. "My civics teacher said this case would fall under the Lindbergh Act and the guy could even get the death penalty."

Robert nodded as he chewed his first bite of the savory stroganoff. "Kidnapping, crossing state lines and victims being killed. He absolutely qualifies for the death penalty."

"That won't bring back the family who died." His wife's soft voice was almost unintelligible. They'd had this conversation many times, and it seemed the two of them would never see eye to eye. He wondered now where his son stood. But he didn't have to wait long.

"Mom, that man needs to pay for his crime."

"There are other punishments than taking a human life." Phyllis stared at her plate as she spoke, not looking at either of them.

Joe reached out and took his mother's hand where it rested on the table next to the fork she had put down, most likely having lost her appetite. "He took life, Mom. If you're concerned about the loss of life, focus on the six lives of those innocent people who did nothing to deserve to die. Billy Cook deserves to die for what he did."

Robert felt himself smiling inwardly. His son had the makings of a lawyer, as he argued his first case with his mother, a staunch anti-death penalty advocate. It had been the only serious disagreement they'd had over the course of their marriage, a disagreement that could not be resolved between the two of them, especially once he attained the position of U.S. Attorney.

He'd given up trying to change her mind though, just finally realizing he needed to accept that they disagreed. He was glad for his son, who argued the point with her.

Phyllis placed her cloth napkin beside the plate while scooting her chair back. "I'm going to tend the dogs." Her voice was gentle as she stood. She wouldn't argue with her son. But she clearly was not changing her position. The hunting dogs were her escape. She wasn't a hunter, but she relished the opportunity to raise the dogs, and she spent time with them often, especially when she had things on her mind. Maybe when this case was over, it would be time for another hunting trip with his son. They could use a diversion. But first, secure the death penalty. It should be an open and shut case once the Southern California district agreed to send Billy Cook here for the trial.

"Dad?" Joe had waited until they heard the quiet click of the back door shutting. He knew she was safely out of earshot. "Why doesn't Mom understand how important this is? She sounds just like the girls in my civics class. Some of them were actually crying about the idea of 'poor Billy' getting killed by our government." He rested both arms on the table, fists clenched, then his voice went up an octave, apparently mimicking the girls. 'He had such a hard life. It's not his fault.'"

Robert watched and listened as the fifteen-year-old version of him slammed a fist on the table, causing the silverware near his place setting to jump and rattle against the plate. How could he scold the boy, when he'd done the same thing, not thirty minutes ago?

"Where is their pity for the little children he killed?"

"Joe," Robert said. "I've never asked you this, but I almost wonder if we might become law partners one day?"

"Are you kidding me, Dad?" The boy smiled, picking up his fork to dig back into the forgotten stroganoff on his plate. "I really never gave any thought to a career yet."

Robert joined him in resuming the meal. He hated for it to go to waste. The least they could do for Phyllis at this point would be to enjoy the fruits of her labor and let her know later how much they appreciated the meal. He looked up after chewing a few bites. "It's just that you remind me of a young version of myself. I had no idea you had such strong feelings about death penalty cases or any type of punishment the courts mete out."

Joe nodded as he shoveled food into his mouth, his appetite apparently not damaged by the serious topic. "I'm not sure I ever gave it a thought one way or the other until it became so personal." He looked over at Robert. "You know what I mean, Dad? Because it started right here in the county where we live, it feels personal to me." He pointed his fork in the air for emphasis.

Good thing his mom wasn't here to see that. He'd add insult to the injury of trying to convince her the death penalty was just. She would not have stayed quiet about his bad table manners. Robert worked hard not to smile at the thought.

"Does it feel personal to you?" Joe continued.

Robert nodded. "Yes, Son, it does. And when I think about that little five-year-old boy, shot in the heart at…" His voice broke. He could feel the tears welling up in his eyes and could not speak the words aloud. The little boy was shot at close range, and every time he read that, he thought of Joe at five years old.

Sometimes he had to fight to hold back the sobs that wanted to rack his body.

Joe seemed to understand why he couldn't finish his sentence. Conversation stopped while they both struggled to continue eating. The only sounds were the clinking of silver against the china plates. Robert watched as the yellow flowers decorating the plates became visible as he finished his meal. He thought of his wife and her insistence on always using her best plates because every meal with her family was a reason to celebrate. And then he thought of the family that would never celebrate together again. About the twin brother who'd had to identify his dead brother. About the parents and adult siblings who would never see their loved ones again. And his determination to win this case grew stronger with each passing minute.

"I wonder if Mom has ever thought about how she would feel if she had to watch someone shoot me in the heart when I was five years old?"

"No!" the anguished wail sounded from the kitchen, alerting them to the fact that Phyllis had come back in without them knowing.

Robert froze, unsure how to handle this moment, but wondering if that would change her perspective. Because it wasn't just Phyllis' objection to the death penalty he was up against, it was the judge, the defense attorneys and the jury. The protesters and the media. Everyone of them had the potential to derail his plans to seek the highest level of punishment for the man who had terrified half the nation.

CHAPTER 51

JANUARY 18, 1951
HAMMOND, ILLINOIS

For over three hundred years, grieving friends and family had gathered at the Hammond Cemetery to bid farewell to those whose lives had been lost whether through illness, accident or worse. But the gathering of people who would soon arrive on this bitterly cold morning was decidedly the most difficult of any in the entire history of this graveyard.

The sun shone brightly in a stark blue sky, with no clouds to block its brilliance. Almost as if the Lord Almighty confirmed the message of hope delivered eight miles away at the funeral chapel by the stocky, bespectacled Reverend Ken Blankenship, the much-loved minister of the local Baptist congregation. If there could be hope in the midst of the pain, then this was it.

"I have no doubt whatsoever in my mind," his loud voice rang out to the packed funeral chapel. Those shivering on the outside who weren't lucky enough to get a seat inside would have to learn of this message of hope broadcast through the outdoor loudspeakers, while those who had arrived early enough to get seats were at least sheltered from the cold. "No doubt

whatsoever," he repeated, "that Carl, Thelma, the boys Ronnie
and Gary and even little Pamela Sue are rejoicing with our
Savior, the Lord Jesus Christ in heaven, right this moment, even
as we weep together here on earth at the loss of their presence in
our lives."

"Think about it," he said as he gestured broadly, both arms
reaching upward, "their joy is beyond measure, because they
believed. Because long ago, they committed their lives to Jesus.
They surely didn't know their lives would be cut short, but they
knew beyond any doubt that whenever their time on earth ended,
they would spend all eternity in heaven with Jesus and all their
loved ones who've gone before them, who also had committed
their lives to Jesus. The Bible tells us in Psalm 16:11 that in
God's presence is fullness of joy and pleasures forevermore. That
means they are experiencing endless explosions of pleasure and
joy. I once heard a man of God put it that way, and I've been
excited to get to heaven ever since."

Lila Ann watched the backs of the family members on the
front rows. Some people raised their heads to nod, while others
hunched over in pain, shoulders shaking with silent sobs. She
hadn't known any of the family personally, only in passing at
the bank, the grocery store and on the rare occasions she went
to church. She wondered if it had been unfair of her to get a seat
inside, when maybe some who didn't make it inside might have
actually been friends. But something drew her here. Some strong
feeling of connection that a young family in her hometown had
their lives so brutally wiped out. She didn't have children of her
own, but she thought she could imagine that unspeakable fear of

watching your children murdered right before your eyes, and she wondered. Who went first? The news reports only ever said the entire family was shot in cold blood. The reports did not say in what order they died. Just pondering the terror of it all caused the tears to flow again.

How could she cry so much for a family she did not know? But that's exactly what she had been doing ever since first learning of their disappearance and even more so once the deaths were confirmed.

And what about this Jesus the minister spoke about? Where was He when that evil man kidnapped them? Why didn't He save them if He is so all-powerful? How could people worship a God who didn't really care that they were suffering and hurting? She didn't think she could ever set foot in that man's church again. Not that she ever went more than once or twice a year, but she knew that an all-powerful God who would let this happen wasn't a God she wanted to hear about ever again. She almost wished she hadn't come today. But she couldn't stay away, and she knew that people showing up for a funeral was an encouragement to the family. She'd leave right now if she could, but she'd have to disturb too many people sitting in her row to reach the aisle leading to the door.

Lila focused on getting her tears under control. She wondered if anyone watching would think she was related to the family, yet when she looked around, most everyone in her range of vision had tears streaming, wiping their eyes and faces with tissue or hankies. This was a crime that had impacted the entire town, and maybe even the nation, if what the newscasters reported was true. A nation with a broken heart, all because of one evil man.

She returned her attention to the front of the chapel, relieved to see the minister had stepped aside and someone she didn't know who, maybe a sister or friend, was sharing memories of the family. Lila didn't know how that person got through it, and she watched as the woman cried on and off while speaking. She shared some fun memories that brought laughter throughout the chapel and seemed to lighten the mood even for the speaker, if only briefly.

Across the chapel, Raymond Baxter listened to the memories shared about the family he barely knew. He'd gone to grade school with Carl, then his family had moved away and he lost touch with his friends from early childhood. In his Arizona home a few weeks earlier, Raymond had watched the news reports about the family's disappearance in stunned silence. He'd followed the reports almost obsessively, having recognized the name of his childhood friend. He didn't know if Carl would have the memories he had, but if he had to name his very first best friend, Carl Mosser would have been the one. A friendly boy, who excelled at sports and his schoolwork, he'd taken Raymond under his wing when he saw him struggling at both. Raymond had never been athletic, and academics still were a struggle for him with his learning disabilities, so he'd been especially grateful to Carl for being such a pal to him. He realized now what a shame it had been that they'd lost touch after the move. But at eight years old, it's hard to keep up a friendship when you're almost two thousand miles away.

He knew, though, it wasn't just his distant connection to Carl that brought the sadness at the loss of this family. With the daily reports of the nationwide manhunt and the days of not knowing what had become of the family, it was as if the entire nation wept together in despair. Raymond was grateful he'd had the means to travel across the country to be here for the funeral. He wondered what was next for him in life. A tragedy like this seemed to make a person question his own existence and reason for living. Carl was gone, but he was still alive. What could he do with his life to make it worth living? To impact others. He wanted this to make a difference somehow.

Lila Ann dropped her head, wishing again that she hadn't come when the pastor returned to the pulpit, probably for more preaching. Really, she thought, wasn't that just hurtful to the family? They just want to remember their loved ones, not listen to a Sunday morning type of sermon. This reminded her why she rarely came to church. She hated for preachers to accuse her with their bold words from the pulpit about a God she wasn't even sure she believed in. She imagined it was particularly bad when you're a family member mourning the tragic loss of a loved one.

"Some of you may wonder the same question that keeps me awake at night," the reverend said, pausing to look over the audience. "Why did God let this happen?"

This unexpected direction in his message got Lila's attention. How could it be that the man read her thoughts? That he had the same question she'd asked to no one in particular? But it had plagued her ever since hearing of the kidnappings and even more so after the bodies were discovered.

"If God is all-powerful, why didn't He stop this tragedy?" The reverend paused and then held up a newspaper clipping. "I don't have the answer, but I found someone who has something to say that may help all of us who are struggling with these questions. He studied the paper for a moment, then surveyed the audience again. "Maybe some of you have heard of the young preacher who has been traveling the world speaking to thousands of people. He's even on the radio. His name is Billy Graham, and he talked about this very topic in an interview with a reporter last summer. While going through my files, deciding what words of hope to bring to the family and friends today, I ran across the newspaper clipping where Mr. Graham answered the very question that is haunting so many of us."

Lila sat up straighter, riveted by the man's words, having forgotten her earlier disdain. She realized now he was a real person, with the same doubts and questions she had. And hopefully he was going to provide an answer to the questions.

Rev. Blankenship adjusted his glasses and glanced around. "I'd like to read to you what Mr. Graham said:

"I've been asked hundreds of times why God allows evil to take place, and I have to tell you honestly that I do not know the answer—not fully.

"But let me tell you three very important truths about evil that might help you. First, the Bible tells us that evil does not come from God, nor can we blame God for all the evils in the world. Evil comes instead from Satan, and it entered this world when Satan deceived Adam and Eve and caused them to turn against God. Both evil and Satan are real, and the two go hand-in-hand.

"Second, the Bible tells us in Matthew 25:41 that someday all evil will be banished. Someday all evil will be cast into everlasting fire, prepared for the devil and his angels.

"Third, the Bible tells us that in the meantime, God can give us victory over evil. This doesn't mean bad things will never happen to us—but even when they do, we can know God is with us, and He will give us strength to stand against them."

Rev. Blankenship paused, taking a deep breath, looked at the family in the front rows, then around to the rest of the people in the room, all silently listening, as if everyone in that place was eagerly waiting for a final word of hope.

"Mr. Graham ends his comments about evil this way: 'Isn't it better to face life's problems with God rather than without Him? No, we may not understand everything that happens to us—but when we know Christ, we know we are on the winning side. Why not commit your life to Him today?'"

Lila Ann dropped her head, studying her hands clasped tightly in her lap. She squeezed them together, feeling the sweat forming in her palms, in spite of the cool temperature outside. She didn't know if she felt better after hearing those words, but she knew she didn't feel worse. Her internal pondering kept her from hearing his closing words, and she was aware of the rustling movement of people around her. She stayed seated as the crowd began streaming out, most likely heading for their cars to make the eight-mile journey to the cemetery. She'd seen enough. She'd heard enough. Rather than follow the hearses that would carry the coffins, she decided to head home. She had much to think about. And her strength was depleted.

CHAPTER 52

JANUARY 21, 1951
SOMEWHERE BETWEEN SAN DIEGO
AND OKLAHOMA CITY

At over six feet tall, U.S. Deputy Marshal Charles Ross towered over the diminutive William Cook. He'd been one of five deputies assigned to accompany the federal prisoners by Southern Pacific Railroad from San Diego to Oklahoma City. Without telling his co-workers, he deliberately maneuvered himself to be closest to Cook on the journey. He was curious if the silent prisoner would do much talking, and if he did, he wanted to be close enough to hear what he had to say.

Fairly soon into the thirty-six-hour journey, he was surprised to see William playing cards with the other shackled passengers they were guarding in the dining car where they spent the daytime hours. During their nighttime hours, each prisoner had their own berth. He and his fellow deputies shared nighttime guard duties, taking turns getting sleep. Three cars on the train were designated for the federal prisoners, with an empty car separating them from the other passengers on the route.

He sat in the lounge area across from the table where William and two others played Gin Rummy. Holding a magazine in his hand, he glanced at it occasionally so the men wouldn't think he was staring, although he often was. He occasionally looked out the window across the way and to the right of where the men played. This way he could enjoy the varying landscapes speeding by, as well as monitor the men, in particular William.

"If your tooth is hurting, you oughta tell them to get you a dentist when we get to Oklahoma." Twenty-one-year-old Joaquin was heading into federal custody for a probation violation, and he'd struck up a friendship with the killer, who was near his age, in the few hours they'd been on the train. "They have to, you know." Joaquin considered the cards in his hands while he talked, then after discarding he looked back at William. "It's the law. They have to take care of us even if we done something wrong and got arrested."

William drew a card from the pile, studied his hand, and without looking at his Gin Rummy partner, said, "No point."

"You said you had a toothache."

This interested Charles. He wondered if he should notify someone that this was going to be a need. Didn't know how that would work, needing to fit a dentist appointment in with the scheduling for the arraignment.

"I do, but there still ain't no point." William looked at Joaquin after discarding a card from his hand. "After you are dead, you don't feel any toothache."

"You figure that's what's going to happen?" Joaquin drew a card, then looked at the other prisoner waiting his turn. The guy didn't seem to be in any hurry to play the winner. So he took his time rearranging the cards in his hand, but he seemed more interested in hearing William's response than he was in paying attention to arranging his cards just right.

For that matter, Charles was pretty interested too. Did this mean William was planning on pleading guilty? He didn't seem to deny his guilt to his fellow passengers.

"I don't know how they kill in Oklahoma, but I bet they do."

Deputy Charles knew for a fact they did. And if that was his sentence, it would be in the electric chair. He didn't offer to join in the conversation with that bit of information. He had some questions he'd like to ask, but thought if he listened long enough, the other prisoners might get around to asking the same things he was wondering.

This match drew to an end with William winning, and Charles couldn't help but wonder if Joaquin was purposely losing. No sense angering a killer, although he hadn't seen any display of anger on this trip so far. In fact, William had been calm, and the previous night had slept right through the night with no disturbances. Maybe the lull of the train's movement and the rhythmic clickety-clack of the wheels on the rails helped him to sleep. Or could it be he had no conscience to bother him and keep him awake? Charles had seen no expression of remorse or of denial or of pride for what he'd done. William just seemed to accept what was coming his way.

"Why did you do it anyway?" Joaquin asked as he shuffled the deck of cards, then shoved them over to the other man waiting his turn to take on the winner.

"It was the tequila and vodka," William said. "Started drinking it Christmas night in Blythe and stayed drunk 'til I caught the ride with that family."

"The tequila did the killing?" Joaquin watched as the new player dealt the cards.

"The woman and children began screaming."

"That why you killed them?"

Getting no response, Joaquin quit asking questions, and Charles figured that might be all he would learn about the killer that he was transporting to face his consequences. He hoped the jury would not be swayed by the sad stories the newspapers were printing of this young man's upbringing. He hoped they'd remember the children and their parents and make their decision based on the horrible way their lives ended.

He couldn't believe a guy could do that and then sit calmly playing cards, ready to face his punishment, even knowing it would likely be the death penalty. At least he wasn't trying to make excuses.

CHAPTER 53

JANUARY 22, 1951
OKLAHOMA CITY, OKLAHOMA

Managing Editor Ed Bradley stood close to his city editor, Georgia Ferguson, still surprised they could get two people from their newspaper into the jail cell press conference. Demand was high, with journalists coming from all over the surrounding states. It paid to have a publisher committed to covering this case in depth. Though it had been a two-hour drive from Osage, they'd been in town for several days, in fact, as soon as his publisher had gotten word that William Cook was being transported from California to Oklahoma.

"Your attention, please." He looked over to the attorney representing William Cook, who'd set up the conference within the jail. It was a first for him to be a part of a news conference for the accused to speak right from a jail cell.

"My client has agreed to make a statement and take a few questions. I must ask you to refrain from talking, shuffling your feet or any type of noise while he is speaking so everyone can hear."

"For the record again, I'm John Connelly, one of the attorneys assigned to represent Mr. Cook. Yesterday, as you may know, my client pleaded innocent to the charges, and we have entered a plea of insanity. He will go on trial March 12." The attorney looked around the room at a group of newsmen and women quieter than Ed had ever heard them.

"And now," John motioned to the sullen-looking young man sitting hunched over on a cot in the jail cell, "Mr. Cook will speak for a few minutes."

Ed wondered if he would talk from where he sat, or at least have the decency to get up and step closer to the bars where they could see him better and possibly hear him better. Kind of a funny word though to attribute to an accused killer. Expecting him to behave decently.

The attorney motioned for Cook to stand and approach him where he was standing on the outside of the cell. He held a microphone as William Cook shuffled over to the bars.

"I didn't kill or kidnap that family," William stared at the floor as he talked. "I never had a friend in all my life. They sent me to a reform school when I was eleven. There they used a rubber hose and beat me all the time. Then I went to the penitentiary, and a bunch of dumb guards hit me on the head every time they saw me." He stopped talking, raised his head and looked around the group before continuing. "Don't try to keep kidding me about people wanting to help me. I hate their guts, everybody and everybody hates my guts."

"What do you remember about the days in question?" One brave reporter spoke up. Ed wasn't sure they had permission to call out questions like they would normally do at a press conference for a non-criminal, but he was glad for this man who boldly asked.

"I don't remember nothing. I got drunk on Christmas in Blythe, where I lived. Next thing I know I was in Mexico. But I never confessed to killing six people. I signed a lot of papers here in the U.S. and in Mexico. Some of them were in Spanish."

"Why did you sign them?" This time, a female reporter spoke up.

"Why wouldn't I?" William said. "They said they were going to hang me."

"Did you kidnap and kill the Mossers?" Ed considered the question to be one of those ridiculous questions reporters asked that addressed a topic that had already been covered, but Cook's answer surprised him. It wasn't something he'd said before.

"I don't know them."

With that, the droopy-eyed, angry-looking man shuffled back to his cot, signaling the end of the press conference.

"How about that?" Georgia said, as they bundled up with their overcoats and hats, down in the jail's lobby, ready to head out. "He wants people to feel sorry for him. He's killed six people, but we're supposed to feel sorry for him."

Ed nodded, watching the angry eyes that accompanied her rant. "He lied, too. He said he never had a friend, did you catch that?"

"Yes, and the man who gave the tip that led them to the bodies was his friend in prison," Georgia said. "What was his name?"

"Harold Suman." Ed held the door for Georgia as they stepped out into the bitterly cold wind. "Glad our motel is only a couple of blocks away."

"Let's stop and get some coffee and a bite to eat." Georgia's teeth chattered as she pulled the scarf around her neck up over her chin, almost to her nose.

"Great plan. I'd love to get an interview with that Suman character. He might have some background stories to tell about Cook."

"I'll bet he's sure glad he didn't follow Cook's goading to accompany him on his road trip."

"You know he is." Ed held the restaurant door open for Georgia and welcomed the warmth as they stepped through. "He'd be sitting in the cell next to him if he had."

"A burger and fries and a large cup of coffee," Ed said as the waitress approached with a menu.

Georgia nodded. "Same here." She watched as the waitress jotted down their order, then left to turn it in to the kitchen. "The other thing about him saying he never had a friend. Remember, we read that the way the deputy in Blythe found him was heading to the motel room where his friend lived?"

Ed nodded, then sipped the hot coffee the waitress put before him. "And there was some talk that he might have had a girlfriend, too."

"I heard that, but I didn't know if that was a rumor."

"Sounded like a pretty solid tip to me," Ed said. "And family. He had at least two sisters who've been involved in his life. I read he lived with one, but then got arrested again, I think for stealing a car or something while living with her. That's where he lived just before he went to the Missouri State Pen."

"I guess it isn't surprising that a man who would kidnap and kill people would also lie."

"He might not be lying about the treatment he got in the reform school and prison–I've heard some horror stories–but I believe he is about never having a friend. And even if the stories are true, it does not give him the right to kill innocent people."

Georgia sipped her coffee, then set it aside to make room for the plate of steaming food the waitress approached with. "And little children," she said. "It's so heartbreaking."

"Y'all talking about that killer they brought into town?" The waitress snapped her gum as she chewed and talked. "It's a crying shame," she said without waiting for them to respond.

"That's exactly what it is," Ed said, watching her walk away, shaking her head. This was a crime that had affected everyone.

CHAPTER 54

MARCH 20, 1951- MORNING
OKLAHOMA CITY, OKLAHOMA

B ut, Momma, you can't protect me forever," Ella Jean pulled on her white gloves, normally reserved for church. She'd determined the courthouse was a very formal place, and formal attire was the best choice.

She glanced at the hat she'd placed on the table near the door and decided against it. She watched her poor mother wring her hands, listening to her moaning. "Why do you need to be exposed to all that talk about kidnapping and murder?"

"Momma, it's been all over the newspapers and television. This is a chance of a lifetime. I've never been inside a courthouse before. And Momma, I'm near 29. That's the age of the poor lady he killed. Least I can do is out of respect for her, go and hear her killer get his punishment. I want to witness justice being done for her and her family."

This is what came of being the youngest in the family. All her siblings had married and moved on, but somehow her momma had convinced her that staying home longer was best. And after losing her papa, she couldn't bear to move on and leave her poor momma alone in this big house. But would she ever get out from under her never-ending instructions?

Lost in her thoughts, Ella Jean was startled to see her mother holding out her best overcoat. "You're going to need this, Ella Jean."

She couldn't believe her mother had given in. Not that she could have kept her home, but at least now she could leave without the guilt of disappointing her mother hanging over her head.

It's funny that such a little thing as going somewhere her mother didn't want her to go could cause her to feel guilty, and yet here was this young man, younger than her, the cockeyed killer they called him. Kidnapping and killing and, according to the reports, not showing any remorse. Didn't he feel guilty for anything he did? What makes some people feel guilty for the smallest thing and others not feel guilty for the worst crimes? And murdering little children? She swiped at the tears starting to fall and hoped her mother didn't see. If she knew how upsetting this was to her, she'd start in again about staying home.

Ella Jean felt her insides shaking as she watched other spectators file in and fill the last of the gallery. She was glad she'd arrived early and been one of the first in line. She knew there were hundreds of others who would never get a chance to set foot inside the courthouse. That's what came of being an early bird. She could thank her mother for that. They always arrived everywhere at least thirty minutes early if not an hour or more, like she'd done for this hearing today.

223

Glancing over at the gentleman seated next to her, she caught sight of the headline on the newspaper in his lap: *Hate-Filled Billy Cook 'Never Had a Friend.'*

"Excuse me."

The man glanced her way, and her heart beat hard. My, but he was nice-looking. She glanced at his hand. No ring. Wouldn't that be something–to find true love at the trial of a kidnapper and murderer?

The man's voice sounded gruff until he cleared it. "Excuse me," he said. "Just getting over a cold."

Was he suffering from a cold, or did the young lady sitting nearby surprise him? Maybe he hadn't noticed her before she spoke. This was ridiculous. She wasn't here to find love. She was here to see justice done. "May I borrow your newspaper to read that article?"

He looked down in his lap, where he had the paper folded over to expose the article. "Sure, it's not a current one. I just ran across it in an old stack of newspapers. It's from January 27." He handed it to her. "But it's an interesting read."

"I can't believe we're actually going to see him brought into court," Ella Jean whispered as the man handed her the paper. Their hands brushed against each other, and she felt a tingle that she hadn't expected to encounter at a murder trial.

She skimmed the article. Handing it back, she said, "Thank you, I just realized I've read that one before."

"I heard he changed his plea to guilty so he wouldn't get the death penalty," the man said. "By the way," he reached over to shake hands, "my name is Dean. Dean Phelps."

She gripped his hand, forcing a little smile. She was happy to meet him, but the surroundings and situation were all so awful. "It's nice to meet you. I heard that too about the plea change. Do you think it's true? He's admitting he did it?"

A hush spread across the courtroom as throat clearing replaced the whispered chatting in the spectator area and all eyes were drawn to the front of the courtroom. The unmistakable features of the short man gave away that he was the defendant, even if armed guards hadn't escorted him. He took a seat at a table while two men in suits and ties sat on either side of him. Ella Jean felt her mouth drop open, as she looked at the man in the neighboring seat and could tell he was in awe as she was at being this close to the accused killer they'd all been reading about in the newspapers for the last few months.

"All rise." A uniformed man she presumed to be the bailiff stood, his loud voice carrying across the courtroom.

"The Honorable Stephen S. Chandler Jr., United States District Judge, presiding."

Ella Jean could hardly contain her excitement at getting to witness this historic hearing. She watched as the black-robed judge directed his attention to Billy Cook.

"I would like to be sure that the defendant at the time he entered his plea understood what the penalty might be."

She felt Dean nudge her elbow as they took their seats, as if to say they were right about Cook changing his plea. She nudged back just slightly, not wanting to take her eyes off the proceedings.

William Cook stood at the prompting of the attorney on his right, who joined him, towering over the man by nearly a foot.

"Mr. Cook," the judge said, "you understand that under a plea of guilty in this case, as to each count, that the penalty could be death, or any term of years, or life imprisonment. I don't know that I called that to your attention. Do you understand what I mean by that?"

"Yes." William sounded unconcerned.

"Now," Judge Chandler continued, "understanding that, as to the first count, where you are charged with kidnapping Carl Mosser, and taking him from one state to another, murdering him, now as to that count, what is your plea, after knowing what the punishment might be?"

"Guilty."

Ella Jean heard a slight gasp around the courtroom, which was quickly silenced by one look from the balding, no-nonsense judge as he shot a disgruntled look over the spectator area.

It hadn't occurred to her that while the proceedings could be terribly interesting, at some points they could be terribly boring as well. She listened as the judge ran through the litany of questions, repeating the same words but replacing them with the names of the victims. Each time, the defendant spoke the same monotone guilty plea.

She watched Dr. Hugh Galbraith get sworn in, take the stand, and explain his qualifications. It surprised her when the judge began the questioning. After going through a diatribe of medical terminology and reading a report into the record that the doctor claimed was short, but with which she disagreed, the judge finally asked a question that enabled the doctor to answer in a way they could all understand.

"Just in plain English, Doctor," Judge Chandler said. "What is this boy's mental capacity, in your opinion, in language we all can understand?"

"He is utterly incapable of making any plans from moment to moment. He is suffering from a disease which makes him live in a world of his own. He is completely incapable of sensing how other people feel. In brief, he has a severe mental illness which psychiatrists recognize as being incurable."

Ella Jean listened as the prosecuting attorney went through some tedious questions of this doctor, including trying to pin him down on his opinion of capital punishment, of which he would not commit to an opinion one way or the other. She wondered whether the doctor opposed the death penalty and if he would rule this man insane to save his life.

After one of the defense attorneys elicited a medical opinion of the defendant as being incurably insane, U.S. Attorney Mr. Shelton, stood, approached the witness and ran through a series of short questions with equally short answers until he broached the subject of whether the defendant was misleading the doctor.

"Doctor," Mr. Shelton said, then turned to look at the defendant before returning his attention to the witness. "Will you describe some of the reactions and emotions upon which you say you based your opinion?"

"When I first met him, he spoke to me noncommittally, shook hands with me feebly. He answered my questions but was incapable of hardly making himself heard. His face was a complete blank, his lips thick, hung loosely in an immobile state, inexpressive. His eyes blinked less often than usual. It is perfectly characteristic of the most severe mental disorders we have."

"Now, suppose Doctor," Mr. Shelton said, "you had evidence that prior to this time this crime was committed, that he held down a job and was jolly and reasonable about his work and that he discussed his family and the people with whom he was associated freely. Would all of those circumstances make any difference in your conclusions?"

Dr. Galbraith's head began slowly turning from side to side. "I would disagree with some of your assumptions," he said.

Mr. Shelton persisted. "Even though my assumptions are true, would you still hold the same opinion?"

Dr. Galbraith nodded. "There are enough variations to invalidate the assumptions, in my opinion."

Why can't he just say yes or no, Ella Jean wondered, regretting positioning herself in a row so close to the front that she could not easily slip out. This case was fast becoming uninteresting to her. She wanted to just get to the end and find out if what she suspected might happen would in fact happen. That the court would declare the man insane and save him from the death penalty. She wished she could get the opinion of her newfound acquaintance, Dean, to see if she was on track with her assessment, but they were not allowed to talk in the spectator section.

Ella watched with relief as the witness stepped down, then saw to the dismay of Mr. Shelton that he was going to be forced to put his witness on the stand before getting to hear the rest of the doctors the judge had appointed to examine the defendant. She wasn't sure, but she had a feeling this judge already knew how this case was going and wasn't doing anything to make the prosecuting attorney's job any easier.

She assumed, since Mr. Shelton was willing to use this next doctor as a witness, that his opinion would be the direct opposite of Dr. Galbraith's opinion of insanity.

Several questions into his testimony, he confirmed her assumptions.

"Have you reached any conclusion with reference to the defendant?" Mr. Shelton directed his question to his witness, Dr. Parker.

"Yes, sir. It is my opinion that this man is a true psychopath."

"Now, tell the Court further," Mr. Shelton said. "Whether or not, in your judgment, this defendant is what the lawyers call criminally insane?"

"I say he is not criminally insane, in my opinion."

"Now, tell the Court whether or not, in your judgment, he knows the difference between right and wrong and the consequences of his acts?"

"Yes, sir. In my opinion he does know the difference and the consequences."

Ella Jean and the other spectators listened as William Cook's attorney then attempted to destroy the testimony of this witness, hammering on the fact that the defendant refused to talk to him. She wanted to clap when the prosecutor came back on redirect

229

with a question that she felt summed up everything that was going on in the defendant's mind.

"Doctor, give your opinion." Mr. Shelton turned to look at the defendant again, taking a few steps away from the witness and then turning back toward Dr. Parker. "Why the defendant wouldn't talk with you, if you have an opinion."

"My opinion," Dr. Parker said, "is that he thought I would be an unfriendly witness, and that he wanted to feign insanity. That is my opinion."

The spectators listened as Mr. Shelton's second witness, Dr. Moorman Prosser, denied that the defendant was criminally insane, labeling him as "crazy like a fox."

Wow, Ella Jean thought. From all she'd read and heard so far, she agreed with both of these witnesses. And ultimately the third witness who also found no insanity in the defendant. Good thing she wasn't the judge, she realized as William Cook's attorneys brought out the juvenile probation officer who knew Billy Cook as a child. Who, in fact, was there when they found him and his siblings in the mine. A sad story for sure, she realized, wondering, did that make a difference in the life of a man who grew up to be a criminal?

"Well, Mrs. Bryson," Defense Attorney Connelly spoke softly to the witness as she recalled first meeting Billy at five years old. "Where was this place located?"

"It was at what we call the White Shirt mine. It was about three miles from the main part of Joplin, and at least a half mile off the highway back in the timber."

"Now, what conditions did you find there?"

"I found these children all alone. The baby was just past a year old. The oldest child was a girl. I think she was near fourteen, and she was playing mother to these children. They had in this cave, a wood-burning cookstove, and they had some homemade furniture. I would say a table made out of boxes. I think they had only one bed. A cheap iron bedstead with a mattress."

"Did you observe any food there?"

"They had a bowl of pancake batter setting uncovered and if the children got hungry, they told Maggie, the oldest girl, and she proceeded to cook them some pancakes. And they were getting water out of a shaft that was about two hundred and fifty feet deep."

"Now, there was an abandoned mine shaft at the place you found the Cook children?"

"That is where they were getting their water. Out of this mine shaft." Mrs. Bryson directed her response to the attorney, but her eyes were on the defendant, who didn't appear to look back at her.

"What kind of a floor did this cave have?"

"It was a dirt floor. The shaft had some boards laid across it. The children, I don't know how they kept from falling into it."

"Did you determine from your investigation there how these children had been living?"

Mrs. Bryson shook her head, a look of disgust crossing her face. "I don't think they had been living. Just existing. Their father had deserted the children, but I was told he was living with a woman that owned a cow and some chickens and when the children would get so hungry, they would go to him for help and they would give them a bucket of milk and some eggs."

"How were the children clothed, Mrs. Bryson?"

"Very meager."

The testimony of Mrs. Bryson drug on, and Ella Jean could feel her stomach rumbling with hunger. To hear this lady talk, Bill Cook wasn't a bad kid when he was little, but it was sure creepy to realize that one of the foster homes he lived in was just a few hundred yards away from the mine shaft where they discovered the bodies of the family he killed. She thought it interesting that Mrs. Bryson said she was probably one of the few people in Joplin who didn't go look at that mine shaft. Ella Jean did not know that the whole town turned out to see the place where they found the family. It was all so sad. She wondered if she should have listened to her mother and not come to the hearing.

CHAPTER 55

MARCH 20, 1951 - 2:00 P.M.
OKLAHOMA CITY, OKLAHOMA

After the lunch break, Ella Jean scooted back into the courtroom in time to get a seat in the back row. She'd hoped to be seated near Dean again, but he'd mentioned he might not make the afternoon session. She scanned the backs of the heads of the spectators in front of her, disappointed not to see him.

She rose with the others as the judge entered and the bailiff recited by rote his name and the names of all parties present.

"I understand there are three gentlemen here from Topeka who made the examination for Dr. Menninger." The judge looked at the front row, where Ella presumed the men were seated. "Dr. Milton Wexler, Dr. Donald J. Watterson and Mr. Martin Mayman. I will call them in that order and put them on instead of Dr. Menninger. Call Dr. Milton Wexler."

Ella Jean wondered if the other nearly two hundred spectators in the courtroom felt as she did, annoyed with these three doctors who all basically testified to the same thing. Sure, the defendant knew murder was wrong, but he was insane. She had grown weary of listening by the time the third doctor took the stand. It was interesting that he would talk to the doctors for his attorneys, but Mr. Shelton brought out in the testimony that he wouldn't cooperate with the doctors for the prosecution. She thought that indicated a pretty savvy guy, if anyone asked her. He certainly knew what he was doing.

But now with this new witness brought on by the prosecutor Robert Shelton she sat up and took note, figuring that he may have a different opinion, especially since the attorney for the defendant was objecting so vehemently to the testimony of the Deputy United States Marshal.

"Describe the nature, the general demeanor, of his conduct and conversation, if you understand what I mean?" Mr. Shelton stood close to the witness, almost as if willing him to get the entire story out there.

"He talked just like any other prisoner would talk to you," Deputy Saunkeah said. "Just the same as talking to other prisoners."

"Tell the Court how he talked to you when you arrived on the scene down there."

"After he tried to rest awhile, we got to talking about some other things."

"Well, now," Mr. Shelton said. "Could you understand what he was talking about?"

"Oh yes. He told me of his trip clear down into Mexico, and back, and how he was brought back by plane, and how they turned him over to the authorities in San Diego."

Ella Jean was surprised when the defense attorney had no
questions and was glad the hearing was moving on a little more
quickly than the morning session. Mr. Shelton called another
witness who worked in the jails.

"Tell the Court in your own way the things you have
observed and describe his conduct while he has been there in
jail."

"Well, he gets up along about nine o'clock in the morning
and brushes his teeth and goes back and plays Solitaire and
reads the magazines, and if he wants something like a magazine
you have, he speaks right up. You can understand him, and if
he wants a shave, he is the same way, but if he wants to ask you
what day it is, he will come up there and you have to ask him
two or three times before you can understand what he wants."

"In other words," Mr. Shelton turned toward the defendant,
then back to the witness. "He speaks out distinctly when he
wants something?"

"That is absolutely right," the witness said. "And another
thing, he reads all the best magazines he can buy."

"Tell the Court some of the magazines he reads."

"*Life,* the *Reader's Digest, Coronet, Esquire, Holiday, Post*
and he reads the *National Geographic* all the time. Reverend
Alexander sent him some, and he studies them from morning 'til
night."

"Did he keep track of his money?"

"He can tell you, I expect, right now, to the penny how much
money he has in the commissary."

"Now, is there anything else you noticed about his conduct there that might be beneficial?"

"The only thing that I noticed about his conduct is," the witness glanced over at the defendant, then back to the prosecutor, "he don't seem to appreciate anything you do for him."

"Now, did you notice any visible difference in his attitude towards the people who endeavored to talk to him there after he had interviewed his lawyers?"

"I did."

"What was the difference?"

"A week ago yesterday, he quit talking to me after Mr. Smith and Mr. Connelly talked to him. Before that, he would speak to me very nearly every day, and from then to this day, he hasn't spoke to me but once."

Ella Jean shook her head as the judge dismissed this witness and the next one, also a jail worker, corroborated all the first one said about the defendant's behavior in jail. That guy could have gone to Hollywood, she thought, if he hadn't chosen a life of crime. What an actor. Not only a murderer, but adept at covering up his capabilities trying to get a lesser sentence.

Ella Jean felt her eyes glazing over as the judges and attorneys discussed the legalities surrounding closing arguments in the sanity hearing. She heard something mentioned about a jury trial, but got the feeling that's not the way this case was going. In any event, the judge ordered the closing arguments to begin the next day. She would follow this through to the end and be back bright and early to secure a seat among the spectators.

CHAPTER 56

MARCH 21, 1951
OKLAHOMA CITY, OKLAHOMA

Robert Shelton tapped his fingers on the attorney table, waiting for the judge to enter. He had a bad feeling about the direction of the hearing. This should have been a jury trial. He would insist on presenting his evidence to the jury today, sticking to his guns.

His worst fears were confirmed when the judge began speaking seconds after entering the courtroom.

"I have heretofore stated to Mr. Smith that I have changed my mind about hearing long arguments unless you gentlemen insist. I have considered the matter carefully, and I think I know what action I should take. Now…"

Mr. Shelton bolted from his seat. "If it please the Court, I want to say that I firmly believe that we ought to take our problems up here at least one by one as they arrive. If the issue here is insanity, then I have not put on all the evidence I have, and the witnesses that I would desire to put on are subpoenaed to be here the 26th day of March and I want the Court to move for a recess until Monday for the proposition of offering additional evidence."

Robert turned as one of the defense attorneys stood, looking in his direction, then back to the judge. "We would like for the district attorney to state into the record, just briefly, what other evidence he proposes to offer and for what purpose."

The judge nodded to Mr. Smith, then turned his attention Robert's way. "Yes, I would like to know, Mr. Shelton."

"I expect to offer the details surrounding this crime, for one thing. The actual murder of these five people. I expect to offer the evidence of Burke and Damron and Waldrip, which will all show the planning and scheming mind of this defendant. Of his boastfulness of the fact that, for instance, when he had Damron and Burke under his gun, that he took from them Jim Burke's identification papers and told him that 'From now on, as soon as I can get over here across the bay, I am going to sell your car and I'm going to be Jim Burke from now on in Old Mexico.'"

He was on a roll, determined to make his case heard, but the judge interrupted him.

"And I understand then, that you want to offer additional testimony as to the mental capacity…"

"Yes, sir," Shelton nearly shouted. "If this is considered a sanity hearing, Your Honor, then I want to ask leave of your court to offer further evidence. I want to further show in the record that when he took into custody, this Deputy Sheriff Waldrip that the conduct that surrounded the defendant at the time he robbed him of his money, of his car, tied him up and left him in the desert.

I want to show that this is the act of a rational man bent on a criminal act. I want to further show that the facts surrounding his conduct at the time that he murdered Dewey and shot him in the back, and other circumstances surrounding that, which shows his mental capacity at that time, and his mental capacity to plan and scheme and to escape. I want to further show the fact that before he left and while he was in El Paso that he went across the border and indulged in fun and frolic and drink and made statements to witnesses that he would like to buy a Mexican girl. The psychiatrists here say that he has no emotions and so forth. I would like to put all that evidence in the record if this is to be considered a sanity hearing, Your Honor. If this is to be considered an absolute sanity hearing, why then I want to respectfully move the Court for a recess until Monday morning."

Robert Shelton took a seat as Mr. Smith, the defense attorney, rose to present a lengthy summary of his own opinion of the purpose of this hearing and how the judge should handle the outcome. Robert could feel his heart sink as he watched and listened, knowing this wasn't going the way it should. He'd be on the phone with the U.S. Attorney General the minute he got out of court. He refocused on the hearing when he noticed the defense attorney took his seat and the judge began talking.

"I have come to the conclusion from a consideration of the evidence and the facts in this case by my own investigation—I think I am in possession of the facts which Mr. Shelton refers to, at least a great amount of them. I have observed the defendant very carefully during this hearing. From consideration of all those matters and the testimony of the doctors, I do not think it could be justifiably said that he has the mental capacity to have committed these crimes with sufficient understanding and premeditated design as to warrant a jury or this court in imposing the death penalty. Further, it is my considered opinion that he did not in any reasonable or legal sense commit these offenses with malice aforethought. I, therefore, deny trial by jury on the question of punishment.

"I am and have always been a firm believer in capital punishment. But the death penalty was designed for persons with sufficient mental capacity and training to be fully chargeable with the consequences of their acts.

"Society stands indicted for the crime of permitting this child to grow up under the cruel and inhuman conditions, only a small part of which are shown by this record, and must take, at least, part blame for these crimes. They might never have been committed had the child, Cook, received civilized care, protection and education.

"Is there any reason why…"

Shelton shot out of his chair. He refused to give up, raising his voice to be heard, even on the street if that was possible. "If the Court please, I want to say as the district attorney in this district, charged with the responsibility of enforcing the law, that I respectfully disagree with every word that this Court has uttered here in the record, and if there was ever a death penalty case in the history of crime in the nation, this is a death penalty case, and I think the Court should, at least, give us an opportunity to present it to the jury. If there wasn't malice aforethought in this crime, I never saw a crime in my life that there wasn't malice aforethought. And the fact that a man is brought up in meager circumstances, in poor surroundings, that don't mean he can't grow up to be a man.

"My mother died when I was five and I lived in a dugout but I didn't commit any murders or crimes and there are other men in this room that have done the same thing and that isn't alone a justification for the murders of six innocent people. The wiping out of an entire family by cold-blooded murder. I want the Court to know, and the community and the public to know, that as far as I stand, that as far as law enforcement is concerned in this area, that I believe the death penalty should be invoked in this case and we should have a jury trial."

"I realize, Mr. Shelton," the judge said, "that this responsibility is fully mine, and you are entitled to believe as you believe. By the same token, this Court is entitled to upon consideration, reach a contrary conclusion."

Not giving up. He was absolutely not giving up. Shelton continued, "Your Honor, I think, if the Court would hear all of the evidence in this case, and was fully familiar with it as we are, I think there is a possibility that the Court might not reach the same conclusion."

"I have considered that carefully," Judge Chandler said, "as I have considered everything about this case. I think I am in possession of those facts. They were available to me. I couldn't conscientiously permit the government to go to the expense of a trial of this case. The expense would be great. It would serve no good purpose where the facts are as I have found them to be, and it was my duty to make a finding of fact, and I have found the fact."

Robert watched as Mr. Smith prompted the defendant to stand, knowing the sentence was about to be pronounced.

"It is the judgment of this Court that the defendant, William Edward Cook Jr. be sentenced to imprisonment in the custody of the attorney general on the first count for a period of sixty years and a like sentence on each count to run consecutively. Now I further recommend to the attorney general, by reason of the fact that sane or insane, unquestionably this man is a very dangerous man, that he be committed to Alcatraz, where there will be no chance of his ever, during his lifetime, escaping and I have tried in my judgment to make it so that he cannot be paroled.

"The responsibility of this case has been great. There is a responsibility to the defendant and a responsibility to society and I believe it is best served in the manner in which I have executed it. Court is in recess."

Robert Shelton, gathered his papers, and shoved his way through the departing crowd, out the back doors, eager to get to the telephone in his office.

"Mr. Shelton?" Reporters' microphones were shoved in his face upon exiting the courtroom doors. "Any comment on the judge's sentence?"

"That is the damndest travesty on justice I have ever heard of, and you may quote me." With that he stormed out of the courthouse.

CHAPTER 57

MARCH 21, 1951
JOPLIN, MISSOURI

Robert Shelton, please. This is Attorney Dale Tourtelot calling from Joplin, Missouri."

"Please hold, Mr. Tourtelot." Loretta, Mr. Shelton's secretary, transferred the call to his private office.

"Dale," Robert's voice came across the wire. "You heard, I take it?"

"I heard. Can we get Cook brought here to face the murder charges?"

"I'm very much in favor of his being turned over to a state where the death penalty can be invoked against him. I can't express how unhappy I am at the turn of events here."

"What's the next step in getting him sent here?" Dale asked, picking up his pen and notepad, ready to write whatever instructions he received from the U.S. District Attorney.

"You need to write to the U.S. Attorney General J. Howard McGrath, in Washington, D.C. and send me a copy of that letter as well. I've already been on the phone with him today, protesting the sentence. In fact, if I had known earlier what I know now, I would have encouraged the attorney general to have this case tried in some other state than Oklahoma."

"I will get those letters out via air mail today. I'm sure we still have time to get to the post office before it closes." He hit the intercom to summon his secretary while still talking to Shelton.

"I will tell you, however," Robert said. "I believe California has a better case against Cook than Missouri. He is wanted there for the January 6 slaying of Robert Dewey."

"I understand," Tourtelot protested. "But we will try him on all five charges in connection with the January 2 slaying of the Mosser family. And we'll be asking for the death penalty as well."

"I'm all in favor of that," Robert said. "Write your letters, and we'll see what the attorney general determines. Bottom line is, at least he will be tried again in one of the two states, with the goal of getting the death sentence."

CHAPTER 58

MARCH 26, 1951
SAN FRANCISCO, CALIFORNIA

The ocean appeared to extinguish the light of the sun as it dropped into the western sky, when the Southern Pacific passenger train rolled into the city, its steel wheels clicking and clacking as they had for the previous forty hours U.S. Marshal Rex Hawks had accompanied the convicted criminal Billy Cook. Two other officers assisted with the transport of the shackled prisoner they were delivering to Alcatraz Federal Penitentiary.

The long low whistle sounded as they passed through what was most likely the last railroad crossing on the city streets of this interstate train ride.

Rex, along with his two fellow guards, watched as the passengers flowed from the other rail cars, some embracing waiting family and friends; others, businessmen no doubt, who'd boarded just an hour or two ago, rushed across the railway platform with their briefcases, heading straight for the Santa Fe depot. Billy Cook sat silent, as he had for the majority of the trip, staring at the floor.

"Looks like fog rolling in." Deputy Sheriff Burks stood, stretching his arms until his hands touched the ceiling. "Going to be good to get off the train for the night."

Deputy Marshal Mike McGrew nodded. "What time do we head back in the morning?"

"Train pulls out at 6 a.m." The platform was nearly empty and a U.S. Marshal stood apart from the few stragglers who were left, looking expectantly into the windows of the cars. Rex motioned for Billy to stand.

He looked forward to sleeping in a real bed that night in the hotel and had been about to say that to the other two men. But not knowing what Billy's sleeping accommodations would be, he refrained from discussing the comfort they would all experience. He believed the man was getting what he deserved, actually not really. He deserved death in Rex's opinion, but the incarceration he was heading toward, was of his own doing, so he felt no pity for the man. However, the manners instilled in him from a young age kept Rex from talking about the enjoyment he and the other officers would experience sleeping in a bed that wasn't moving that night. Glancing at his watch, he figured they had about thirty more minutes at the most until this assignment was over for them.

Warden Edwin Swope waited on the deck of the prison launch as the sedan carrying the prisoner and all four officers pulled up and parked at the San Francisco waterfront. Rex watched as the warden disembarked from the boat to meet them.

"Any trouble with our new resident?" Edwin shook hands with Rex while they watched the officers in the back join them.

Before Rex could respond, Deputy Burks spoke up, "We had handcuffs and leg irons on him all the time. He gave us no trouble."

Swope nodded, then turned back to Rex, motioning toward the back seat at the young man staring down at the floor. "Was he like this the whole trip?"

"Sure was. Words he uttered wouldn't add up to a five minute conversation over the last forty hours."

Rex's eyes took in the bay and the island. The incongruity of the situation struck him as odd, all this beauty, yet the reason for being here was one of untold ugliness and evil. And no doubt the prison was filled with men with the same kind of backgrounds. Almost couldn't enjoy the beauty. He watched as Billy sat stone still, waiting for orders. Shackled, an overcoat in his lap covering the handcuffed wrists, totally uninterested in the beautiful scenery so different from where he was from.

Warden Swope motioned to the Marshal who had met them at the train station. "Let's get him ready to get on the launch."

Rex nodded, then turned to the deputies he'd traveled with. They would help shackle the prisoner to the U.S. Marshal for the trip across the bay.

Rex accepted the good-bye handshake from the warden.

"We'll treat him just like the rest of them." Edwin turned and followed the odd pair, a foot difference in height, down the ramp and onto the prison launch, ready to start the longest sentence in the history of Alcatraz.

CHAPTER 59

MARCH 30, 1951
ENID, OKLAHOMA

Milton B. Garber, Vice President of the Enid Publishing Company, stood at the lectern ready to call to order the weekly meeting of the American Business Club. His hunger for news to report combined with the passion for justice instilled in him by his father, the founder of the publishing company. Before starting the newspaper, Milton C. Garber had served in politics as well as practiced law, even advancing to a judicial position as a judge in several districts. He knew for a fact his father would have been as unhappy as he was at the ruling Judge Stephen Sanders had issued just a few days ago. He glanced at his watch, then tapped the lectern with the small gavel.

"May I have your attention, please?"

The rumble of voices died down as all eyes turned his way.

"I am most honored to introduce our distinguished guest this evening. Before I do so, a little background, though most may find it unnecessary if you've been following this case closely in the news."

He scanned the audience, then continued, "Just a week ago when the press announced the sentence conferred upon William E. Cook Jr. a wave of disappointment swept through the land. The public felt that if ever a man deserved to pay the supreme penalty, Cook was such a man. While the case as handled in our jurisdiction is closed, one voice remains to speak out against the action of Judge Stephen A. Chandler. The voice of Robert Shelton, U.S. Attorney." He motioned for Robert to stand, and the crowd stood as well while offering thunderous applause.

"Thank you very much," Robert said, stepping to the lectern, as Milton took a seat in the first row.

"In the days since this sentence was handed down, a legal opinion has turned up which indicates the five counts in the indictment against Cook may be considered one offense. Judge Chandler sentenced Cook to serve sixty years for kidnapping and murdering each of the five members of the Mosser family. In other words, it appears as though there might be some legal loopholes as a result of Chandler's unpopular disposition of the case. It is possible that Cook's three hundred years may be just one sixty-year term with the possibility of parole after twenty years. And if left to the Alcatraz lawyers, they will certainly find this loophole."

He stopped as the uproar in the place drowned out his words, the reality sinking in that this man, a killer of six people, could be free in twenty short years.

"I direct your attention to the photos I have on display, depicting evidence I would have presented at the jury trial. At the close of my talk, feel free to look at these photos, just know that some will be gruesome. The blood-splattered Mosser family car, as well as the blood-splattered car of Mr. Robert Dewey. The gruesome photos of the firefighters recovering the bodies, beginning with two-year-old Pamela Sue from the mine shaft, even down to their little white family dog. All dead at the hands of this killer."

He let his eyes roam to the photos, shaking his head at the frustration of not being able to present the massive evidence he had compiled to argue his case for the death penalty before a jury.

"This evidence should have been considered by the Court, but it was not. And not just photos, but reams of testimony, even statements from Cook himself, which showed that the killer knew right from wrong and was actually an astute criminal. I will take every opportunity I can get to speak before groups of people and to accept interviews with the press to get the word out about the evidence that was not allowed to be presented, all because of one lone judge."

He took a deep breath, then continued. "This decision, to deny the prosecution an opportunity to present evidence before a jury, was based on the findings of some psychiatrists, who disagreed among themselves, and the judge's own rather peculiar philosophy of jurisprudence—society is to blame for producing such people. This was the type of thinking that led to Chandler's decision."

Encouraged by the attentiveness of the audience, Robert continued, "Two points I would like to make today, and every chance I get to speak on this matter, I feel should be seriously considered by our congress at some future date.

"Number one, there is a tendency on the part of the federal judiciary to get away from jury trials, and number two, the appointment of federal judges for life has its disadvantages as well as advantages." He looked around the audience, motioning to include them all. "I ask each of you to take it seriously when called upon to exercise your right to vote and to be heard in the public arena. The leaders we choose can make a life or death difference for some of the people in our society.

"The federal courts have always stood for strict enforcement of the law, and the FBI and the federal courts have always been feared by criminals. If I had known what I know now, I would have encouraged the attorney general to have this case tried in some other state than Oklahoma. And I am relieved to know this isn't the end. The Department of Justice has announced it will turn Cook over to California authorities on state charges of murdering Robert Dewey."

The audience stood, offering resounding applause and shouts of agreement as Robert took his seat. Milton resumed his place at the lectern.

"We must admire District Attorney Shelton's bulldog determination to keep at least a flicker of the national spotlight on the Cook case, which he considers a travesty of justice. In so doing—may potential killers be deterred—and may federal judges be aroused into taking a look at themselves in retrospect."

CHAPTER 60

MARCH 31, 1951
ALCATRAZ FEDERAL PENITENTIARY

Associate Warden Paul Madigan removed his glasses and cleaned a smudge while waiting for the shackled inmate on the other side of his desk to respond to his question. He didn't necessarily see a smudge, but was doing his best to encourage the despondent man to talk. He'd been told that on a trip across the county with three law enforcement officers, the man had barely uttered a word. Not amounting to more than five minutes of talking over the forty-hour trip is the way it was explained to him.

He replaced his glasses, picked up his pen and repeated the question. "How did you plead to the crimes you were charged with, William? I need to include that in my intake report."

"Guilty."

"You pleaded guilty?"

William Cook nodded, almost imperceptibly.

"Can you tell me about the offenses you were pleading guilty to?"

No response. Paul wondered whether he should ask again. Decided against it and moved on to the next question. "Can you tell me about your early history? Your childhood and growing-up years?"

"It's all been given before," William said without making eye contact. "Should be in the records."

"Are you married?" Paul wasn't sure why he bothered with that question, when given the amount of time this man had been incarcerated in the last ten years he highly doubted he'd had an opportunity to be married.

"Hard to say." William looked up and surprised him both with the response and the eye to eye connection.

"Can you explain what you mean by that?"

"Hard to say."

This was a new answer. He'd never asked an inmate about their marital status without a definite yes or no.

"Have you been married in the past at some point?"

"Could have been."

"Can you help me understand? Where is your wife, or the woman who might have been your wife, residing at this time?"

"Don't know."

"Where were you married?"

"If I am married, it might have been in Blythe."

"Would that have been this year? In 1951."

"Nah. Last year. I worked in Blythe for a while at a restaurant. A girl came to my cabin when I got off work at night."

"And you think you might have married her?"

253

"She said I did."

"You don't recall?" Paul felt encouraged. While this was the most confusing answer to marital status he'd ever received, at the same time, it was the most words he'd gotten out of the inmate yet.

"Nah. I was drunk."

"You got married when you were drunk?"

"She said I did. I got drunk one night, and the next morning I woke up. I was still in bed and she told me we got married."

"Did she have proof of that?"

"Showed me a paper with my name on it." William tilted his head and seemed to ponder the incident. Then shrugged. "Don't know, really."

"What is her name?"

"Can't say."

"You don't know her name?" Paul stared, holding his pen, waiting to fill in more info.

"Of course I remember her name, but you're not getting it!"

Paul held back a chuckle. It was the most emotion he'd seen the young man display. He wondered if the tattoos the record showed had any bearing on this supposed marriage. Maybe the one with the anchor and the initials "R.S.S. and W.E.C." had something to do with this relationship. He moved on to the next question and simply wrote "unknown" under marital status.

"Ever been in the military?"

"I tried to enlist when I got out of the Walls, but they rejected me because of my record."

254

"When you say 'The Walls,' are you referring to Missouri State Penitentiary?

"Yes."

"So that would have been in the summer of 1950?"

William shrugged. "Guess so."

"How old are you, William?"

"About twenty-three years old, I guess."

"What kind of work have you done?"

"Railroad construction."

"As a laborer?"

"Yeah. Picked fruit in California and washed dishes at the restaurant for a couple months."

"That was in Blythe?"

He nodded.

"Would you like to advance your education while you're here? Take some classes?"

William shrugged, and Paul could read his demeanor. This inmate was quite finished with the interrogation for today.

CHAPTER 61

APRIL 2, 1951
CLOVIS, NEW MEXICO

Dear, who are you writing to so diligently over there? You know your supper is waiting."

Laverne Kershner had put in a long day at New Mexico Nurseries, the business he and his wife owned and operated. He thought he'd come home, eat supper and fall asleep. But instead, he felt an urgent need to act upon something that had been wearing on him pretty near all year. He'd followed the trial of the "Cockeyed" Killer, as some had called Billy Cook. His heart broke for the loss of lives, but what really weighed on him now was the lostness of this Cook character.

"He needs to know the Lord," Laverne said.

"What, Dear? Who are you talking about?"

Laverne blocked out the background noise, focusing fully on the letter he had composed multiple times in his mind. He'd already located the address of the warden of Alcatraz. It had taken some doing and a long-distance phone call that wasn't cheap, but he got the address and they said it was okay to write to the prisoner.

Dear Mr. Cook: I am enclosing a Bible for you to read. I wonder if you have thought about where you will spend your life someday after you are dead and gone? We all have to make the choice, and I want to tell you how to choose to go to heaven. You have to tell Jesus you are sorry for your sins, of which you have committed many, and ask Him to forgive you. Ask Him to be your Savior. That is all there is to it. He will love you, and He will forgive you no matter what you have done. You can write me back if you would like to, and I will write to you again. Yours truly, Laverne Kershner, Clovis, NM.

He felt someone standing near him and looked up to see his wife. "You startled me, Dear."

"I've been talking to you, and you're a million miles away."

"Not a million, just about a thousand or so."

"Whatever do you mean? You're not making any sense."

"My mind is on that boy, the one that killed all those people." Laverne folded the paper and wrote William Cook on the outside, then pulled another paper from the cubbyhole in his desk. He had one more letter to write.

"You're writing the young man in Alcatraz a letter?"

"Yes, and I'm sending him a Bible. I'm worried about his soul."

She patted him on the shoulder. "You're a good man, Laverne. I'll keep supper warm."

Dear Warden, I am enclosing a letter addressed to Bill Cook. This poor wretch has nothing to look forward to in this life, and his only hope is through salvation for the next world and I am interested in his soul. Altho he is a disgusting failure but possibly there was some good in him and it is possible that he might have been a good citizen if he had been raised under a different environment. Maybe it is because he is one of the most unfortunate persons that I know at present and that has aroused my interest. Yours truly, Laverne Kershner, Clovis NM

CHAPTER 62

APRIL 13, 1951
TULSA, OKLAHOMA

Robert Shelton sat immobilized at the head table of the County Bar Association luncheon. The plateful of food before him looked enticing, but his mind remained back in the courtroom, listening to the judge deny his request for a jury trial. He pondered the mountain of evidence he'd been ready to present to the jury and still felt enraged that the judge had issued the verdict of his own choosing without even hearing all the evidence.

"Looking forward to hearing what you have to say, Robert," the attorney sitting to his right said to him. "I agreed with you that the verdict was a travesty."

Startled from his pondering, Robert picked up his fork to attempt to eat some of the food, if for no other reason than to not appear ungrateful for the delicious lunch the preparers and servers had provided. He was most grateful for the opportunity to be invited to speak and tell his side of the story before the attorneys gathered today at the luncheon.

By the time introductions started, he'd nearly cleaned his plate, but his anticipation ran high as he subtly scooted his chair back to be ready to take the podium at the appropriate time.

Ignoring the applause, he jumped right in with the bold statement that had been replaying in his mind since the day they walked out of the courtroom after the disappointing conclusion to what amounted to a non-trial.

"I come before you today to denounce what can only be described as a one-man justice by a federal judge. In fact, a close study of federal court processes will convince almost anyone that the jury system as a fact-finding body has virtually been eliminated."

He watched as heads nodded, and a smattering of clapping sounded from the back of the room.

"I am making no personal attack on Judge Stephen S. Chandler or any person of the judiciary, and I am not approaching the Cook case in a vein of anger, but I do rebel against any judge, state or federal, who will not give you a complete and full hearing on a case. I further rebel when a judge rules out the jury system. The Cook case was the first time in criminal jurisprudence that a prosecutor's request for a jury trial was turned down."

He watched as shock showed on some who had not followed the case carefully, perhaps not realizing just what had actually happened in the courtroom. "Let's not have one-man justice or summary proceedings. We ought to rebel and say the jury system should be maintained as a fact-finding body in federal and all courts."

Robert paused and looked around, encouraged by the interest on the faces in his audience. He continued with the thought that had plagued him the most since the case ended. "How can a judge or jury pass on the brutality of a killer or kidnapper without hearing all the evidence?" He pictured the volumes of files and witnesses he had subpoenaed, still frustrated he was denied the opportunity to present any of this before a jury.

"This was a $250,000 international manhunt. The FBI agent in charge here in Oklahoma, D.A. Bryce, was linked with every phase of the widespread hunt by teletype machines, telephones and other forms of communication. Following on maps every place the killer had been spotted, Bryce had estimated the approximate time Cook would be captured. This man, who can draw a pistol and fire it with deadly aim faster than perhaps any man alive, probably chafed in his Oklahoma City office, preferring instead to be in on the capture."

Understanding nods caused Robert to believe many of the men in the room had the same feeling of wanting to have been in on the capture, even when their jobs are to prosecute, or in some cases to defend, as opposed to hunt down and capture.

Nearing the end of his speech, he shared the details of the kidnapping of Deputy Homer Waldrip, who unintentionally sabotaged the capture of Cook at Blythe when he went ahead on his own to pursue Cook rather than following the FBI instructions to wait for the team.

"And finally, I'd like to share a few details about the Damron and Burke kidnapping that I would have brought out in trial, details probably no one is aware of, as the FBI had blocked these

261

two men from sharing their story with the media while this was an ongoing case."

It may have been his imagination, but the listeners seemed to lean forward, growing even more interested.

"Cook was having car trouble in the car owned by Robert Dewey, his sixth murder victim, and stood by the roadside to flag down help. Once Burke and Damron pulled over shortly after getting in the car, he pointed his revolver at them, effectively taking them hostage. After they had driven down the road at the point of the revolver, he made them turn around and go back to the Dewey car for guns and other property.

"When he took charge of these men, he had one of them drive and the other put up his arms where they could be seen. While Damron was putting his arms up, one dropped out of sight, which startled Cook. He quickly pulled the trigger at the head of Damron, but the hammer fell on an empty cylinder, and Damron escaped with his life. Cook quickly spun the cylinder and cursed, then said, 'it'll work next time.'"

Robert breathed deeply. That part of the story got to him every time, imagining the fear that had coursed through Damron and Burke at that moment. "Cook's plans went awry in Baja California when he missed a ferry which would have taken him to the mainland of Old Mexico and a chance for further escape. There was little doubt that Cook planned to murder the two before trying to flee into the mainland."

He watched as the listeners shook their heads and whispered feedback to the others at their tables.

"I cite these examples to show how rational a person he was." It still galled him that the judge believed the man to be insane and incapable of understanding his actions.

"Thank you for the invitation to speak. Since I could not air the evidence in court, this is my only means of getting the truth out."

CHAPTER 63

Detective Carl Nutt and his wife stood outside the nursery window at the hospital, beaming at their brand new baby girl. In just a few days, they would take her home, and she would really be theirs.

He thought back to that afternoon in the office just a few weeks ago when the very pregnant young mother walked into the Joplin Police Station and asked for him by name.

"I heard you were kind to children," she said after he introduced himself.

He nodded. It was hard to keep his eyes from being drawn to her large belly. She looked ready to have this child any day.

"I have to put my baby up for adoption, but I want to make sure the baby goes to good people." At that she stopped talking, her chin quivering, eyes glassy. She stared at Carl.

He and Goldie had wanted children for a long time, but the good Lord hadn't seen fit to bless them with any. Was this how it was to happen? A young woman walks in off the street to give them the greatest blessing of their lives?

She must have read his expression, somehow knowing what he was thinking.

"Would you?" she whispered. "Would you and your wife adopt my baby?"

Feeling near tears himself, he assured the girl they would love her baby like their own.

Carl rushed home to share the news with Goldie, the love of his life, and wife of four years.

Weeks later, when the young woman gave birth to a beautiful baby girl, Carl looked into her sweet face and recalled the horror experienced by another sweet little girl. He'd never forget finding Pamela Sue in the watery mine shaft with the rest of her family, just a few months before.

There was no doubt what they would name their brand new baby girl. This little baby would be a living tribute to her namesake. A few days later, Pamela Sue Nutt joined her new parents at home, completing the circle of love in their household.

And for Carl, this helped to numb the ache that still filled his soul. He shared the anger of U.S. Attorney Shelton, who'd argued the case before the judge in Oklahoma just last month. Anger that Cook had escaped the death penalty by claiming insanity. It was the grossest travesty of justice. He'd be eligible for parole in fifteen to twenty years if the reports he'd read were correct. And the surviving family members? The death sentence for their loved ones was for all eternity.

It couldn't end this way. It just couldn't.

CHAPTER 64

MAY 4, 1951
ALCATRAZ FEDERAL PENITENTIARY

Warden Edwin Swope surveyed the group gathered to discuss the evaluation of inmate William E. Cook Jr. at the six-week mark of his incarceration in their facility.

"Let the record show that this is the meeting of the Classification Committee to share impressions and make recommendations regarding the prisoner William E. Cook Jr., Inmate #918-AZ." Edwin looked around the room at the others in attendance. "Please state your name and title for the record."

"Paul Madigan, Associate Warden."

"Dr. Milton Meltzer, Chief Medical Officer."

"Arthur M. Dollison, Superintendent of Industries."

"Bob Bristow, Chief Steward."

"R.F. Winkelman, Protestant Chaplain, I go by Bill."

"Alfred Kaeppel, Records Clerk."

"We will discuss our findings and recommendations before bringing in the inmate for interview." Edwin looked across the conference table. "Dr. Meltzer, can you share your findings to date?"

"Yes, a psychiatric board consisting of myself, Dr. Leon J. Whitsell and Dr. George Johnson have examined Cook." He looked up at Edwin, then around the table to the rest of the participants. "I should say I attempted to examine. He hasn't proven very cooperative."

Looking back down at his notes, Dr. Meltzer continued, "While he refused to submit to tests, our clinical examination reveals that he appears to be of at least average intellectual endowment. He has been interviewed on several occasions since his admission, and he presents as an unattractive, tense, sullen-looking young man who consistently refuses to answer the examiner's questions. In each interview, he indicated verbally his refusal to be questioned, stating, 'I have answered all this before; look in the record.'"

"Any information about his behavior since he has been incarcerated here on the island?"

"Yes, Warden, we do have information we've gathered on that. According to our notes since admission, he has shown no evidence of any bizarre or inappropriate behavior. He has cooperated with prison routine and has done a small amount of work, under direction, in the cellhouse. He has kept himself apart from all social contact with inmates and personnel. It has been noted that he usually will answer questions when they are put to him by other inmates or personnel, but he never is spontaneous or willing to elaborate on his comments."

"Anything else to add?"

"His effective capacities are markedly impaired, and he seems to be living a barren, isolated, emotional existence.

It is noteworthy, however, that chronic anxiety and tension appear to make him extremely suspicious of being harmed. A diagnostic impression is difficult to make, but if the notoriety and newspaper data are disregarded, it appears that he is a schizoid character of long standing, as evidenced by his behavior during interview and observations here. The prognosis for his institutional adjustment is just fair. He will need close custody."

"Thank you, Doctor." Edwin looked around the group. "Does anyone have questions for Dr. Meltzer?"

"Yes," Bill Winkelman said. "Can you explain in layman's terms what you mean by the term 'schizoid'?"

"I wondered that too," Arthur chimed in. "It will help me as I find a place to plug him in for regular duties here."

"Yes," Dr. Meltzer turned to Arthur sitting on his right side. "Schizoid is a personality type characterized by emotional aloofness and solitary habits."

"That is definitely what I've seen so far," Associate Warden Paul nodded in agreement.

"Arthur," Edwin said, "what are your findings as far as plugging this inmate into one of our industries? Have you made a determination or had any success with that?"

"Mr. Cook has expressed an interest in plumbing. While confined at the Missouri State Penitentiary, he worked in the plumbing shop and apparently thoroughly enjoyed his apprenticeship. He is definitely opposed to working in our clothing factory and alluded to a background also at the Missouri State Pen in that area. But for now, the plan is for general maintenance in the cellhouse, with perhaps eventually assigning him to something in the Industries, possibly laundry, since the clothing factory won't be a suitable option."

"Reverend?" Edwin turned his attention to the gentleman directly across from him at the end of the conference table. "Do you have any feedback on his religious interests?"

"From what I'd seen in the intake information, it looks that he has no interest. He resents being forced to attend Sunday School as a child in the various homes and institutions he was in, I've read. But I've also heard from some of the guards that he cherishes a Bible someone sent him in the mail. Whether he reads it or not, I do not know."

"Has he attended chapel services since arriving?" Edwin asked.

Bill shook his head. "No, but I hope to meet with him soon. I know he won't come to me, so my plan is to find him in the rec yard in the not too distant future and see if I can engage him in a conversation."

"You won't find him taking part in any vigorous activities," Associate Warden Paul Madigan said. "He goes for board games, so that will be the place to look for him. He doesn't seem to be interested in any activities involving physical exertion."

"What about other reading material?" Dr. Metzler asked of the group. "Is anyone aware of whether he does any reading in his cell?"

"Yes," Paul said. "I've also heard from the guards that he reads adventure-type fiction and travel magazines."

"Bob," Edwin turned to the man seated next to him. "Any diet concerns? Have you had to oversee special food preparation?"

"None, he is on a regular diet."

"So, the overall plan is to keep him in maximum custody. He has an escape history, and also there are continued detainers for him, which we will discuss with him at the conclusion of this meeting." Edwin looked over to Bill. "Reverend, great idea to find a casual meeting place. Maybe you can encourage him to attend chapel services." He looked around the table. "Does anyone have anything else to add before we bring Mr. Cook in?"

With no response, Edwin nodded to his associate warden, Paul, to escort William Cook in.

As the young man entered, the shackles on his feet clinked against each other and bumped the metal chair legs when he took the seat Paul escorted him to. He sat, handcuffed hands in his lap, clearly uncomfortable being the center of attention in the roomful of men.

"Mr. Cook," Edwin said, "do you have any questions for us regarding your time here at Alcatraz so far?"

"No." He stared at the table in front of him, rather than making eye contact with any of the men assembled.

"How are the programs and assignments you've been involved in?"

"All right."

"Do you have any complaints about your time here thus far?"

"No."

Edwin, as well as, he assumed, the others, strained to hear the responses, but he noted they were forthcoming immediately upon being asked and he took it as a good sign there was no evasiveness.

"Do you have any special requests?"

"No."

"Mr. Cook, do you understand that detainers have been issued from the State of California and the State of Missouri regarding further pursuit of your case?"

"Yes."

"Do you understand what that means?"

"Yes."

"Do you care to explain for us what that means?"

"No."

"But you are aware that you are likely to be transported at some point in the future to another county, possibly another state, for an additional trial on your charges?"

"Yes."

"And do you understand that you might possibly receive an additional sentence that could be life imprisonment or even death?"

"Yes."

"And do you have any questions about these procedures?"

"No."

The entire interview of the inmate had taken less than five minutes. "Gentlemen, if there are no further questions for Mr. Cook, we will dismiss at this time."

William Cook stood, the living embodiment of his intake description: an awkward, small, underdeveloped twenty-three-year-old male with poor posture and bad skin. Acne, more reminiscent of an adolescent than a young man, sprinkled across his face, and needle marks on his arms bore witness to his drug use during a previous incarceration. Staring at the floor, he shuffled his way to the door, the picture of hopelessness.

CHAPTER 65

MAY 5, 1951
MCALESTER, OKLAHOMA

The defense attorneys appointed by the court originally entered a motion to test their client's sanity." Robert looked over the audience of the Pittsburg County Bar Association. He made it his mission to inform not only the public but fellow attorneys what the truth was behind the scenes about how their state handled this case while the case proceeded in another state. Hopefully, to change a future outcome if a similar case arose and most definitely to make sure other attorneys knew of the potential risks of trying a case such as this one.

"The defense attorneys employed the services of a psychiatrist and a psychologist in Oklahoma City. These two examined Cook. And the defense attorneys then went back into court and withdrew the motion for a sanity hearing. I have since talked to this psychiatrist and psychologist and learned that it was their judgment that Cook was not insane.

"So, where did the insane diagnosis come from then, if not from the defense attorneys' witnesses? The judge himself appointed two psychiatrists to examine Cook on behalf of the

Court. These experts reported that the slayer of the five members of the Mosser family was 'mentally ill and had the mind of a three-year-old and could not premeditate murder.'"

Satisfied by the shocked looks on the faces of the attorneys present, he continued, "The experts I obtained upon advice of the medical society in Oklahoma County, testified that Cook did have the faculties to distinguish between right and wrong and to know the consequences of his acts. We later learned that one of the psychiatrists requested by the Court to examine Cook is known to be a man opposed to capital punishment. It is my sincere feeling that we should have been afforded a jury trial, and that the Court certainly abused its discretion in refusing us one. I brought out the fact that if William E. Cook was insane, then he was not competent to enter a guilty plea to a crime for which he could hang. But the Court still held that he was insane and also accepted his guilty plea and assessed the sentence on that basis."

"Mr. Shelton?" Robert turned to Ewing Sadler, the program chairman, speaking from his front row seat. "Some of the members have asked if you're open to receiving questions?"

"Absolutely, what would you like to know?"

A young attorney three rows back stood. "Mr. Shelton, can you tell us about some of the evidence that you were planning to present?"

"Absolutely," Robert said. "All of Cook's relatives and his associates at the time he was in Missouri State Training School and the Missouri State Penitentiary were questioned about his behavior. Without a single exception, they told us there was no evidence of insanity or abnormalcy. His seventh grade teacher told us he was respectful to her, his deportment was good and he made above average grades. He has an I.Q. of more than ninety. He was medium to superior in reading, writing and arithmetic. He read the best magazines while he was in jail in Oklahoma City, and he kept an accurate record of the money he had left with the jailer."

An older attorney stood near the back. "May I ask what your thoughts are on why he let the remaining two men live? Damron and Burke, I believe the names were."

"That was not his original plan," Robert said. "He had taken James Burke's billfold and identification papers and had planned to kill the two prospectors, take the car deep into Mexico and sell it, then live under the assumed identity of one of his victims."

"I'll share one more example. This one was related to me by the FBI agents who questioned Cook when he was brought back over the border. When apprehended, he was brought to a jail in the little town of Santa Rosalia, Mexico. There were no FBI men there, no officers from the United States. Cook told the FBI that a group of Mexican soldiers was floundering around the jail, appeared to be drunk, and left the door to his cell standing open. Cook said to the FBI agents, 'I didn't fall for that old trick. Then one of them set a rifle down within my reach—with the door still open. I didn't fall for that old trick either.'"

With that, Robert thanked the listeners and took his seat. Mr. Sadler took the podium and looked across the room. "What do you think, men? Did this young man have the mind of a three-year-old?" Snorts of derision sounded across the room.

He looked over at Robert and closed the meeting with this final statement: "On behalf of the Pittsburg County Bar Association, we commend you for your courageous stand in your efforts to have Cook tried by a jury."

CHAPTER 66

JULY 10, 1951
ALCATRAZ FEDERAL PENITENTIARY

Rev. Bill Winkelman stepped into the recreation yard and let his eyes roam. He had a particular inmate in mind he hoped to engage with on this unusually sunny day. Spotting the men playing basketball, he watched a bit of the sport he'd always loved. He'd been told William did not prefer physical recreation, but opted for table games. Bill hoped it was something simple like checkers, so he could focus on the conversation he wanted to have as opposed to chess, a game he'd never excelled at, that would require his full concentration.

Across the yard at an isolated corner table, he spotted the frowning young man sitting alone. Perfect. As he approached, he saw he got his wish. William appeared to be playing a solitary game of checkers. He wondered if he would welcome a partner.

Bill pulled out the chair across from William, noting that the inmate never lifted his head to make eye contact.

"Mind if I play checkers with you?"

"Suit yourself." William tipped the board, letting all the pieces slide off onto the table. Before Bill could choose a color,

William began sorting out the black checkers and placing them on his side of the board.

Once Rev. Bill had his checkers in place, he motioned. "Do you want to start?"

William moved his first piece without speaking.

Bill wondered if it would be an easy game, and if so, should he let William win, but to his surprise, he found his partner to be adept at the game, and he concentrated hard as he realized William was quickly collecting his red playing pieces.

He wondered if winning would put a smile on the man's face, but rather doubted it. He'd heard and read in the reports that no one had ever seen him smile. And such was the case as William got all his remaining pieces on the board crowned, then proceeded to wipe Bill's playing pieces off the board, easily winning. So much for thinking he would have to let him win.

Bill watched as William placed his playing pieces back in form, ready to play another round.

"I must say," Bill organized his playing pieces, then looked up at William. "I didn't expect to get beaten so badly."

William still did not make eye contact, but uttered something that sounded like "hmmpf."

Trying harder this go-round, Bill was determined to capture some of the black pieces before his pieces started flying off the board and, to make the game even more challenging, he also chose this time to engage William in conversation.

"I never see you at chapel."

William jumped one of his pieces and ignored his comment.

Better to use a question that needed a response than just making a statement. This guy obviously was not a willing conversationalist.

"Would you like to attend chapel this Sunday?"

"No."

That was a quicker response than he had expected. He'd been hoping, of course, for a positive answer, but he felt any answer was progress.

"Why not?" Bill wasn't usually so blunt with men he was inviting to chapel, but the occasion seemed to call for it in this instance.

"Had enough of that stuff rammed down my throat." He still did not make eye contact, and continued to clear the board of the reverend's red playing pieces.

"Rammed down your throat here at Alcatraz?"

"No."

Rev. Bill had given up trying to win a game. "Where then?"

William finally looked at him, if only to show his disgust, with a deep sigh accompanied by a scowl. "People. When I was a kid. Foster homes. Reform school. Always trying to stuff religion down my throat. I had enough of it."

While the answer dismayed him, Bill was encouraged by the longest stream of conversation he'd ever heard out of the man. "Well, I'm sorry to hear about that," Bill said. "We don't cram religion down people's throats at chapel. We sing praise songs and hear short messages that teach us how to grow close to God."

"Hmmpf." William was again placing his pieces in their spot so he could win a third game.

Bill followed his example, determined to win this time, emboldened by the success he was having getting William to respond to his questions.

"I heard you have a Bible in your cell," Bill tried to sound nonchalant as he moved his first playing piece, trying to copy William's moves, in the hopes he could finally win.

William dropped his playing piece and looked up at him. "Yeah, what's it to you if I do?"

Bill met his gaze and shrugged. "Just interested. Who gave it to you?"

"Some guy mailed it to me."

"Do you ever read it?"

William stood and shoved his chair into the table, bumping the board and sending the pieces scattering across the table. "None of your business."

Reverend Bill sat and watched William Cook shuffle out of the recreation yard. Well, he'd mark this as a successful visit, despite the outcome. At least he got the man to answer his questions.

CHAPTER 67

NOVEMBER 19, 1951
EL CENTRO, CALIFORNIA

Aggie Dahm listened as the court clerk called the names of all the prospective jurors, then moved to take the seat assigned to her as they called her name. She knew already she would not get seated on this jury for the trial. She'd heard enough already to know what her position was. Much as she'd like to vote with the jury, she had listened to the questions the judge began asking once they were all seated and she'd be honest when they got to her, even though that honesty would keep her from getting to vote on the outcome.

"Mrs. Dahm, you heard the statements in reference to what the issue of the case is?"

"Yes."

"And is there anything that you don't understand, my statements about what this case is about?"

"No."

"You understand the duties of the jury in this case, what the issue that has to be decided is?"

"Yes." Aggie knew very well the issue to be decided wasn't if the defendant committed the crime, but if he was sane and knew what he was doing. Of course, the young man knew what he was doing. It was hogwash, in her opinion, that the defense attorneys were trying to protect this young man by claiming he didn't know, just like that judge did in Oklahoma.

"Now," the judge continued, "if I were to ask you the same questions I asked Juror Number one, would your answers be substantially the same?"

"No."

"What?"

She wanted to chuckle at the surprised look on the judge's face, but knew that wasn't appropriate behavior in a courtroom, so she simply repeated her first answer. "No."

"In what way would your answer be different? As to that question, I mean."

"Well, I have discussed it and I have formed my opinion, and I don't feel I would be a fair juror."

"Well, Mrs. Dahm, before you took your place in the jury box, were you familiar with this definition of insanity which I gave you?"

"No."

"Well," the judge appeared to be reading from notes, "in view of that fact, have you such a preconceived idea—and remember that the only issue in this case is the issue of whether the defendant was insane or not insane at the time of the commission of the act—do you have any preconceived idea which would interfere in any way with your giving a fair and impartial consideration to the evidence in this case, bearing in mind the definition that I gave you of insanity, and bearing in mind that the only issue is as to whether he was sane or insane at the time of the commission of the act?"

Oh, for Pete's sake, Aggie thought, does this man not get the point of my answer? She couldn't continue listening to his drivel. "Well, that is the way I feel, Your Honor."

"Well," he was not to be deterred, "as I stated before, the Court is only interested, and I feel confident that the attorneys are only interested, in getting twelve men and women as jurors who will impartially consider the evidence and return a verdict after considering that evidence, and applying the law to the facts as they find them to be from the evidence. Now, if you sincerely believe that you cannot impartially do that, why I don't think you should act as a juror. You honestly feel that you cannot?"

"I honestly feel that way." Aggie nodded for further emphasis.

"You cannot impartial—you have such a conviction that you can't sit here with an open mind and consider this evidence?"

"That is right, Your Honor."

She watched as the judge turned his attention to the attorneys. "I think this juror should be excused."

"I believe she should be." C.F. Sturdevant Jr., the assistant prosecuting attorney, agreed. Aggie wanted to jump up and tell him she was on his side. She fully believed this young man knew what he was doing, and was fully deserving of the death penalty.

Mr. Connelly, the defense attorney who she heard had traveled from Oklahoma, most likely hoping once again to get

William Edward Cook declared insane, thus avoiding the death penalty, also agreed that she, Mrs. Agnes Dahm, would not make a good juror. "I believe in view of her last statement, she is disqualified."

"You will be excused." The judge turned from her to the clerk. "You may draw the name of another juror."

Aggie stepped down wondering if the judge would recognize her when she returned the next day to sit in the gallery to observe what she hoped would be a quick trial ending with a sentence of death.

CHAPTER 68

NOVEMBER 20, 1951
EL CENTRO, CALIFORNIA

Aggie Dahm had skipped out on the morning session of court once she realized they were still deep into the tedious and time-consuming task of choosing jury members. However, when she came back after the lunch recess, she had missed the opening statements from the attorneys and some of the testimony as they re-called Mrs. Bryson, the lady who worked for the child services division when Billy first came to their attention, to resume her testimony after the lunch recess.

Her mind wandered as the defense attorney grilled Mrs. Bryson on the early years of Billy's life. She had read much of this testimony in the newspaper articles from the first trial in Oklahoma. But now they were venturing into something she hadn't heard about before, and she sat up to pay closer attention.

"Now, is there anything further that you haven't said that you base your opinion on?" Mr. Connolly probably hoped for further proof that the witness was correct in her assessment of the defendant being insane.

285

"Yes, because I feel the shock that he received when he was four years old would affect his entire life."

"What was that?"

"Finding his mother's dead body. Walking in unexpectedly and finding his mother either accidentally killed or murdered, and blood all over her face." Mrs. Bryson looked at the judge, then back to the defense attorney, as if gauging whether they comprehended the horror this would have been for a child. "It seems to me that it would be such a shock that he could never recover from it."

"Well," Mr. Connolly said, "was it ever determined how his mother died?"

"Not definitely so," Mrs. Bryson said. "The coroner said that apparently she was chopping wood, and a stick went up in the air and came down with force enough to kill her; which I don't believe, for I think a woman who has strength enough to chop green wood and for it to come up and hit you with force enough to kill you. I just don't think it is possible."

"Are there any further facts, Mrs. Bryson, that you base your opinion of insanity on?"

"Well, the boy had the worst case of inferiority complex of any child I ever had dealings with. I thought perhaps it was to some small extent due to his eye, and I had a doctor—I had this done myself—I had a doctor to operate on that eye, and while he never could open it in the beginning, after the doctor operated on it, he tied it up short, and he never could close it again. So he has still got a bad eye."

Aggie pulled out a roll of lifesavers, peeled the paper back and offered one to the spectators on either side of her, then plucked the next one out for herself. Red, her favorite color. It gave her something to do, enjoying the lifesaver, as they got through the rest of Mrs. Bryon's testimony wherein she tried to prove Bill Cook was insane. The following witness would do the same, she discovered as the defense attorney began questioning a doctor who had come in from Oklahoma. He seemed to go by the same playbook that had worked successfully for them in his home state. She wondered how that would play out here, with a jury listening and making the final decision.

She enjoyed the cross-examination by the Deputy District Attorney more than the questioning by the defense attorney.

The psychiatrist's next words appalled her.

"I don't think this man would have been shot if he had kept his mouth shut or had said the right thing."

Aggie couldn't believe this doctor was blaming Robert Dewey himself for being murdered.

He continued, "There was a sheriff in Los Angeles, for instance, who was subjected to the same situation he was, who said to him, 'Bill, take me out in the desert and tie me up and leave me there, and make your getaway.' Bill did that. This man, instead, responded by saying, 'Well, I am not afraid of a gun. I was in the Army. I have been shot several times.' So, bang, bang! Bill shoots him."

"Well, suppose the defendant, after shooting this man, makes an effort to escape," Mr. Sturdevant said, "would that indicate to you an awareness of the possible consequences of his act of shooting?"

"If it were true, which I doubt, that he made an attempt to escape –"

"We are simply assuming for the purpose of the question that he does make an effort to escape from the scene where the shooting took place," the prosecuting attorney said.

"He was already escaping from another place," Dr. Galbraith said, "I mean, he was going about his business, traveling. It was just a continuation of something that he had been doing before."

Aggie nearly dropped her lifesavers as she struggled to stay seated while she longed to jump up and scream "objection." Did this doctor really want them to believe this guy was just traveling? In a stolen police car?

So disgusted at this line of questioning, she missed much of the dialogue that followed, but tuned back in as the judge had a few questions to wrap up this witness. After a long-winded preamble, he got down to the nitty-gritty of what he wanted to ask the witness. "Have you an opinion as to whether the defendant was insane or sane on January the 6th, 1951?"

"Yes," Dr. Galbraith said, speaking right to the judge. "I would say that he was one of the most insane men I ever met."

After much wrangling between attorneys and the judge, they decided the prosecution would begin presenting their evidence right after the mid-afternoon break because the defense's last witness wouldn't be available until the next day.

This ought to be good, Aggie thought as court reconvened and they called Deputy Sheriff Homer Waldrip to the stand.

Finally, she thought, we're getting to hear from one of the
kidnap victims. She was pretty sure this man would not say the
defendant was insane and acting without knowledge of what he
was doing.

After all the introductory questions and learning of his
personal knowledge about the defendant, having known him
before the day of the kidnapping, Mr. Sturdevant brought up
the important question. "Now, taking into consideration your
acquaintance with Mr. Cook before January 6, 1951 do you have
any opinion as to whether on the 6th of January 1951 he was
sane or insane?"

"Objection!" Mr. Connolly was on his feet before the
question was complete. "We object to that as being incompetent,
irrelevant and immaterial, the witness not being qualified to
answer the question."

"We are offering the testimony, Your Honor, as that of an
intimate acquaintance."

After several more back-and-forth exchanges between the
attorneys, judge and witness, it was determined that Deputy
Waldrip was not qualified to determine sanity. But the narration
of what happened while in the defendant's captivity surely
convinced Aggie, and, she would imagine, most of the jury as
well, that the man knew what he was doing. Knew he was in
the wrong and knew he needed to escape. That seemed to be the
qualifier for this insanity game changer they were trying to pull.

It was getting late in the afternoon, and Aggie was tempted to
slip out so she could get home to make dinner, but then she heard
the name of the next witness being called. This was Hazel's boy.

They weren't close, but she remembered doing volunteer work with her a few times at the PTA Clothes Closet some years back when their kids were still in school. She couldn't imagine how hard that was on her when her son was missing for those eight days.

After the clerk swore in the witness, the district attorney, Mr. Bitler, jumped right in with questions.

"Do you know the defendant," Mr. Bitler looked over at the defense table, then back to the witness, "William Edward Cook?"

"Yes, I do." Forrest had no smile when he said that, and Aggie wondered if William made eye contact with him when he responded.

"When did you first meet him?" Mr. Bitler said.

"January 7th, Sunday, en route to San Felipe, Mexico."

"What time of day or night was it?"

"It was in the neighborhood of six o'clock in the morning."

"How did you happen to contact Cook?"

"We saw parked across the road on the opposite lane of traffic—that would be the east lane of traffic—a Buick, a blue Buick sedan parked at approximately forty-five degrees across the road. Beside it, in our lane, was a man waving what looked to be a one-gallon gasoline can."

"Who was that man?"

"At that time I didn't know," Forrest said. "We later discovered him to be William Edward Cook."

Aggie imagined there must have been great regret and much fear when the two young men made that discovery.

Forrest explained the circumstances of picking the defendant up, moving the car that was stranded, all under the direction of the defendant. Interesting, Aggie thought, that William Cook seemed to take charge immediately.

"Did he speak in an audible tone, so that there on the road where all three of you were, you could understand what he said?"

Forrest looked over at the defendant, then back to Mr. Bitler. "Absolutely."

Hmmpf, Aggie thought. Just as she suspected, the killer is putting on an act when he pretends he can't speak up.

She checked her watch, knowing she needed to leave soon, but continued to listen as Forrest detailed the drive all around Baja California from one town to another, even down to changing shirts with Forrest's friend James so the defendant could hide his identity. She hoped that psychiatrist from Oklahoma was listening to all of this and realizing how wrong he was in his assessment.

Forrest had gone through nearly the entire eight days of their captivity, and it seemed like the district attorney was ready to wrap it up for the day with a few last questions.

"Was he at any time, to your knowledge, without possession of one of the pistols or revolvers?"

"He was never to my knowledge at any time during the trip without possession of one or the other of the pistols or revolvers," Forrest said.

"Did you do anything down on that trip without the sanction of Bill Cook?"

"We did not."

Mr. Bitler turned to the judge. "That is all right now."

"Ladies and gentlemen of the jury," Judge Mouser said, "before taking our evening recess, I admonish you that you shall not discuss the case with anyone."

Aggie was the first out the door, rushing to get to her car. Dinner was going to be late tonight.

CHAPTER 69

NOVEMBER 21, 1951
EL CENTRO, CALIFORNIA

Day three. Fifty-nine-year-old Charles Hilt was many things, a World War I veteran, a widower, a member of the Sons of the American Revolution, a former immigration officer and even after retiring from civil service, he found himself serving as a bailiff in the Superior Court of El Centro. He loved to travel. Had lived all over the United States, but returned to El Centro to work for a few more years before really retiring. His destination would be Florida with his second wife, who had found her way into his life after several years of mourning the loss of his first wife.

But today, in fact, all this week, the week of Thanksgiving, he was not feeling very thankful. He was, if the truth be told, feeling angry. He stared at the emotionless defendant in his customary place at the defense table, eyes focused down while one of his kidnap victims, Forrest Damron, continued his testimony from the day before.

Thankfully, in all his years of law enforcement and civil service, he had learned to mask his emotions. So his anger toward this defendant did not show. He had been steaming mad inside ever since reading about the ex-con killing a veteran last January. And leaving him lying face down in the road. The disrespect for the body of a man deserving only honor for serving his country. Charles came from a long line of patriots who had served in various wars, himself included. He supposed that was why after reading this in the newspapers so many months ago he had abruptly ended his retirement, returned to El Centro, and applied for the bailiff position. Maybe deep down inside he knew the trial would eventually make its way back here. And he wanted to be there, to hear it for himself, when the judge pronounced the death penalty. It was the only punishment in his estimation that equaled the horrific nature of this man's crimes.

He supposed most people in the courtroom never gave the bailiff a second thought. Never imagined a bailiff might have an opinion on the case, or might even pay close attention to this case. But he was. He surely was. That is, when his mind wasn't wandering, anticipating what the future verdict and sentence would be.

"That is all," the district attorney said upon finishing up the questioning of Forrest Damron. "Cross-examine."

Charles watched as Mr. Connolly, the defense attorney, stood. "Now, if the Court please, we move that all of this witness' testimony be stricken for the reason it is incompetent, irrelevant and immaterial, does not apply to the sanity or insanity of this defendant."

The judge's decision came swiftly. "The motion will be denied."

Charles listened as the attorneys finished with Forrest Damron, then questioned the FBI agent who discovered the buried license plates the defendant had instructed his captives to remove from Robert Dewey's car. Next, the Sheriff's Department Chief of Identification testified about searching Dewey's car in Mexico and finding a change of clothes.

When the second kidnap victim, James Burke, came along, Charles felt his anger ratcheting up as he discovered that this man too was a veteran, having served in the U.S. Army during World War II. He was especially incensed at the way the defense attorney attempted to mock him.

"Now, after you picked this boy up down here, near Mexicali, it was more or less of a lark, wasn't it, for all three of you?" Mr. Connelly said.

Charles wanted to cheer at the look of hate in Burke's eyes as he silently stared down the attorney without answering.

But Connelly didn't give up. "What I mean, when you got down to that last town, you went in and out of places and walked up and down streets like tourists, didn't you?"

Burke nearly came out of his seat, shooting daggers with his eyes. "If you can consider the gosh-darn trouble that my wife and my family went through, it certainly isn't a lark. It is far from a lark."

Charles felt his head shaking, something he knew was a big no-no. Showing no reaction was part of the rules. He wouldn't let it happen again, but what was the worst that could come of it? He'd be heading to Florida sooner than he planned.

After Burke's testimony, he listened as FBI Agent Plaxico gave damning testimony of the defendant almost boasting about what he'd done, including his plans to act crazy if he got caught, to get a lighter sentence. He almost shook his head again, but didn't want to push it, and risk there being a mistrial for inappropriate behavior by a court employee.

After the lunch break, the rest of the day consisted of listening to various doctor testimonies, and Charles was excited to learn that both attorneys were ready to rest their cases mid-afternoon. They could head home for Thanksgiving, knowing that the trial was almost over. Just a matter of hearing closing arguments, and then, hopefully, prayerfully, a quick verdict by the jury. Perhaps they could wrap up this case by the weekend.

CHAPTER 70

NOVEMBER 23, 1951
EL CENTRO, CALIFORNIA

Judge L.J. Mouser surveyed the courtroom, letting his eyes roam over the members of the jury, the spectators silently watching from the gallery and the attorneys. He settled briefly on the defendant, recalling the opportunities he'd had to question him in the earlier proceedings while the man sat silent, refusing to respond.

He turned back to the prosecuting attorneys and gave a slight tip of his head. "You may proceed with your closing argument."

Deputy District Attorney C.F. Sturdevant stepped from behind the table and approached the jury box, then turned and faced the judge. "May it please the Court." He adjusted his body position, now facing the defense attorneys, "Counsel," and finally turned his attention back toward the jury. "And ladies and gentlemen of the jury. You have been told by the Court, and I believe it has been mentioned by counsel heretofore, that the sole issue before you, as the jury in this case, is the issue of the sanity or insanity of this particular defendant at the time of the killing of Robert Dewey."

Judge Mouser listened as the deputy D.A. debated the conflicting testimonies of the witnesses regarding the mental capacity of the defendant.

C.F. paused, looking deliberately into the eyes of every juror, before continuing. "The sum and substance of Mrs. Bryson's testimony was that this boy had an extremely hard early life. I think we can accept the fact that he did. But I think we also can accept the fact that if everyone who had a difficult youth, had hardships while they were growing up, were permitted to carry out the act with which the defendant here is charged, this world would be an extremely difficult place to live."

C.F. turned to look at the defendant, so long that throat clearing could be heard throughout the courtroom as the silence became uncomfortable. Yet still the defendant remained stone-faced. Turning back to the jury, he continued, "The psychiatrists appointed by the Court, took into consideration the acts, conduct and statements of the defendant and all three of them gave the opinion that the man was sane at the time the acts were committed, which as I said before, is the only issue which we are to consider here."

Judge Mouser noted with appreciation the attentiveness of the jury as the deputy district attorney reiterated much of the testimony given by the various witnesses, spelling out all the steps carefully taken by the defendant to carry out his plan and cover his tracks. He saw sorrow on the faces of some women as once again they heard the details of Robert Dewey's last moments as he was passing through their county. Watching with the poker face he had perfected over his many years on the bench, he did not allow himself to make a decision. He felt he was less likely to inadvertently manipulate the findings of the jury by using biased words when he gave his final instructions before they went out to deliberate.

His attention was drawn back as he could sense the deputy D.A. wrapping up the first round of the closing statements.

"Considering that we know that up until the moment of his capture when he had a gun in his hand, he was active, he was observant, he made all the plans necessary for his escape and he carried them out exactly as he planned. I think we have to agree that he planned them very cleverly. Yet, at the moment of his apprehension, he ceased to be active, ceased to be observant, he has nothing to say, his position has changed radically."

C.F. turned sideways, pointing boldly toward the defendant, while continuing to face the jury. "I say this to you, that all of these things indicate one thing: that he is doing exactly what he said he was going to do; that he was clever enough to choose the defense of not guilty by reason of insanity, and the only answer for his complete change in personality demonstrates conclusively that he has taken up that course of conduct in connection with his plan." He paused again, doing another individual look at each juror, turned to the defendant, then back to the jury, where he slammed his fist on the ornate panel separating the jury box from the attorney area. "He is still putting his plan into effect here in this courtroom."

The judge watched as C.F. took a deep breath, looked his way, then one last time to the jury. "Thank you," he said before taking his place at the attorney table next to the district attorney.

Attorney John Connolly remained at his desk during the ten-minute recess after the deputy district attorney finished the prosecution's first round of closing statements. He'd been at a slight disadvantage this entire case, never having practiced law in California. The judge had been lenient and helpful along the way as he inquired of procedure. He'd come into this case confident, after their successful outcome when he and the co-attorney argued the case in federal court in Oklahoma, convincing the judge the defendant was insane and avoiding the death penalty. However, the court-appointed psychiatrists in California had put him at a disadvantage with their assessment of sanity.

He looked over his closing statement notes. He needed to deliver this statement flawlessly, speaking to the heart and sympathy of each juror, convincing them of his client's inability to have planned and pulled off this crime.

"The case of the People of the State of California against William Cook."

Connolly looked up, startled, so deep in thought he had missed the return of the jury and the judge at break's end.

"May it be stipulated that the defendant is in court and the jury and alternate juror are in their seats and that you are ready to proceed, gentlemen?"

He and the district attorney stood simultaneously.

"So stipulated," Attorney Bitler said.

Making direct eye contact with the judge, Connolly responded simply and confidently. "Yes."

"You may proceed, Mr. Connolly."

Coming around the table, John Connolly approached the jury, careful to make eye contact with each juror, including the alternate. After his opening statements he was ready to deliver his best.

"I defended this boy in Oklahoma City in federal court when he stood trial for a horrible crime. The federal judge in that case sentenced this boy to five terms in Alcatraz of sixty years each, to run consecutively, meaning that when he finished one sentence, he started on the other one, and on down the line. The federal judge, in his wisdom, made it impossible for this boy to ever see the light of day, or get out of the dungeon of Alcatraz. No one was more surprised than myself when I read an AP report in the Oklahoma City paper that Don Bitler was bringing this boy from the Alcatraz dungeon to try him in California. I couldn't see any reason for it."

He paused to take a reading on the pulse of the jury. Pages and pages of notes were before him, and he knew he would base how much of it to present on how long he could hold their attention.

"In the case in Oklahoma City, four eminent psychiatrists were called by the federal court as his witnesses, and they convinced everyone there that this boy was totally insane. All right, now let's see what happened right after Judge Mouser appointed these California State doctors."

He launched into the narrative he'd planned to show the jury how biased the D.A. had been in this case, how he'd unfairly swayed the opinion of the psychiatrists and tweaked the testimony of the witnesses. Connolly was determined to convince the jury of the unfairness of this trial. "He heard a rumor that he was being criticized for trying this case, for dragging this boy out of the dungeon up there where he was spending the balance of his life. What did he do about it? Cunning, scheming, he made arrangements to be invited to the Kiwanis Club and other civic organizations, all through the valley. He takes his stooge, Damron, with him, and he tries this case before all the civic bodies. Why? To inflame the minds of the people against this boy."

Good, he still had their attention. He kept going, spending another ten minutes hammering on what he perceived as misconduct by the district attorney. He had to make these jurors understand that the man was not to be trusted.

Then, holding his notes in one hand, he slammed his palm down hard on the railing of the jury divider, so hard, he saw some of them jump. Maybe he'd overdone it, but he meant business. He had to get through to these people. He had to do damage control.

"I say, shame on you, Don Bitler." Connelly turned and pointed right at the opposing counsel. "Shame on you!"

Turning back, he saw one or two jurors stifle a yawn. He went into overdrive, reiterating the psychiatrists' testimony and his opinion of their findings versus the Oklahoma doctors. He hammered on the pitiful and poverty-stricken upbringing, and the rehearsed testimony of Damron and Burke. One or two glassy-eyed looks from jurors and his heart beat harder. The speed of his words increased as they poured out, urging the jurors to see his side and recognize the inability of this boy to plan such a diabolical crime as they were accusing him of committing.

And finally, his big guns. He saved this for last. "I believe society, more than anything else, is responsible for this boy." Waving his finger at several vulnerable jury members and then back at himself, he continued. "I think you and I are responsible. I think everybody in the United States is responsible for this boy's condition.

"I am firmly convinced that this boy is absolutely insane. I believe by your verdict of insanity in this case that you should send him on back there to Alcatraz. That is where he belongs."

John Connolly breathed a silent sigh of relief. "I thank you," he said, directing his comment to both the jury and the judge, before returning to his seat.

District Attorney Don Bitler had spent the lunch recess going over his closing statement notes. As he suspected would happen, the defense attorney had spent a good portion of his time attacking him personally. He would not let this trial end with the jury having a mistaken impression of what type of man he was, especially when weighed against the defendant, who was the one on trial here.

He was the first to return to the courtroom and watched from his position at the counsel table as the other attorneys and the jury filed into the room, and finally, as they all stood upon the entrance of Judge Mouser.

"The case of the People of the State of California versus William Edward Cook. May it be stipulated that the defendant is in court and the jury and alternate juror are in their seats, and you are ready to proceed, gentlemen?"

John Connolly, his adversary, was the first to respond. "Ready."

"So stipulated," Don said and remained standing in preparation for his portion of the closing statement.

Judge Mouser nodded. "You may proceed with your final closing argument."

"May it please the Court, counsel and ladies and gentlemen of the jury." Don looked in the direction of each as he spoke, then settled on the jury, where he would cast his attention for the duration of his comments.

"Many years ago, I had the pleasure of knowing Clarence Darrow, of whom most of you have heard described as a great criminal lawyer. They attribute to him this advice to a young attorney: he said, 'if the facts are on your side, argue the facts; if the law is on your side, argue the law; and if you haven't either of them, attack the district attorney.' Now, that is what has been done in this case."

Bitler studied the faces of the jurors, gauging whether they got the point of his introduction. He continued, encouraged by the slight nods of a few.

"Counsel talked to you, a nice forcible argument. He talked to you by the clock, which you have a right to notice is in the room here, for thirty-five minutes. Exactly seventeen of that thirty-five he talked about the district attorney." Don turned to look at the opposing counsel, then back to the jury, pausing to let his words sink in. "You can draw your own conclusions."

"Mr. Connolly stated that public demand in Imperial County was against the trying of the case. He is a good lawyer, I think, but he didn't know that under California law the district attorney is bound by his oath to assist in the apprehending and prosecution, of people who have violated our state law. And I want to say to you ladies and gentlemen, in handling this case, it is exactly what I would do again. I acted under my oath as district attorney to bring this charge and to bring it to trial in this manner.

"Counsel also stated that this case should never have been brought to trial. He sort of suggested that Mr. Cook—I speak of him as 'Mr. Cook' because I think he is a grown man, even though counsel has called him a boy throughout. He is twenty-three or four years old, by record. He stated that Mr. Cook had been put away permanently for three hundred years by the judge in federal court in Oklahoma. Therefore, his suggestion is that there was no reason for trying him for murdering a man in Imperial County, in violation of California law. He decried the statements that have been made that he could be paroled in fifteen years.

"I am afraid that Mr. Connolly has been so busy back in Oklahoma, and maybe on this trial, that he has not heard of or read the bill called Public Document 98, adopted by Congress this summer, and signed by the President on July 31, 1951, which says very plainly that any federal prisoner on good behavior throughout his sentence can be paroled after serving fifteen years of a life sentence, or of a sentence over forty-five years; and that is one of those over forty-five years. Therefore, it is the law of the United States Government that this defendant is eligible, if he behaves, after fifteen years, eligible to go out on the street."

Looking at the clock, judging how much time he had left, the district attorney proceeded to attack the opinions of the psychiatrists who testified in Oklahoma, comparing their findings to those of the doctors in California, all the while watching the eyes of the jurors, to see if they were following him, or losing interest, or, heaven forbid, falling asleep. Encouraged to see he had their rapt attention, he continued, moving onto a new and just as important topic.

"You have had some suggestions made by the witness, Mrs. Bryson, a nice old lady, who used to be a juvenile officer. She says in Missouri she knew Cook and because of the fact that she knew him up to about seventeen or eighteen years ago, somewhere back in the thirties when she saw him, and then she saw him maybe again along about '43, she believed that he was insane because of the hardships that he had in his earlier youth."

Mr. Bitler motioned to all the members of the jury, then around the courtroom, taking in even the spectators. "I don't know the experience of the members of the jury, but I never have seen twelve men and women assembled in any manner, as a jury, or anywhere else, that you could talk to them, that they didn't have certain hardships in their youth that they would rather not have, that they resented, that they didn't seem to enjoy. And still I don't see so much result from it in the effect on your later life because the tendency of most people is to get on the right track regardless, and not rely upon their early hardships to get out of it."

He shared examples of famous people, such as Abraham Lincoln and William Henry Harrison who had hardships as a youth, yet went on to do great things.

"Now the picture of this case boils down very finely to the question of whether you have a right, in deciding your verdict, to allow a person of this kind to avoid punishment because you personally might believe he is insane. I say you must handle it as a group, as a citizen, as a member of society yourself; and don't be stampeded, no matter how long it takes to argue it out, don't be stampeded by the thought that you are harming him if you decide one way; that you are not harming him if you decide the other."

He turned and approached the defense table, attempting to make eye contact with the defendant, but his expressionless face with downcast eyes prevented that. He looked at the defense counsel briefly, then returned to where he paced the rail of the jury box while he spoke.

"The point is that you should think of the harm that might be done if you bring the wrong verdict, the harm that might be done to society itself. We have more than ten million people in California, and when I speak here, I am speaking for them. That is our society. People have a right to be members of society if they observe these laws that we have on the books that prescribe our rule of action. You have a right to consider that angle, which should control whether you believe this man is sane or insane."

Lest the jurors forget some of the ample evidence, he reiterated the changing of shirts with Mr. Burke, the removal of license plates to bury and hide them, and the planning for what they would do when arriving in Santa Rosalia.

"It is probably one of the strangest cases in legal history out there. But you heard the evidence of Burke and Damron, just what happened, that he carried these boys night and day under his gun for the entire trip, and they never had a chance to get away from him. The vigilance, the planning, the perception of the defendant in all these movements—doesn't that appear to be the work of a person of canny nature, or deliberation? Mind you now, we are not talking about now, sitting here in the courtroom in this manner." He turned sideways, motioning to the defendant, hopefully encouraging the jurors to take a look at the persona the defendant now presented, so different from who he was when on his murderous rampage.

"We are not talking about now," he said, returning his attention back to the jury box. "We are talking about January 6 and the following week, 1951. I would think that nobody would be in a better position to talk as a witness than two men who traveled with him under that situation for eight days, under that tenseness, under that strain. Talk about hardship?

"Cook had no difficulty talking audibly so they could all hear him. He issued orders, sometimes shouted at them. He has a voice, he knew what he was doing. Because he doesn't see fit to speak at this stage of the game, that doesn't prove that he was insane January 6th and the following ten days. Oh no, that speaks for itself, I think.

"And then, ladies and gentlemen, we go to Mr. Plaxico. You heard his testimony. In all my experience, I have never heard a more straightforward piece of testimony that rang with accuracy and convincingness than was given by Mr. Plaxico. You have heard it. I don't need to repeat, but he ended with the one statement when he asked Cook, 'What are you going to do to beat this deal if you go back to Oklahoma?' First, Cook says 'How high do they hang them back in Oklahoma?' Then he went on to say he would pretend he was crazy and try to develop public sympathy.

Bitler tucked his notes under his arm, clasped his hands together, and after a brief pause, said, "Ladies and gentlemen, I think that just about covers it. You have a very important duty to perform, and all we expect is that you do your duty, not alone to the defendant, mind you, but to the State of California. It's up to you. Thank you."

CHAPTER 71

NOVEMBER 23, 1951 - 4:02 P.M.
EL CENTRO, CALIFORNIA

Fifty-four minutes after entering the deliberation room, the twelve members of the jury filed back into the courtroom where attorneys, defendant, spectators and judge awaited. The sun was low in the western sky, and most everyone in the courtroom, except for the defendant, was probably looking forward to getting home to Thanksgiving leftovers. But uppermost in the minds of everyone except the twelve jurors was the question of what the verdict would be.

Judge L.J. Mouser ran through the recital of people present, and after receiving appropriate stipulations from the attorneys, he asked the question that would lead to the answer the entire trial hinged on. "Ladies and gentlemen of the jury, have you arrived at a verdict?"

The jury foreman stood. "We have, Your Honor."

"You may hand the verdict to the bailiff, and he will transmit it to the Court."

The silence, thick with anticipation, permeated the courtroom as the judge received the verdict, then handed it over to the clerk.

"The clerk may read the verdict to the jury and ascertain if that is their true verdict."

The court clerk stood. "In the Superior Court of the State of California, in and for the County of Imperial, verdict No. 5326. The People of the State of California, plaintiff, versus William Edward Cook, also known as William E. Cook, defendant. We, the jury in the above-entitled cause, find the defendant, William Edward Cook, sane at the time of the commission of the offense charged in the indictment on file herein. Dated November 23, 1951. W.A. Tondro, Foreman."

"Ladies and gentlemen," Judge Mouser turned his attention to the jury. "Is this your true verdict?"

Speaking as one, all twelve voices rang out in unison, "It is."

He might have imagined it, but District Attorney Don Bitler thought he heard a collective sigh of relief throughout the courtroom. He refrained from looking at the defendant, but suspected nothing would have changed in his demeanor.

CHAPTER 72

NOVEMBER 28, 1951
EL CENTRO, CALIFORNIA

Dismissed juror, Aggie Dahm, once again settled into the seat she claimed for herself in the gallery on day one of the trial. She was pleased with the trial's progress, and the jury voted just as she would have if she had been serving. And now the day for sentencing had arrived. Would Judge Mouser choose the sentence she and many others had already chosen in their minds?

She watched the back of the defendant as the judge droned on with the usual opening statements. She'd heard them so many times in the last week she could take the judge's chair and recite them herself. As she suspected, the defendant, from behind, appeared to be his same insolent self, staring at the floor, slouching in his place at the defense table.

"The record may also show that the defendant is in court with his attorney, M.M. Cline, who is associated in this case as an attorney of record at the request of Mr. Connolly, and with the consent and approval of the defendant."

Aggie watched as the new kid on the block nodded his head. She figured Connolly had headed back home to Oklahoma, maybe for a late Thanksgiving with the family.

The judge continued. "Today, gentlemen, is the day that has been set for the pronouncement of judgment and the imposition of sentence in this case. The Court has read and considered the pre-sentence reports which has been submitted by the probation officer. Have either of the attorneys anything to say before I arraign the defendant for sentence?"

The district attorney, Don Bitler, stood. "May it please the Court and counsel, I have a statement I desire to make, and may I read it, Your Honor? It is not very long."

Aggie groaned inwardly. This man could talk. If he said it wasn't very long, she knew it was long. She just wanted to get to the sentencing.

Judge Mouser nodded. "You may proceed."

"I concur fully in Your Honor's determination that this is a case of murder of the first degree under the California statutes," he read from his notes. "The slaying of Robert Hilton Dewey by William Edward Cook was done in the perpetration of robbery, which the law pronounces murder of the first degree. This killing was also of a cruel and aggravated character. It was willful, intentional, deliberate, premeditated assassination, cowardly and unnecessary—thus, under our laws, making it doubly a murder of the first degree.

"For more than forty years..."

Aggie surreptitiously slipped her paperback out of her handbag at that statement. If this man was going to cover the past forty years of his life, she was going to sneak in a few pages of reading while he reviewed his legal history and the facts in the case.

"Cook shot a fine man," Bitler later said, prompting Aggie to look up from her book. "A fine man who had served with an honorable record in the United States Army while Cook, the killer, was serving time in a Missouri reformatory and penitentiary. He shot a man who had done him no harm, a man whom Cook did not even know ten minutes before the killing."

Aggie shook her head. Her devoted appreciation for men who'd served in the armed forces caused her even more anger at the reminder that Dewey had fought in World War II.

"Dewey apparently was in the confines of Imperial County hardly three hours before he met his death at the hands of Cook," Bitler continued. "Dewey had told his father in La Mesa that he wanted to go through the desert to see the place where he had trained with General Patton, to call on comrades at Blythe. Cook himself was in the county barely an hour before he killed Dewey. In that hour Cook committed many crimes against the State of California, including two counts of kidnapping, two of grand theft, two of robbery, two of possession of a gun by an ex-convict, and then finally, murder, with Dewey his helpless, unarmed victim."

Her eyes drifted back to her book, as Bitler again reiterated testimony about the insanity plea and the doctors, reminded the judge how quickly the jury returned a verdict of sanity and while Aggie simultaneously tried to read her book while listening with half an ear, she could tell he might be winding down. Closing her book, she returned her attention to the district attorney.

"Although personally we may feel great sympathy for the defendant for the position in which he now finds himself, officially we believe, without reservation, that defendant Cook has wholly forfeited his right to be a member of society. We believe the people of Imperial County and the ten million citizens of California would agree to this statement. Cook is not the type of man who has the right to live in the society whose laws he flaunts with such impunity, and with such an abandoned heart, such a cold-blooded lack of feeling, such an inconsiderate appreciation of other people's right to live. We cannot feel that he can blame anyone but himself—his own acts, his belief that he is above the law—that have brought him at last to the 'bar of justice.'

"Therefore, Your Honor, we, in the name of the People of the great State of California, recommend that in the sentencing of this defendant, he be given the fullest penalty provided by law."

Aggie clapped in her mind, since the rest of the room stayed silent. She was pretty sure that wasn't proper decorum in the courthouse. But she also felt like belting out a shrill whistle in support.

"Have you anything to say?" Judge Mouser turned to the newcomer.

"Your Honor," Mr. Cline said, "I feel compelled to object to Mr. Bitler's statements upon the ground that most of his remarks were not in the nature of argument but were in the nature of unsworn testimony, and I ask that they be stricken from the record for that reason."

"Your motion asking for them to be stricken from the record will be denied."

More clapping and whistling went on in Aggie's mind. She even withheld the chuckle that tried to sneak out.

"I want to assure you," Judge Mouser appeared to address his comments to the defense table, "and the defendant, that any statements made by Mr. Bitler in his statement to the Court will in no way interfere with the decision that I have reached in this case. Which I have reached through my independent consideration of the case and the investigation as presented by the probation officer. Have you anything more to say, either attorney?" He turned to the district attorney at his last question.

Mr. Cline shook his head. "No, Your Honor."

"No," Mr. Bitler echoed.

"You may stand, Mr. Cook, if you will please," Judge Mouser looked straight at the defendant.

Aggie fully expected the killer to stay seated, but was surprised as he slowly stood. She wondered how the man managed to stay standing as the judge recited all the legal mumbo jumbo required before he ever got to the point of the sentencing. She considered pulling her paperback out again, but she did not want to miss the most important part.

Minutes later, the judge got to the part Aggie and everyone in the courtroom, and across the country were waiting to hear.

"William Edward Cook, you having been charged with murder by the indictment filed in this case, by going to trial on your single and sole plea of not guilty by reason of insanity have admitted the commission of the act charged in the indictment, and a jury having returned a verdict finding you sane at the time of the commission of the act charged, you now stand before this Court convicted of the crime of a felony, to wit, murder of the first degree. Now therefore, it is the judgment, order and decree of this Court that you, the said William Edward Cook, in punishment of the offense of which you have been convicted, suffer the punishment of death for said crime.

"It is the further order of the Court that the said defendant, William Edward Cook, be delivered by R. W. Ware, the sheriff of Imperial County, within ten days from this 28th day of November, 1951 into the custody of the warden of the California State Prison at San Quentin, to be held pending the decision of the Supreme Court of the State of California upon the appeal of the said defendant, William Edward Cook, and until the further order of this Court.

"That is all, gentlemen."

Aggie breathed a sigh of relief as she knew millions around the nation following this case would as well.

CHAPTER 73

ONE YEAR LATER
OCTOBER 10, 1952
EL CENTRO, CALFIORNIA

Deputy Clerk Barbara O'Guinn left the warm weather behind as she stepped into the air-conditioned lobby of the courthouse on her way to meet with Judge Mouser. She was glad the brutally hot summer weather had ended, but still found ninety degrees to be a bit too warm for her liking. Fall weather came late to their desert town every year.

"Mrs. O'Guinn, thank you for filling in for the county clerk today. He said he knew as soon as he left on vacation the word would come down from the Supreme Court."

Barbara chuckled, taking a seat across from the judge at the ornate, oversized desk in his chambers. "I'm happy to do it. I'm actually glad to be a part of seeking closure in this case. My family has known the Damron family for years, and I still remember the fear for everyone when the news reported that Billy Cook had kidnapped Forrest and James."

Judge Mouser nodded, then slipped his glasses on. "I, too, am glad to see this case come to an appropriate end. I never agreed with the judge in Oklahoma finding him insane and itched to get to try him."

"I saw that the Supreme Court denied the appeal and request for a new trial."

"Yes, and now it's back in our court and time to set the execution date." Looking down at his notes, he said, "This should be brief. I'd like to get it filed right away and then sent out by registered mail today to the warden at San Quentin."

Barbara nodded, "Will do." She held up her pen. "I'm ready to take notes."

"I had most of it dictated, but this is the pertinent info that needs to be filled in, where I indicated, I was waiting for the exact info from the Supreme Court."

"Okay, I'm ready."

"It is the further order of the Court that you, H.O. Teets, Warden of San Quentin Prison, carry the judgment into effect and impose and carry out said sentence of death hereinafter specified on the 12th day of December, 1952, being a day not less than sixty days nor more than ninety days from the time of making this order, between the hours of sunset and sunrise, at San Quentin Prison, et cetera, et cetera." He looked up at Barbara. "It's all on the dictaphone. This is just the part I'd left blank."

He took his glasses off, leaned back in his chair, and slowly nodded his head. "It's a burdensome responsibility."

"Setting the date to end a man's life?" Barbara said.

Judge Mouser nodded. "But it's what must be done."

"He did it to himself when he chose to kill people."

CHAPTER 74

OCTOBER 24, 1952
SAN RAFAEL, CALIFORNIA

Sheriff Walter B. Sellmer stared at the postcard the mail room had delivered to his desk. In his thirty-two years as sheriff of Marin County, he'd never seen anything like it. A convicted death row killer from San Quentin writing to someone, in fact a group of someones, he believed would also end up on death row.

This Bill Cook character obviously did not realize that Louis E. Blair, who he had addressed the postcard to, had been released just about the time Cook was writing and mailing the card. Further investigation had proven Louis wasn't the mass killer of this father and three children. They were already on the trail of the other suspects in what had become known as the Chester Murders. And William Cook was right in using the term "en masse" in his address. This was most likely a group of killers working together, just not including the wrongly accused Louis Blair.

He pondered the phrase "en masse" and wondered about the death row convict knowing the proper usage of that term.

The typewritten postcard most likely was prepared in the library at San Quentin. Walter took a seat at his desk, slipped his reading glasses on and slowly read the curious and confusing prose of the San Quentin prisoner:

Overlooking My Palace of Despair!
The finger of guilt is pointing at you for the dirty crime you committed up in Plumas County. Me too was the victim of Lust and Revenge for someone that questioned my authority. That fake Lie-Test you had in Reno will only temporarily keep you free from punishment. Sleuths will keep you covered like they did me. Hounding your very soul should you go back to Chester to live. Maybe the first night the citizens will burn you alive. Better follow me and confess so you and myself can be sent to the Gas Chamber for the same nature Mass Murders you deserve just like myself. The moans of those innocent little kids will haunt you from now until the authorities get your confession. Sneaky lawyers that take your money cannot protect you from God, and the demands of society. Pay for your crime like a man. Hope to see you soon—Brother-in-Slaughter.
Bill Cook—Arch Killer, San Quentin.

Sheriff Sellmer shook his head as he stared at the typed words. This killer in San Quentin was reading the newspapers and must have closely followed the arrest and crime Louis was accused of. He mentioned the moans of the children. He knew then that three little children had been murdered. He also knew they administered a lie-detector test to Louis.

He found it interesting that William Cook referred to the moans haunting the killer and wondered, never having admitted that to anyone, was this the true state of his mind, haunted by the cries of the children he murdered? Or had the haunting stopped when he confessed? And his mention of God? Did he know that no matter what judgment the courts meted out, he still would stand before the Almighty God? It did indeed sound as if he was aware of that.

He pondered all that he'd read of the first trial of William Cook in Oklahoma, where he was found not to be responsible for his crimes due to insanity. This man certainly did not have the mind of a three-year-old as the psychiatrists in his first trial had testified. The writing on this postcard proved that.

CHAPTER 75

NOVEMBER 15, 1952
SAN QUENTIN PRISON

Harley Teets re-read the letter from prosecuting attorney Gene Frost in Jasper County, Missouri, while waiting for FBI Special Agent John Arends. He had chosen John specifically for this task. The young, energetic, likeable agent was just getting his career started and seemed destined to make a success of it. He had a way with people, and if anyone could get to the bottom of this mystery, he figured Arends could do it. His perpetual smile drew people in, even the harshest of criminals. Although Arends had never yet had occasion to interview Billy Cook, Harley hoped he would succeed where other agents had failed in drawing information out of the tight-lipped death row inmate.

The quick rat-a-tat rapping on the frame of his office doorway signaled the arrival of the FBI special agent.

Harley stood, motioning for the man to step in through the open doorway. He often kept his office door open, extending a welcome to visitors, both prison staff and outsiders, who had reason to visit him. The more he reached out to people, the more information he could take in, which helped him do his best job of running a prison that could offer rehabilitation and, he hoped, ultimately benefit society.

"Sir." John's firm clasp when Harley extended his hand of greeting was yet another thing to like about the man. He exuded confidence. "I hear you have a challenge for me."

Harley motioned to the double set of padded chairs across his office. He preferred to talk to his visitors face to face without his desk dividing them, and he'd specifically chosen comfortable chairs. Often the topics discussed in the warden's office were difficult ones, so no sense in having the visitors uncomfortable while conversing.

"We do. I don't believe you've had occasion to interview William Cook. He's scheduled to be executed in just a few weeks, but a matter has come to my attention that we need to investigate. And I'm glad I received the letter in time."

Once they were both seated, Harley handed the letter to John. "I'll let you read it, and then we can discuss it before I have them bring Cook into the interview room."

Harley watched John's eyes flit back and forth across the page, quickly consuming the surprising contents.

"Boy, what are the chances Cook will confess to this?"

"Slim to none," Harley said, but we need to try. "If what they say is true, this Harold Suman needs to be tried for murder, as well."

"I followed this case in the news last year, before I became a special agent, so I'm fairly familiar with it," John said. "I know some reporters had speculated that Cook must have had help to get all the bodies of the Mosser family into the mine shaft, but I'd never read they thought Harold Suman was the accomplice."

"They were in prison together in Missouri, at the same penitentiary Suman is in now. I looked into that, and he just started this sentence recently, also for aiding in a kidnapping and robbery."

"Same M.O. as Cook, except without the murder. That's interesting."

"The prosecuting attorney is eager to get some evidence to find out if the way Harold Suman knew where the bodies had been hidden was because he helped to put them there."

John shook his head. "What a shame if that's the case, and then he's so bold, to come forward and help in the search and collect part of the reward money." John looked over the letter again. "So they think William Cook told someone at some point that Suman helped him?"

"That's not clear to me in this letter," Harley said. "Something about someone's brother. Whether it was Cook's brother or Suman's, I'm not sure. But he would have had to communicate that to them before he was captured."

John stood. "In any event, I'm eager to begin the interrogation."

Harley stepped over to his desk, activating the intercom. "Maureen, can you notify a guard to bring William Cook to an available interrogation room?" He looked back at John. "I will warn you, if you get information out of him, you will be the first to do so since he arrived here last December. Cook wouldn't even answer the intake questions to give any background information. He has maintained his refusal to answer questions throughout this entire time. He also refuses interviews with reporters."

John's smile encouraged Harley, and he felt his own lips curling up at the corners. "And that, my man, is why I chose you. I figured if anyone could get information out of him, it would be you."

"I'm eager to try, sir." He stepped toward the door. "Show me to the prisoner."

CHAPTER 76

NOVEMBER 20, 1952
SAN QUENTIN PRISON

Harley slid the letter from attorney Gene Frost across the desk to his secretary. "You'll be able to get all the address information from here."

Maureen glanced at it, then sat, back erect, perched on the edge of her chair, steno pad in hand and pencil poised. She was a top-notch secretary, and her attention to detail aided him immensely in his daily administrative duties.

"Today's date." Harley glanced at the calendar hanging on a nearby wall. "Let's get it out in today's mail and hopefully they can receive it before Thanksgiving. Although it will probably spoil their Thanksgiving, since it will be of no help to their investigation."

"I'm curious to hear the letter," Maureen said. "I'll get right on it as soon as we finish the dictation."

Harley leaned against his high-backed office chair, his eyes focused on the three dots on the ceiling he always seemed to stare at while dictating. If the maintenance department ever painted the ceiling, or worse, added the popcorn texture, he'd lose his point of focus. He shook his head to eradicate the frivolous thoughts and get to the task at hand.

"Dear Sir. Pursuant to your communication of November 8, 1952, our condemned inmate, William Cook, A19569, has been interrogated but is completely uncooperative and refuses to discuss this, or any other matter. He has been consistent in this attitude since we received him and refuses to talk to special agents of the Federal Bureau of Investigation who attempt to interrogate him regularly.

"I regret that we are unable to assist you and am of the opinion that your officers would meet with the same situation if they should come to California."

He sat forward, looking at Maureen. "The usual closing, and I'll wait here in my office to sign when you're finished."

"I'll get right on that." Maureen stood, shook out the wrinkles in her skirt, tucked the pencil behind her ear and disappeared into the outer office.

CHAPTER 77

DECEMBER 12, 1952 - 9:30 A.M.
HOLDENVILLE, OKLAHOMA

Martha, if you were going to send a telegram to the young man, don't you think you should have planned ahead and not waited until the morning he is set to die?"

Martha Nelson stared out the windshield as her husband drove her to the Western Union office. She wondered the same thing he did. Why did she wait? Probably because she kept putting it off. Thinking it wouldn't do any good. Afraid to share her faith. Always thinking she had one more day to decide. Then she woke up that morning and realized, this was the day set for execution. She wasn't sure of the time, but she thought it was noon. Whether that was noon her time here in Oklahoma, or noon in California, she did not know, but she knew after breakfast and her Friday morning chores, she could not put it off any longer.

She pondered what to say while she defrosted the freezer, then went in search of her husband in his workshop. His woodworking business kept him busy, but she hoped he'd take time out to drive her to the Western Union office. She was not in a frame of mind to drive herself this morning.

Martha counted the words she'd written on the notepad, trying to keep it short, since they would pay per word. Plus, she realized that in waiting so late to send it, she would probably have to pay more to get it sent as an urgent message. She wondered if once it arrived at San Quentin, would they get it to the man in time? She didn't know what their priorities were.

All she knew is, she'd felt this niggling in her soul for a week now that she should do this, and even though she'd put it off too long, she had to do it this morning before she regretted the rest of her days not trying to get a message to the young man before it was too late.

The pat on her knee startled her, and she jerked her head in her husband's direction. "It's okay, Martha. Whatever it costs, it will be okay."

She felt tears forming, grateful for her husband's support in doing what she had to do.

"Can I help you?" She was glad that the clerk was friendly. Once before she'd sent a telegram and got a grumpy old man who didn't like his job. This young clerk seemed enthusiastic.

"Yes, please. I need to send an urgent telegram to San Quentin Prison in San Quentin, California."

The clerk turned shocked eyes her way as he handed her the notepad to compose the message.

"Don't believe I've ever sent a telegram there."

"And this needs to be an urgent message, so it gets there as soon as possible."

"Okay, ma'am, he pulled out his rate card, that will be…"

"Never mind," her husband interrupted. "Just let us know the total when it's complete. We'll pay it."

Martha wiped at a tear that slipped out and showed the clerk the notepad she'd already composed her message on.

"This is going to Billy Cook at San Quentin."

"Let me read this back to you before I input it into the teletype."

She cringed, wondering how her message would sound being read out loud and what the clerk and her husband would think of it. But still she knew it was what she wanted to say.

"Trust Billy, your soul with Jesus. Have peace with God before noon. See a chaplain, call on God. John 3:16. A friend to souls."

She felt her husband's hand on her shoulder and appreciated the gentle squeeze of encouragement.

"Yes, that's correct. Can you send it immediately?"

"It's as good as gone, ma'am."

She sighed, as a burden lifted. She'd done what she'd been led to do. Whether the young man ever saw it, she guessed she would never know this side of heaven.

CHAPTER 78

DECEMBER 12, 1952 - 9:50 A.M.
SAN QUENTIN PRISON

Is there a typical way to die in the gas chamber? Or was each killer's death as individual as their heinous actions?

Brander Harrison didn't know why he'd been chosen to be in the witness gallery. Luck of the draw, he guessed. He didn't even know why he'd thrown his name in the hat. Just had to see for himself that this madman could no longer terrorize innocent people. But could he actually watch someone die? He was about to find out.

He listened to the murmuring of nearby voices and figured out that the two men standing near him were military. Air Force, he believed it was they told the man who seemed to be a greeter of sorts.

Glenn Boydstun had shaken his hand when Brander took his place near the railing in the back. "This is my partner Andrew Grimes," Glenn said after introducing himself. "We're from Temple, Oklahoma, and came here to claim the body." He handed a business card to Brander. "The body will be on display in my funeral parlor for the townspeople who'd like to get a look

331

at him." Brander thought that was odd, but then could it be any odder than him coming here to see the actual execution.

Glenn turned back to the military men who stood just in front of them. "What brings you fellows here? Are you for this or against it?"

"I feel if any guy should be executed, he should get it, on account of the kids more than anything."

"This here is Master Sergeant Howard Morris from Oklahoma City," Glenn said to Brander. "He serves in the Air Force with his friend Technical Sergeant Vance King." Brander shook hands.

"They're both from Oklahoma, too," Glenn said. "You know that's where that family got picked up."

A hush fell across the spectator area as movement inside the green-walled execution chamber caught everyone's attention. The door opened, and William Cook, flanked by two guards, with another following, entered the chamber. Cook never made eye contact with any of the spectators. Brander was shocked at the lack of emotion showing on his face, as if he were bored with the whole procedure.

The guard helped him into the execution chair. He looked around the eight-sided room while the guards strapped him in and never even seemed aware of the fifty or so witnesses standing two and three rows deep in a semicircle outside the chamber.

When the guards exited the chamber, William Cook clenched his hands, and the infamous H-A-R-D L-U-C-K tattoo on his fingers was clearly visible, one letter on each finger carefully spelling out the two words. Brander wondered if the others noticed it as he did.

At 10:03 the gas began filling the chamber. Though not visible, the reaction of William Cook was evident, his head held back, he inhaled deeply of the fumes. Brander, along with the others, cringed as they watched him take three big gasps. The only change in his expression was the frown that flickered across his face with the first gasp. No one spoke in the witness chamber, as they watched life ebb out of the man who once callously inflicted evil on so many, both those who lost their lives, their families and friends and the thousands across the nation who grieved with those personally involved.

At 10:13 a.m. doctors listening at the witness window through a stethoscope attached to Billy's chest nodded to each other, while one stood, facing the small group who were observing and pronounced him dead. It had taken ten minutes.

CHAPTER 79

DECEMBER 12, 1952 - 11:00 A.M.
SAN QUENTIN PRISON

"Maureen," Warden Harley Teets spoke into the intercom. "I need you to take a letter."

Moments later, she sat poised near his desk with her dictation pad and pen waiting quietly for the letter she knew was to come.

"Today's date, file number is COOK A-19569. Address it to James V. Bennett, Director, Bureau of Prisons, Washington, D.C.

"Dear Sir,

"This is to report that William Edward Cook, No. A-19569, was this date legally executed within the walls of this institution in accordance with the Warrant of Execution issued by the Honorable L. J. Mouser, Judge of the Superior Court of the State of California, in and for the County of Imperial, under date of October 10, 1952.

"Copy of the death certificate is attached for your file. Very truly yours."

He paused, she held her pen in place awaiting more instructions. Henry picked up the death certificate on his desk, looking it over to see that every "i" was dotted and every "t" crossed. Looking back at Maureen, he resumed, "Copies to the usual, James Boyle, U.S. Marshal, Los Angeles; Edmund Brown, Attorney General; Richard McGee, Director and Warden E.B. Swope, Alcatraz Island. That's it, and you know the urgency."

"Yes, sir. I'll get this out before lunch and bring it in for your signature."

He nodded. One of the difficult parts of his job. He was thankful it was over and glad there were success stories of prisoners who'd been rehabilitated within their walls and gone on to successfully complete their parole. Not everyone by far, but there were some. And it made the job worthwhile. It wasn't just about the executions. And it wasn't he himself taking a man's life, nor the judge, nor the state. He firmly believed it was the prisoner himself who committed the crime that resulted in this sentence. He would forever be thankful for those prisoners who succeeded. It made a day like today just a little easier to cope with.

CHAPTER 80

DECEMBER 14, 1952
COMANCHE, OKLAHOMA

Comanche Funeral Home director Glenn Boydstun stood over the body of the young killer, satisfied with the work of his skilled employees. His employees dressed the body in a dark blue suit and a carefully knotted black tie. His hands were plainly in sight on his chest, and mourners streaming by would clearly see the tattooed motto of his life "H-A-R-D L-U-C-K" on his fingers.

"A smile?" His employee, Albert, said. "You put a smile on him? Why not the snarl seen in every news photo? Why not just let him look more like who he really was?"

Glenn shrugged. "It's not in me. I believe our job is to present every deceased person in the best light."

He walked over to the glass doors, stunned to see lines of people waiting for the doors to open. "That line must be two blocks long," he said to Albert, who had joined him at the door.

"It's ironic, isn't it?" Albert said. "The guy who said he hates everybody's guts is now the center of attention. Imagine if he could know, all those people he hated are waiting to walk by and bid his body farewell."

Glenn pulled the keys out of his pocket, ready to unlock the door and unleash the crowd. "It's hard to say what draws people here in a time like this. Probably different reasons for every person in that line."

"It looks like the news media is here, too," Albert said. "You going to let them in?"

"No, I'll just suggest they keep their reporting focused on the crowds outside. I don't want photographers and reporters in here with the body and the mourners."

"Do you really think these people are mourners who are coming in to look?"

"Well," Glenn inserted the key into the door, watching people outside take notice at the sound of the lock clicking. "If not mourning for Billy Cook, certainly mourning for the six lives he ended."

CHAPTER 81

DECEMBER 15, 1952
JOPLIN, MISSOURI

Bertie Mae Adams had told herself she would not turn on the television. She would not watch the news. No matter how curious she got. No matter how much her neighbors told her about the streams of people flowing by the casket of the killer. No matter how engrossed they were in watching the spectacle. None of her neighbors knew of her connection. She'd never breathed a word to anyone. No one but Jackson. What a saint he was. He'd kept her secret. He'd never talked to her about it again after that summer day when she thought the telephone would never stop ringing. Even approaching his twenty-fifth birthday, he protected her, came to check on her, stayed the night when he could get away from his night watchman's job. She loved that young man as if he were her own. Even though she'd had no kids of her own, she imagined the love she felt for Jackson to be the love a real mother felt.

He'd told her once she was his real mother. She'd taken him in after his own mother had abandoned him at the Children's

Home. He'd been so easy to love. Was that the meaning of love? To love the ones who are easy to love?

Lost in thought, she hadn't even noticed when little Tobias joined her in the small living room, until she heard the sounds of voices coming across the television. She should have realized it was almost time for his show. That boy lived for Howdy Doody, but he couldn't tell time yet and didn't know he had twenty more minutes.

The news reports drew her in, no matter how strong her vow had been to avoid them.

She watched as the throngs of people waited to get through the doors to view the casket, appalled they would even air something like this on the television news. But unable to draw herself away.

She heard the front door open and close gently as she stared transfixed. "Momma," Tobias hung on her arm, snuggling close to where she sat on the sofa, "why all those ladies crying?"

She felt the sofa move as someone joined them and looked over to see Jackson wrapping an arm around Tobias' shoulders. "You shouldn't be watching this, big guy," he said. "Why don't you go play 'til your show comes on?"

"But Momma, why they crying?"

Bertie Mae struggled to control her own tears that threatened to fall. She looked over at Jackson. He nodded towards the television. "That him?" he whispered.

She could only nod.

"A bad man did something wrong, and he got killed for it," Jackson said. "Those ladies are probably crying for all the people the bad man hurt."

"Maybe that bad man never had no one to love him," Tobias said.

Bertie Mae's insides went cold. "He needed someone like you to love him," Tobias tried to reach his little arm around the back of his foster mother. "Then maybe he wouldn't have done nothin' bad to hurt people."

She couldn't help it now. A cry escaped her lips, and she was thankful for Jackson's visit at the perfect time. As if God Himself brought him here. He scooped up the young boy and whisked him out of the room. "I bet Momma's got cookies hidden somewhere," was the last Bertie heard as the two left her in peace to cry out her heart to God.

"God, I never loved that boy. I never did," she sobbed out the words, with her hands buried in her face as she remembered the trials of trying to care for Billy Cook when he was a young boy. It was as if evil had already invaded his body and controlled his every thought and move. "I tried to, but when he was so mean to Jackson, I just couldn't take it no more." Her shoulders heaved with heavy sobbing, backed up by the sobs of the women waiting in line.

"Oh God, is it my fault all those people got killed? Would it have helped if I could have loved him? What if I caused all of this?"

"No, Momma, no." She heard the gentle whisper of Jackson and hoped to heaven Tobias was not with him. "You did all you could."

She didn't know he had heard her ask God if it was her fault. "You're not to blame, Momma. Look what you did for me, for all the others, for Tobias. Momma, you're not a miracle worker. You couldn't change what was in his heart. You did what you could."

She held tight to his hand until he stepped over and shut off the television set.

She sat unmoving, tears subsided, and listened to the sound of laughter from the kitchen where Jackson had returned to occupy little Tobias.

The face of another little boy, his deformed eyelid, his perpetual snarl, haunted her as she closed her eyes and continued to pray for forgiveness and for comfort for all who had been hurt by an angry little boy who grew up to be an angry man, blaming everyone in his path for his awful life. Hard luck. They said he had it tattooed on his fingers. It was his life's theme, and he followed that bitter path to the end, leaving broken hearts in its wake that extended across the nation and back.

Shortly, the time arrived for Howdy Doody's daily joyous interlude, and Jackson led Tobias by the hand from the kitchen. He blocked the entire television screen with his body as he knelt down to tune in Howdy Doody, most likely not wanting to risk the news coming up again to upset his momma.

With Tobias settled in front of the set, he turned and reached for his momma's hand where she remained on the couch. "Come in the kitchen with me."

Once there, Jackson pointed to a small plate of cookies on the table, a glass of milk close by and the ever-present napkin. She smiled, already understanding what her son was doing.

"It's what you always did for us, Momma," Jackson said. He led her to the chair. "Sit. Just like you'd tell us. A cookie will fix everything."

Bertie Mae smiled, the memory warming her heart. Not so much her own memory, but realizing it was a special memory for him brought her joy. Maybe she had done some things right, and it was time she stopped focusing on what she felt was her failure.

Jackson took a seat across from her at the small table. His face grew somber as he stared into her eyes. She placed the cookie back on the plate and finished chewing the small bite she had taken to please him.

"Momma, I thought of something that you and me probably never thought of in all these years since Billy lived with us."

"What's that, Jackson?" She flinched inwardly just hearing the name. She hadn't heard Jackson mention his name since that day eleven years ago when she'd been confronted by the social worker about abandoning Billy outside the Children's Home.

"I remember his threats."

Momma Bertie nodded. She supposed he did. She remembered at the time he'd scoffed at them. Said he was older and bigger than Billy, and there was nothing Billy could do to hurt him.

"Momma, I know I told you back then, he didn't scare me none." He paused and stared across the room, then looked back at her. "But that wasn't true. There was something in his eyes. And that one eye that never closed—I know it wasn't his fault, but there was something so scary about that eye, too. But Momma, in that good eye, the evil that showed through there. I didn't want you to be scared back then, but the truth is I was always afraid of him."

Bertie Mae reached across the table for Jackson's hands and took hold of them tightly. She had no words.

"Momma, you've been looking at this wrong, thinking you done something bad." He gripped her hand back, squeezing it hard. "I coulda been his first victim."

She gasped and brought both her hands to her mouth.

"Momma, you've been looking at this like it was your fault all those other people died just because you couldn't love him like you thought you shoulda, but Momma, what if you actually saved my life and stopped him from killing long before he started?"

"Oh, Son. Oh, Jackson," she murmured. Tears rolled down her face, but this time tears not of grief and remorse, but of gratitude.

CHAPTER 82

A ttorney John Connelly sat across his desk from the siblings of the man he and his partner, Gomer Smith, defended the previous year, saving him, at that time, from the death penalty. The case was out of their hands once the attorney general transferred it to the state of California, where Billy Cook was unable to escape the death penalty a second time.

He listened as Juanita, the distraught sister-in-law of Billy, begged for help. "We think we have been double-crossed. We resent the whole thing and demand that it be stopped immediately."

John looked at Billy's brother Joe and sister, Bertha, sitting on either side of Juanita. "And you two agree with what she says?"

"Absolutely," Bertha said. "When the funeral director got permission from my father to claim the body after execution, we had been assured the service would be quiet and inconspicuous and that there would be no publicity whatsoever. We're shocked and hurt at what has happened."

Joe Stevenson placed an envelope in front of John. "These are the letters he wrote to us, with his intentions. He said a wealthy community member, who had a wayward son, had offered to pay for the embalming and the funeral service, and he wished to remain anonymous."

"But you weren't expecting it to turn into a Roman Holiday affair, is that correct?" John skimmed the letters before him as he responded.

"Most definitely correct," Joe said.

John looked at the three of them. "Who would like to be the spokesman? We'll give Glenn Boydstun a call right now and demand this be stopped."

"I'll do it," Bertha said.

John dialed the number of the funeral parlor listed on the letterhead and then dropped the handset into the amplifier on his desk so everyone could hear the conversation.

By the fourth ring, a woman's voice came through, "Comanche Funeral Home. May I help you?"

John nodded to Bertha.

"I'd like to speak to Glenn Boydstun. This is Bertha Massingill. I am the sister of William Cook."

"Oh!" The woman sounded startled. "Yes, ma'am, I will locate him for you."

Within seconds, the jovial voice came across the telephone wire. "Glenn Boydstun here, how may I help you, Mrs. Massingill?"

"This display of my brother's body needs to be stopped immediately. I want you to load up my brother's body right away and take it to the Galena Funeral Home and don't put out anymore news! We never agreed to anything like this. You have violated our trust."

"I assure you, I was not expecting this level of interest, Mrs. Massingill."

"Hello, Mr. Boydstun, this is John Connelly, attorney representing William Cook's family."

"Oh yes, sir, I did not know they had representation."

"Can I assure these folks that you're going to do what they want? I think this would be a good point to stop it, don't you?"

"Yes, sir," Boydstun said. "We will close the doors now and be on the road within thirty minutes."

"We want people to know we never agreed to anything like this, Mr. Boydstun," Juanita said. "We have been tricked into a publicity stunt. We're shocked and hurt at what has happened."

"Believe me," Mr. Boydstun said, "I don't understand myself why so many people wanted to see the body of this young man. I will lock the doors and arrange transportation as soon as we end this phone call."

"Thank you," John said. "See that you do. Good day, sir."

CHAPTER 83

DECEMBER 17, 1952
COMANCHE, OKLAHOMA

G lenn Boydstun headed to the viewing room and watched as a group of kids of all ages streamed past the inexpensive wooden coffin holding the body of the mad-dog killer, as people had been calling him.

He approached the group, knowing he needed to bring the viewing to a close. A man who appeared to be accompanying the school-age children shook his hand. "Thank you for making it possible for us to bring our students here. It's a great educational experience that I hope will teach them that crime does not pay."

Glenn gripped his hand, thankful for the news that this was indeed helpful to some. "I'm glad your group got here in time. At the request of the deceased's family, I must bring the viewing to a close immediately."

"Is it time for the funeral preparations? I've heard that it's been a windfall for the economy here in town. We stopped at a restaurant outside of town, and it was packed, and they said it had been for three days."

Glenn nodded. "I've heard the same, gas stations, motels, grocery stores. They're all benefitting. I never imagined the interest this man's body would garner."

"I know for us, it was a very realistic way to show kids what can come of a life of crime. We explained how this young man didn't just wake up one day and become a murderer. It started at a young age." He motioned toward the kids still passing by the coffin. "Some of them are already the age Cook was when he first got in trouble with the law."

"To answer your question about why, it is because the family has requested we stop. I just don't think they realize how this crime has impacted thousands. We've had over ten thousand people through here in the past three days and from what I hear they are from all over the U.S. Some of them are curiosity seekers, some are heartbroken at the crimes committed, and some just are angry and want to see that this killer got what he deserved."

The man began herding his crowd out the door, as Glenn followed them to the door, to speak to those in line outside who would not be able to get in.

"I apologize profusely to those of you who have come from far away, but at the demand of the family we have been given orders to shut down the viewing and immediately transport his body to an undisclosed location."

Groans of frustration sounded, but Glenn closed the door on the protestations, knowing it was out of his hands. Nothing he could do about it now. And he had an obligation to fulfill as he made the arrangements for one of his employees to deliver the body to the funeral home requested by the family.

CHAPTER 84

DECEMBER 17 1952 - LATE NIGHT
JOPLIN, MISSOURI

Forty-three-year-old Reverend Dowe Booe stood tall, head held high, as he stared into the black night pondering a different day. Nineteen years earlier, he had officiated over the burial of William Cook's mother, Laura May. He'd only been a minister for one year at the time and as a young man of twenty-four hardly knew what to say as he had surveyed the family of eleven children ranging in age from three to twenty-six and a father who looked like he'd had too much to drink.

What would his grandfather, the founder of their church, have done with that family of youngsters who'd lost their mother and been abandoned by their father? Could he himself have done something differently?

The few people present had gathered in the dark of night to prevent crowds of curiosity seekers. A day earlier than the public expected the burial to be, they came to an undisclosed location on the outskirts of Peace Cemetery, an ironic name for the burial place of a man who destroyed the peace of anyone he came into contact with.

In the lantern light, Billy's father, his sister Bertha and a sister-in-law waited as the coffin was lowered into the grave. Off in the distance, a lonely police cruiser watched like a silent sentinel on standby to prevent trespassers. Cemetery workers shoveled dirt in as the somber group watched and listened while the dusty clumps hit the wooden box, slowly filling the hole. Once complete, those standing there looked to Reverend Booe.

"Friends, tonight we are all gathered together as I have been called upon to perform one of the hardest tasks I have ever had to do, as I have been so closely acquainted with several of you for so many years." Rev. Booe looked around at the small group before continuing.

"We do not understand why some things have to happen to some families, as some families have more than their share of trouble, but we do know that God understands all of our trials and all of our heartaches. It seems like some people are born into this world for more than their share, but God said He would bear our burden.

"As far as Billy is concerned, God knows and understands more than any of us. We do not know, but maybe in the still calm hours of the night, the thought and prayer, that he might have repented out to God. And this we know, we are leaving him in the hands of a just and merciful God and to the family I would say, God said, 'Come unto me all ye that are weary and are heavy laden and I will give you rest.'

"And as we depart for our different homes tonight, if we can put our trust and confidence in God, I am sure that His love will suffice for this hour."

Whispers of "amen" echoed as they all turned and walked away from the grave without a backward glance.

CHAPTER 85

DECEMBER 18, 1952
JOPLIN, MISSOURI

C arl Nutt watched his little daughter staring mesmerized at the Christmas tree. Goldie joined him near his chair, where he sat enjoying the little one's pleasure. Once they discovered the tree lights held a special joy for little Pamela Sue, they'd started a tradition of turning them on each afternoon when he got home from work, so they both could share in her excitement.

"Supper is almost ready." Goldie wore her favorite Christmas apron, the one covered in red poinsettias. She glanced at the newspaper in his lap. "Do you want to eat now or after you read the paper?"

He reached out for her hand, where she stood close by. Quietly they watched as Pamela Sue arranged her baby doll in the bed near the Christmas tree, so the baby doll could also see the colorful lights.

"I'll just glance at this for a bit, then I'll be ready."

Leaning back in his recliner, he held the newspaper at arm's length, looking for the article that would confirm what he knew had taken place the night before, not five miles from the police department.

There it was at the top of page one in the right-hand column. *Badman Bill Cook is Buried at Night at Peace Cemetery.* Carl breathed a deep sigh of relief, for the first time in nearly two years.

William Cook was dead and buried. It was finally really over. He watched Pamela Sue playing and his mind wandered to the surviving members of the Mosser family. Of course it would never be over for them, never again would they get to enjoy Christmas with their loved ones. The children would have been four, seven and nine now. Their aunts, uncles, grandparents and cousins now facing a second Christmas without them. He wondered if the punishment of death for the killer had given them any closure. And he wondered if it would be of any comfort to them, to know his own precious little daughter was named after their Pamela Sue.

"Goldie?" Carl folded the newspaper and tucked it into the pocket of his recliner, then went in search of his wife.

"Yes, Dear?" She met him at the kitchen doorway.

"You mentioned last week something about a news item about the Mosser family relatives talking about the execution." He watched the puzzled look on her face, realizing she hadn't been inside his head, she didn't know what he'd been thinking, he wasn't even sure if she knew about the burial last night. Then a look of understanding spread across her face.

Goldie nodded. "Follow me." She headed back into the large kitchen. "I put it here on the kitchen table. I thought you would want to read it when you had time."

Carl sat at the table where family and friends had gathered over the years for meals and fellowship. So many good memories. He almost hated to delve back into the evil his life had been immersed in over the past couple of years, but he had to know. Picking up the newspaper, he studied the article, appreciating that Goldie had left the paper folded with the article easily visible for him.

This must have been a hard interview for the reporter, he thought, as he read of the tears flowing from Thelma Mosser's sister, Alice. "Cook should have died for killing them if he died at all," Alice told the reporter. Carl nodded, he understood. The Oklahoma judge not condemning the killer to death for the murder of the Mossers still rubbed him the wrong way. "A prison sentence wasn't enough," Alice continued. "Even if it was three lifetimes. Of course he should have had the death penalty. But I don't know. I shouldn't say anything." He disagreed with her. He felt losing a sister in that horrible way entitled her to say anything and everything that was on her mind.

The reporter also talked with the twin brother of Carl Mosser. No tears here, according to the article. "I'm tickled to death about his execution," Chris said. "We don't need a man like that in circulation. This is what we wanted."

When asked about the rest of his family, Chris told the reporter that his mother "was over here Wednesday. She still thinks a lot about Carl's family, but she's just awful glad the killer was punished." He said his three brothers and five sisters felt the same way.

Even with a large family, the death of Carl and Thelma Mosser and their three children left a huge hole in their hearts.

Carl Nutt hadn't realized tears were rolling down his cheeks until he heard his little daughter.

"Daddy cry?"

He felt her hand resting on his knee, her blue eyes pools of concern. She was his miracle. His and Goldie's. Carl reached down and pulled her into his lap, embracing her. "Tears of joy, little one," he whispered, while peppering her soft hair with kisses. She giggled, then squirmed to face him, wrapping her little arms around his neck. "Love daddy."

Carl's heart swelled with joy and the knowledge that it was going to be all right. Life goes on, just like he learned after the war. Life goes on and sometimes, wonderful things come along to take your mind away from the awful things.

It had been a difficult two years, not only for him, but for hundreds out there who had been involved in this case, and the families who had lost their loved ones.

But his little Pamela Sue was a reminder to him of the miracles of joy that spring up when you least expect them. He still remembered the day her birth mother came into the station looking for him, on the verge of giving birth to a child she could not care for. Just weeks after he'd made the grisly discovery of the poor Mosser family.

Thank you, Lord, he breathed silently, still hugging his little girl. *Thank you for miracles in the midst of the pain. Thank you for giving everyone the strength to ride out this storm.*

Epilogue

Jacob Booe had been a circuit-riding preacher in the late 1800s. Firmly committed to the work of the church, he began a ministry in 1901 in the Smelter Hill area of Joplin, Missouri.

Jacob's ministry was devoted to the poor, the elderly and the mine workers of the area. He died in 1916. Seventeen years later, Billy Cook and his siblings were abandoned in a cave near a mine shaft in the Smelter Hills area.

Jacob was a willing servant of the Lord for his generation. What if Billy had been born in that same generation and been discovered by Jacob? Would that have changed the course of history in Billy's life and all of those lives he destroyed?

Maybe it would have. But perhaps not.

We can never know how many lives we will touch in a good way, how much evil we might prevent, if we but offer ourselves up as willing servants of the Lord to our own generation.

SEPARATING FACT FROM FICTION

T he majority of the people in this book are real people with real histories. Some characters are completely fictional to flesh out the story and very likely could represent what might have happened. Others have fictional conversations attributed to real people, but based on facts that are true.

The characters that are fiction, but very likely represent real people include (listed in order they appeared in the book): Bertie Mae Adams, Jackson, Verna Wilson (child services worker), Gus Madison (gun store owner), Jed Wilson (Tulsa police officer), Leona (FBI clerk), Liza Hodges (clerk in Imperial County sheriff's office), Arthur (law clerk in Oklahoma), Miranda (El Centro police department dispatch clerk), Lila Ann and Raymond Baxter (attending Mosser family funeral), Ella Jean and Dean Phelps (attending Oklahoma City hearing), Loretta (Robert Shelton's secretary), Maureen (Warden Harley Teet's secretary), Brander Harrison (attending execution), Albert (funeral home employee), Tobias (foster child).

All other characters are real, including mention of extended family members.

The church service led by B.N. Simmons is imagined, but B.N. and the church were real and the newspaper article about the governor's order for people to help search, read by B.N. was real, so it's very likely a service could have taken place just like that one.

The funeral for the Mosser family was led by Rev. Ken Blankenship and it was reported it gave a message of hope in Jesus Christ. The service and message as written was imagined however the quote from Billy Graham was factual.

Baby Pamela Sue was a real character as was her birth mother who sought out Detective Nutt to adopt her child. All chapters with the baby are imagined how they may have happened.

Nearly all conversation between William Cook and victims Homer Waldrip, Robert Dewey, Forrest Damron and James Burke are word for word according to court transcripts. Conversations between William Cook and the Mosser family are imagined based on news reports and law enforcement interviews with Cook.

All court testimony is verbatim from court transcripts.

The prison chaplains are real people, conversations imagined, except for the conversation at Alcatraz during the six week review, that was verbatim. The Missouri State Pen chaplain did remodel the chapel.

Letters and telegrams written to William Cook are verbatim with the exception of the letter Laverne Kershner wrote to William, that was constructed from facts in the records while the letter Kershner wrote to the warden is verbatim. The postcard Cook wrote to another suspected killer was verbatim.

Aggie Dahm was a real prospective juror and the conversation while being considered for jury duty is verbatim. However, having her stay as a spectator and her thoughts on the trial are imagined.

Bailiff Charles Hilt was a real person and his history was real. His thoughts were imagined how he might feel based on his history as a veteran.

The conversation between Attorney John Connelly, Cook's siblings and funeral home director Glenn Boydstun is verbatim based on newspaper reports. The reactions of visitors to view the body and the economic impact on the town is factual.

The graveside service for William Cook is based on newspaper reports and the message by Pastor Dowe Booe was verbatim based on a newspaper account.

All newspaper articles referred to or quoted are factual.

APPENDIX

A few interesting tidbits connected to this story

Tijuana Police Chief Francisco Morales donated his portion of the reward paid out by the families of Damron and Burke to the Tijuana Children's Breakfast Committee charity.

C.F. Brown, a 62-year-old Joplin Missouri firefighter, was one of the crew members recovering the bodies of the Mosser family from the Joplin mine shaft. Forty years earlier in January 1911, he recovered the body of a slain night watchman from an abandoned mine shaft in that same area.

The body of a tiny infant accompanied Cook's body when it was transported from California to Oklahoma. The month-old son of an Oklahoma serviceman had died while the family was in San Rafael, California and the parents could not afford to have his body transported to their Oklahoma hometown. Glenn Boydstun, funeral director, transported the infant's body at no charge to the parents.

Glenn Boydstun, who was originally appointed to handle the body of William Cook had his license suspended for one year when the State Board of Embalmers and Funeral Directors ruled in February 1953 that he had solicited the burial of the executed murderer. Two days later Boydstun filed a suit in district court appealing the ruling. Two months later Boydstun filed a $300,000 lawsuit against The Rangeley-Holden Funeral Home for alleged slanderous statements made about him during the time his license was being examined. In April 1953 The Oklahoma Supreme Court temporarily lifted the suspension of the license of Glenn Boydstun. In May 1954 The Oklahoma State Supreme Court overruled the State Board of Embalmers in suspending the license. The Supreme Court ruled that the legislation covering funeral directors does not keep them from legally soliciting business. Later that year Boydstun requested that the district court dismiss the $300,000 lawsuit against his competitor. ($300,000 in 1953 is equivalent to approximately $3.6 million in 2025.)

Lee Burd Archer, the first kidnapping victim of William E. Cook was in fact a criminal himself. Between the years of 1932 and 1960 he was convicted seven times, at least two of those times were for car theft and transporting across state lines, and also for kidnapping.

Lower California was the actual terminology used in the newspaper archives and court transcripts. We used the name it goes by in modern times – Baja California – to prevent confusion for the reader. Baja is the Spanish word for lower.

Book Club
Discussion Questions

1. "Hard Luck" is tattooed on Billy Cook's fingers—what do you think this symbolizes in the context of his life and crimes? Does it evoke sympathy, warning, or something else?

2. Which of the victims' stories or experiences hit you hardest? How did the author help bring them to life beyond just being names?

3 The murder of a whole family—parents and three young children—is especially horrific. How did the author handle this sensitive content? Was it respectful, too graphic, or appropriately balanced?

4. The story doesn't end with Billy's capture—it delves into the legal and societal aftermath. How did that deeper exploration affect your perception of justice in this case?

5. The Mosser family's decision to help a stranded motorist ultimately led to tragedy. How does the novel handle the theme of randomness or fate, and did it change how you think about everyday safety?

6. What did you think about the contrast between Bertie Mae's lifelong guilt and Billy's apparent lack of remorse?

7. Which victim or side character's perspective stayed with you the most, and why? How did the book give humanity to those often reduced to "crime statistics"?

8. The ripple effects of trauma are a central theme. In what ways did the book show how a single person's violence spreads beyond their immediate victims?

9. How did the pacing and structure—particularly the use of short chapters—affect your reading experience? Did it enhance the urgency and tension of the story for you?

10. After finishing the book, what lingering emotions or questions were you left with? Did it change how you think about crime, justice, or evil in real life?

Acknowledgements

First of all I thank our grandson Wyatt Kukla. Without his suggestion this book would never have been written. He was a great encourager during the process, delving into the things discovered during the research whenever he visited, and showing genuine interest throughout the project. He was a great inspiration.

Thank you to the following court and government personnel who helped during the court transcript and inmate records search:

The National Archives team at Fort Worth; Twila Gore, National Archives and Records Administration; Ivan Ramirez, Court Services Assistant I, Superior Court of California in Imperial County; Sean Heyliger, Archivist, National Archives of San Francisco; Timothy Wilcox, Archivist, National Archives at Kansas City; Brendan O'Brien, Reference Archivist, California State Archives; Chris McGreanor, Office Assistant, California State Archives and Criminal Records, Superior Court of California, Imperial County.

I am also very grateful to my first readers, Tracy Kerchner and Deanna Mosier, who were the first to lay eyes on the manuscript and helped with errors as well as giving feedback on the story as it was written.

The scenes taking place in Missouri State Penitentiary were made possible by watching the very informative tours of the museum and narration by Harvey Seidel, who has personal knowledge of this prison, on the Harvey Talks Prison YouTube channel. Harvey also graciously responded to the request for him to read an advance copy and provide a review.

Superior Court Judge Poli Flores Jr. who currently serves in the 100-year-old courthouse where William Cook's final trial was held, read an advance copy, writing an early review and taking time to discuss the book and how it relates to his hometown community of Imperial County, California.

Cassy Kerr, U.S. federal stenographer working in the Western District of Oklahoma pointed me in the right direction for obtaining court transcripts from the Oklahoma hearing. Then, when the manuscript was complete, she read an advance copy and helped with correct court terminology as she explained the difference between the federal and state court systems, as well as catching a few other errors. Her help is much appreciated.

Shawn Presley, granddaughter of Detective Carl Nutt, agreed to read an advance copy and provide feedback. I am especially grateful for her being willing to delve back into a difficult part of her grandfather's life and the family's lives. The sorrow did not go away after the execution. This was a terrible tragedy that he remembered for the rest of his life.

Dr. David Jeremiah from Shadow Mountain Community Church in El Cajon, California and his in-depth teaching every Sunday gave me ideas for two of the spiritual sections. Specifically, in Chapter 50, the phrase that says in heaven they are "experiencing endless explosions of pleasure and joy" came from Dr. Jeremiah's sermon titled *Won't Heaven Be Boring?* on May 18, 2025 and in the epilogue the concept about "offering ourselves up as willing servants of the Lord to our own generation," was from his message about King David entitled *Passing on the Torch,* April 13, 2025.

And to my husband, I am forever grateful for his support and for his patience in listening to me talk about this book and the research non-stop for the entire six months of bringing this book to life.

And finally, thank you to my Savior Jesus Christ for the gift of creativity, for the wisdom and direction He supplies in our daily lives and for salvation.

Not TRUE CRIME but CRIME just the same

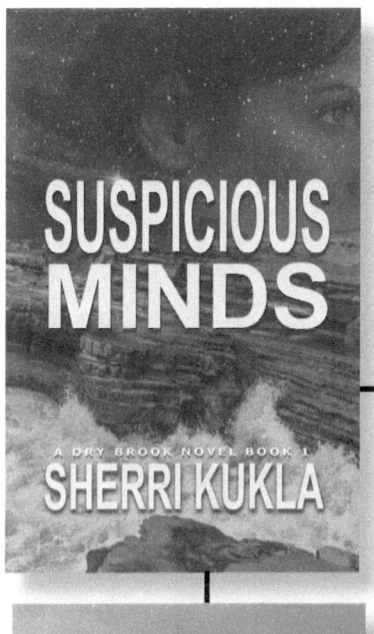

DRY
BROOK
MYSTERY
SERIES

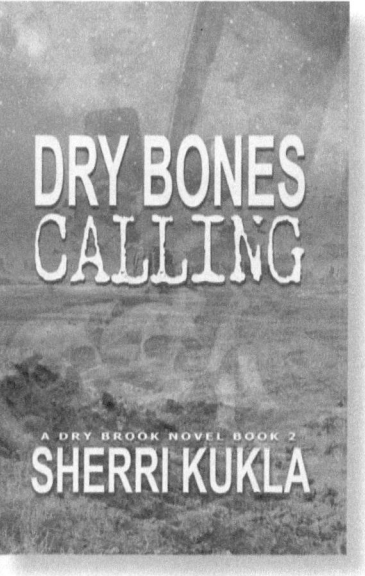

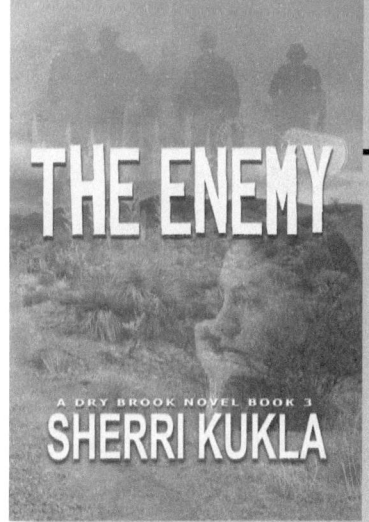

S&S Publishing Inc.
Visit us at
www.sspublishinginc.com
www.sherrikukla.com

And for the YOUNGER READERS
who enjoy MYSTERIES

MotoMysteries
The Skeleton and the Lantern
Book 1
SHERRI KUKLA

MotoMysteries
Ghost Lights of Dry Brook
SHERRI KUKLA

MotoMysteries
Phantom Ship in the Desert
SHERRI KUKLA

MotoMysteries
HARBOR POINT HAUNT
SHERRI KUKLA

MotoMysteries
THE LADY IN WHITE
SHERRI KUKLA

S&S Publishing Inc.
Visit us at
www.sspublishinginc.com
www.sherrikukla.com

www.ingramcontent.com/pod-product-compliance
Lightning Source LLC
Chambersburg PA
CBHW021212130626
46554CB00004B/1183